1001 FAST EASY Recipes

1001 Fast Easy Recipes

1st Printing January 2007

ISBN: 978-1-931294-96-6
Library of Congress Number: 2007920452

Illustrations by Nancy Bohanan

Edited, Designed and Published in the
United States of America
Manufactured in China

Cookbook Resources, LLC
541 Doubletree Drive
Highland Village, Texas 75077
Toll free 866-229-2665
www.cookbookresources.com

cookbook
resources® LLC

Introduction

Believe it or not, there are still 24 hours in each day. However, these days we spend more time away from home and our families. However late we arrive home from our busy day, there are still meals to prepare, dishes to clean, lunches to make, homework to be done and laundry that will need folding.

We can't help with the laundry or homework. We can help you save time in the kitchen, by offering you **1001 Fast Easy Recipes**. Time saved is time earned!

And, with 1,001 different recipes, moms will never-again hear the dreaded moan of "We're having this again?".

Included in this book are timesaving recipes guaranteed to please even the most discriminating of palates (read: children). These delicious recipes use ingredients that can be found in your own pantry. No long grocery lists needed!

Whether you are putting together an impromptu party or feeding your family on a weeknight, **1001 Fast Easy Recipes** is your quick-look book for easy, affordable meal ideas.

With all the time you are saving, you can finally follow through on 1998's New Year's resolution or start on that honey-do list somebody's been nagging about. Better yet, take the time for yourself. It's okay, we won't tell.

Contents

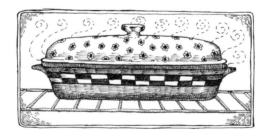

Contents

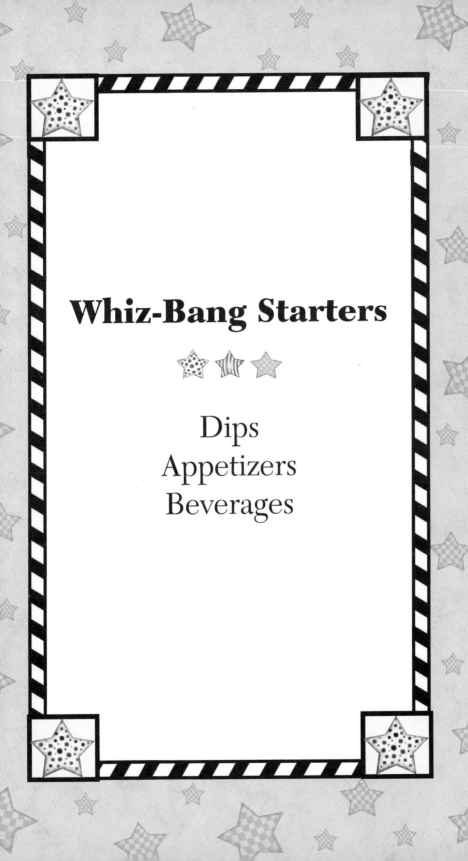

Whiz-Bang Starters

Dips
Appetizers
Beverages

Creamy Onion Dip

2 (8 ounce) packages cream cheese, softened	2 (227 g)
3 tablespoons lemon juice	45 ml
1 (1 ounce) packet dry onion soup mix	28 g
1 (8 ounce) carton sour cream	227 g

- Beat cream cheese until smooth. Blend in lemon juice and onion soup mix. Gradually fold in sour cream until it blends well. Chill. Serve with chips, crackers or fresh vegetables.

Cottage-Ham Dip

1 (16 ounce) carton small curd cottage cheese, drained	.5 kg
2 (6 ounce) cans deviled ham	2 (168 g)
1 (1 ounce) packet dry onion soup mix	28 g
½ cup sour cream	120 ml

- Blend cottage cheese in blender or mixer.

- Add ham, soup mix and sour cream and mix well. Serve with crackers.

Crunchy Asparagus Dip

1 (15 ounce) can asparagus spears, drained, chopped	425 g
½ cup mayonnaise	120 ml
¼ teaspoon hot sauce	1 ml
½ cup chopped pecans	120 ml

- Combine all ingredients in medium bowl and chill. Serve with wheat crackers.

Hot Crab Dip

1 (8 ounce) package cream cheese, softened	227 g
3 tablespoons milk	45 ml
½ teaspoon Worcestershire	2 ml
½ teaspoon hot sauce	2 ml
2 teaspoons prepared horseradish	10 ml
1 tablespoon instant onion flakes	15 ml
2 (6 ounce) cans crab, drained, flaked	2 (168 g)

• Preheat oven to 375° (190° C). In mixing bowl, combine cream cheese, milk, Worcestershire, hot sauce and horseradish, beat on low speed until all ingredients are well blended. Stir in onion flakes and crab and spread in small, buttered ovenproof dish and bake for 15 minutes. Serve warm with crackers.

Hot, Rich Crab Dip

1 (10 ounce) can cheddar cheese soup	280 g
1 (16 ounce) package cubed Mexican	
processed cheese	.5 kg
2 (6 ounce) cans crabmeat, flaked, drained	2 (168 g)
1 (16 ounce) jar salsa	.5 kg

• In microwave-safe bowl, combine cheese soup and processed cheese. Microwave at 1-minute intervals until cheese melts. Add crabmeat and salsa and mix well. Serve hot with chips.

Elegant Crab Dip

1 (6 ounce) can white crabmeat, drained, flaked	168 g
1 (8 ounce) package cream cheese	227 g
½ cup (1 stick) butter	120 ml

• In saucepan, combine crabmeat, cream cheese and butter. Heat and mix thoroughly. Transfer to hot chafing dish. Serve with chips.

Cucumber Dip

2 seedless cucumbers, peeled, shredded, drained
1 (8 ounce) carton sour cream   227 g
2 teaspoons white vinegar   10 ml
2 teaspoons olive oil   10 ml
1 teaspoon minced garlic   5 ml

- After shredding cucumbers, drain well on several paper towels. Add sour cream, vinegar, olive oil, garlic and 1 teaspoon (5 ml) salt, mixing well and chill. Serve with wheat crackers or pita wedges.

White Bean Dip

1 (3 ounce) package cream cheese, softened   84 g
2 (15 ounce) cans cannelloni (or navy) beans, drained   2 (425 g)
1 heaping teaspoon prepared minced garlic   5 ml
¼ cup extra-virgin olive oil   60 ml
2 teaspoons fresh, minced rosemary   10 ml
Grated zest of 1 lemon

- Place cream cheese, beans, garlic and salt to taste, in bowl of food processor. Turn machine on and add olive oil in a steady stream and process until smooth. Place mixture in bowl and stir in minced rosemary and lemon zest. Chill.

Talking Tomato Dip

1 (10 ounce) can tomatoes and green chilies, drained   280 g
1 (8 ounce) carton sour cream   227 g
2 teaspoons horseradish   10 ml
Chips

- Combine all ingredients and 1½ teaspoons (7 ml) salt. Chill and serve with chips.

Warm Cheddar-Onion Dip

1 (3 ounce) package cream cheese, softened, cut into chunks	84 g
⅔ cup mayonnaise	160 ml
1 sweet yellow onion (Vidalia if available), finely chopped	
1 (12 ounce) package shredded cheddar cheese	340 g
½ teaspoon dried thyme	2 ml

• Preheat oven to 350° (176° C). Beat together cream cheese and mayonnaise, until mixture blends well. Stir in onions.

• In bowl, combine onion-cream cheese mixture, cheddar cheese and dried thyme. Spoon into a shallow baking dish; cover and bake 20 minutes. Cool slightly and serve with round buttery crackers.

Whip-It-Up Dip

1 (2.5 ounce) jar dried beef, coarsely chopped	70 g
1 (8 ounce) package shredded cheddar cheese	227 g
⅔ cup mayonnaise	160 ml
⅔ teaspoon garlic powder	3 ml

• Combine all ingredients and mix well. Serve with crackers.

Velvet Dip

2 (16 ounce) packages cubed Mexican processed cheese	2 (.5 kg)
2 cups mayonnaise	480 ml
1 (4 ounce) jar chopped pimentos, drained	114 g
1 (7 ounce) can chopped green chilies	198 g

• Place cheese in saucepan and melt over low heat. Add other ingredients and mix well. Serve with chips.

Speedy Cheese Dip

2 (10 ounce) cans cheddar cheese soup   2 (280 g)
1 (10 ounce) can diced tomatoes and green chilies   280 g
1 (10 ounce) can cream of chicken soup   280 g
Pinch of cayenne pepper

- Mix all ingredients in saucepan. Add ½ teaspoon (2 ml) salt to taste. Serve hot. Serve with chips.

Five Minute Dip

1 (8 ounce) package cream cheese, softened   227 g
1 cup mayonnaise   240 ml
1 (1 ounce) packet ranch-style salad dressing mix   28 g
½ onion, finely minced

- Combine cream cheese and mayonnaise and beat until creamy. Stir in dressing mix and onion. Chill and serve with fresh vegetables.

Egg and Cheese Dip

5 eggs, hard-boiled, mashed
1 cup mayonnaise   240 ml
½ cup shredded Monterey Jack cheese   120 ml
½ teaspoon prepared mustard   2 ml

- Combine all ingredients in bowl and mix well. Add salt to taste and chill. Serve with wheat crackers.

Cottage Cheese Dip

1 cup small curd cottage cheese	240 ml
½ cup crumbled feta cheese	120 ml
1 teaspoon dried oregano	5 ml
¼ teaspoon lemon juice	1 ml

• Combine all ingredients in blender and process until smooth. Pour into small bowl and serve with celery sticks, fresh broccoli florets or baby carrots.

Beer and Cheese Dip

1 large onion, finely chopped	
2 tablespoons butter	30 ml
1 cup beer	240 ml
1 (2 pound) box Mexican processed cheese	1 kg

• In large saucepan, cook onion in butter, but do not brown; add beer. Cut cheese into large chunks and add to onion and cook on low heat, stirring constantly until all cheese is melted. Serve with tortilla chips.

Easy Cheesy Bean Dip

1 (15 ounce) can refried beans	425 g
1 teaspoon minced garlic	5 ml
1 cup milk	240 ml
1 (16 ounce) package cubed Mexican processed cheese	.5 kg

• In large saucepan, combine beans, garlic and milk and stir on low heat until smooth. Add cheese and stir on low heat until cheese melts. Serve warm with chips.

California Clam Dip

1 (1 ounce) packet dry onion soup mix	28 g
2 (8 ounce) cartons sour cream	2 (227 g)
1 (6 ounce) can minced clams, drained	168 g
2 tablespoons chili sauce	30 ml

- Combine onion soup mix and sour cream and mix well.

- Add clams and chili sauce and chill.

Velvet Clam Dip

1½ (8 ounces) packages cream cheese	1½ (227 g)
¼ cup (½ stick) butter	60 ml
2 (6 ounce) cans minced clams, drained	2 (168 g)
½ teaspoon Worcestershire sauce	2 ml

- Melt cream cheese and butter in double boiler. Add drained minced clams and Worcestershire sauce. Serve hot.

Party Shrimp Dip

1 (8 ounce) package cream cheese, softened	227 g
½ cup mayonnaise	120 ml
1 (6 ounce) can tiny, cooked shrimp, drained	168 g
¾ teaspoon Creole seasoning	4 ml

- Blend cream cheese and mayonnaise in mixer. Stir in shrimp and seasoning. Mix well and chill. Serve with chips.

Hot Cheesy Bean Dip

1 (15 ounce) can Mexican stewed tomatoes	425 g
1 (15 ounce) can pinto beans, drained	425 g
1 (15 ounce) can refried beans	425 g
¼ teaspoon ground cumin	1 ml
¼ teaspoon oregano	1 ml
1 cup shredded cheddar cheese	240 ml

• Preheat oven to 350° (176° C). In bowl, combine tomatoes, pinto beans, refried beans, cumin, oregano and ¼ teaspoon (1 ml) salt. Spoon into 7 x 11-inch (18 x 28 cm) baking dish, cover and bake 15 minutes. Remove cover and sprinkle cheese over top of bean mixture. Return to oven to 5 minutes. Serve with tortilla chips.

Pep-Pep-Pepperoni Dip

2 (8 ounce) packages cream cheese, softened	2 (227 g)
1 (3.5 ounce) package pepperoni slices	100 g
1 (10 ounce) bottle chili sauce	280 g
1 bunch green onions with tops, chopped	

• In mixing bowl, beat cream cheese until creamy. Cut pepperoni slices into smaller pieces. Add pepperoni, chili sauce and green onions to cream cheese and mix well. Chill and serve with chips.

Spinach-Feta Dip

1 (8 ounce) carton sour cream	227 g
1 (8 ounce) package cream cheese, softened	227 g
¾ cup crumbled feta cheese	180 ml
1 (10 ounce) package frozen chopped spinach, thawed	280 g

• In mixing bowl, beat sour cream, cream cheese and 1 teaspoon (5 ml) salt. Fold in feta cheese. Using several paper towels, squeeze spinach until all liquid is drained. Stir into cheese mixture, adding 1 teaspoon (5 ml) minced garlic if you like.

Creamy Sausage Dip

1 (16 ounce) roll sausage	.5 kg
1 teaspoon minced garlic	5 ml
2 (8 ounce) packages cream cheese	2 (227 g)
1 (10 ounce) can tomatoes and green chilies	280 g

- In skillet cook sausage over medium heat until it is slightly brown. Drain well. Stir in garlic, cream cheese and tomatoes and green chilies. On medium heat, stir until cream cheese melts and dip is thoroughly hot. Serve with chips.

Black Bean Dip

2 (15 ounce) cans black beans, rinsed, drained	2 (425 g)
1 sweet onion, finely chopped	
1 green bell pepper, finely chopped	
1 (4 ounce) can chopped pimentos	114 g

Dressing:

3 tablespoons olive oil	45 ml
2 tablespoons red wine vinegar	30 ml
2 teaspoons minced garlic	10 ml
2 teaspoons sugar	10 ml

- Place 1 can of beans in bowl and mash second can with fork and add to whole beans. Add chopped onion, bell pepper and pimentos. In small bowl, combine olive oil, vinegar, garlic, sugar and salt to taste. Stir into bean mixture. Serve at room temperature with tortilla chips. Refrigerate any leftover dip.

Crab Dip Kick

1 (8 ounce) package cream cheese, softened	227 g
3 tablespoons picante sauce	45 ml
2 tablespoons prepared horseradish	30 ml
1 (6 ounce) can crabmeat, drained, flaked	168 g

- In mixing bowl, beat cream cheese until creamy; add picante and horseradish and mix well. Stir in crabmeat and chill. Serve with assorted crackers.

Broccoli-Cheese Dip

1 (10 ounce) can broccoli-cheese soup	280 g
1 (10 ounce) package frozen chopped broccoli, thawed	280 g
½ cup sour cream	120 ml
2 teaspoons dijon-style mustard	10 ml

- In saucepan, combine soup, broccoli, sour cream, mustard and ½ teaspoon (2 ml) salt and mix well. Heat and serve hot.

Broccoli Dip

1 (10 ounce) package frozen chopped broccoli, thawed	280 g
1 (10 ounce) can cream of chicken soup	280 g
1 (12 ounce) package shredded cheddar cheese	340 g
1 (7 ounce) can chopped green chilies	198 g

- In saucepan, cook broccoli for 5 minutes in butter and about ½ teaspoon (2 ml) salt. Add soup, cheese and green chilies and heat until cheese melts. (If chilies are not hot enough, add several dashes of hot sauce.) Serve with tostados.

Red Pepper Artichoke Dip

1 (14 ounce) can artichoke hearts, drained, chopped	396 g
1 cup mayonnaise	240 ml
1½ cups shredded mozzarella cheese	360 ml
½ cup roasted red peppers, drained, chopped	120 ml

- Preheat oven to 350° (176° C). Combine all ingredients and place in greased 8-inch (20 cm) baking dish. Bake 25 minutes or until thoroughly hot.

Steamy Hot Artichoke Dip

1 (14 ounce) can artichoke, drained, chopped	396 g
1¼ cups mayonnaise (not light)	300 ml
1 cup grated parmesan cheese	240 ml
2 teaspoons minced garlic	10 ml

- Preheat oven to 350° (176° C). In bowl, combine artichoke, mayonnaise, parmesan and garlic, mixing well. Spoon into an 8 or 9-inch (20 cm) pyrex pie pan and bake uncovered for 25 minutes. Serve hot with wheat crackers.

Artichoke Bean Dip

1 (14 ounce) jar marinated artichoke hearts, reserving liquid	396 g
2 (15 ounce) cans garbanzo beans, rinsed, drained	2 (425 g)
4 fresh green onions, sliced	
⅓ cup mayonnaise	80 ml

- After artichokes have been drained, coarsely chop artichoke and set aside. In blender, combine beans, green onions and reserved liquid; pulse until smooth. Combine mixture from blender and stir in mayonnaise and a little salt and pepper. Serve with crackers.

Special Guacamole

4 medium avocados, peeled	
3 tablespoons sour cream	45 ml
1 tablespoon hot sauce	15 ml
1½ teaspoons garlic salt	7 ml
2 teaspoons lemon juice	10 ml
2 tablespoons Italian salad dressing	30 ml

• In bowl, mash avocados to desired smoothness and stir in sour cream, hot sauce, garlic salt, lemon juice and Italian dressing. You may want to taste to determine if you need extra salt. Serve with chips.

Party Hearty Dip

2 (15 ounce) cans black beans, drained, mashed	2 (425 g)
1 (16 ounce) jar mild salsa	.5 kg
1 (8 ounce) package shredded Monterey Jack cheese	227 g
2 teaspoons ground cumin	10 ml
1 teaspoon garlic powder	5 ml
1 (4.3 ounce) package real crumbled bacon	114 g

• In saucepan combine beans and salsa (use hot salsa if you want more spice), stir in cheese, cumin and garlic powder. Heat on low-medium, stirring constantly until mixture is hot. Stir in crumbled bacon and transfer to serving bowl and serve with chips.

Holy Guacamole

4 avocados, peeled, seeded	
½ cup salsa	120 ml
¼ cup sour cream	60 ml
Tortilla chips	

• Mash avocados with fork and mix with salsa, sour cream and 1 teaspoon (5 ml) salt. Serve with tortilla chips.

Dipping Sauce for Leftover Ham

¾ cup smooth peanut butter   180 ml
2 tablespoons soy sauce   30 ml
½ cup honey   120 ml
3 tablespoons lime juice   45 ml

- In bowl, combine all dip ingredients, mixing well. Cut ham in bite-size chunks and use toothpicks for ham and dip-dip-dip!

Quickie Shrimp Dunk

1 (8 ounce) package cream cheese, softened   227 g
1 (10 ounce) bottle of cocktail sauce   280 g
1 teaspoon Italian herb seasoning   5 ml
1 (6 ounce) can tiny shrimp, drained   168 g

- Place cream cheese in mixing bowl and beat until smooth.

- Add remaining ingredients and chill. Serve with crackers.

Cream-Cheese Dip for Apples

1 (8 ounce) package cream cheese, softened   227 g
2 tablespoons powdered sugar   30 ml
3 tablespoons orange juice concentrate, thawed 45 ml
1 teaspoon ground cinnamon   5 ml

- In mixing bowl, combine all ingredients and mix until well blended.

Caramel-Apple Dip

1 (8 ounce) package cream cheese, softened	227 g
1 cup packed brown sugar	240 ml
1 teaspoon vanilla	5 ml
½ cup chopped dry-roasted peanuts	120 ml

• With mixer beat together cream cheese, brown sugar and vanilla until creamy. Stir in peanuts and chill. Serve with crisp apple slices.

Peachy Fruit Dip

1 (15 ounce) can sliced peaches, drained	425 g
½ cup marshmallow cream	120 ml
1 (3 ounce) package cream cheese, cubed	84 g
teaspoon ground nutmeg	.5 ml

• In blender or food processor, combine all ingredients. Serve with assorted fresh fruit.

Curried Cheese Spread

2 (8 ounce) packages cream cheese, softened	2 (227 g)
1 (10 ounce) jar mango chutney	280 g
1 (5 ounce) package slivered almonds, toasted	143 g
2 teaspoons curry powder	10 ml

• In blender, combine cream cheese, chutney, almonds and curry powder until creamy. Cover and chill. Shape into round balls. Serve with assorted crackers or apple slices.

Hot Artichoke Spread

1 (14 ounce) can artichoke hearts, drained,	
finely chopped	396 g
1 cup mayonnaise	240 ml
1 cup grated parmesan cheese	240 ml
1 (1 ounce) package Italian salad dressing mix	28 g

- Remove tough outer leaves and chop artichoke hearts. Combine all ingredients and mix thoroughly. Pour into 8-inch (20 cm) baking pan. Bake at 350° (176° C) for 20 minutes. Serve hot with assorted crackers.

Devil's Spread

1 (4 ounce) can deviled ham	114 g
¾ cup mayonnaise	180 ml
1 tablespoon grated onion	15 ml
1 (4 ounce) can chopped green chilies, drained	114 g

- Mix all ingredients. Spread on wheat crackers.

Black Olive Spread

1 (8 ounce) package cream cheese, softened	227 g
½ cup mayonnaise	120 ml
1 (4 ounce) can chopped black olives	114 g
3 green onions with tops, finely chopped	

- Blend cream cheese and mayonnaise until smooth. Add olives and onions and chill. Spread on slices of party rye bread.

Sweet Cheezy-Garlic Spread

2 (8 ounce) packages cream cheese, softened	2 (227 g)
¼ cup apricot preserves	60 ml
1 teaspoon minced garlic	5 ml
¼ cup finely chopped walnuts	60 ml
3 fresh green onions, finely chopped (only green portion)	

- In mixing bowl, combine cream cheese and apricot preserves and beat until well blended. Stir in garlic, walnuts and green onions. Refrigerate. Serve with assorted crackers.

Artichoke-Cheese Spread

2 (8 ounce) packages cream cheese, softened	2 (227 g)
1½ cups grated parmesan cheese	360 ml
1 tablespoon lemon juice	15 ml
1 teaspoon garlic salt	5 ml
¼ cup finely chopped green onions	60 ml
1 (14 ounce) can artichoke hearts, drained, chopped	396 g

- In mixing bowl, beat together cream cheese, parmesan cheese, lemon juice and garlic salt. Stir in green onion, artichoke hearts and mix well. Chill and serve with wheat crackers.

Pineapple-Island Spread

2 (8 ounce) packages cream cheese, softened	2 (227 g)
1 (8 ounce) carton sour cream	227 g
1 (8 ounce) can crushed pineapple with juice	227 g
½ cup finely chopped pecans	120 ml

- In mixing bowl, combine cream cheese and sour cream and beat until creamy. Fold in pineapple and pecans and mix well; chill.

Shrimp Squares Deluxe

1 (6 ounce) can shrimp, drained, chopped	168 g
1 cup mayonnaise	240 ml
1 cup shredded cheddar cheese	240 ml
10 - 12 slices white bread, trimmed, cut in 4 squares	

- Combine shrimp, mayonnaise and cheese. Spread shrimp mixture on bread squares and broil until bubbly.

Avocado Olé

3 large ripe avocados, mashed	
1 tablespoon fresh lemon juice	15 ml
1 (1 ounce) packet dry onion soup mix	28 g
1 (8 ounce) carton sour cream	227 g

- Mix avocados with lemon juice and blend in soup mix, sour cream and salt to taste. Serve with chips or crackers.

Chili-Cheese Bites

6 slices white sandwich bread	
1 (14 ounce) package shredded cheddar cheese	396 g
½ cup (1 stick) butter, softened	120 ml
¾ teaspoon chili powder	4 ml

- Trim bread crusts and cut each slice into 4 squares. Combine cheese, butter and chili powder and mix well. Place heaping teaspoonful (5 ml) of mixture on each bread square and place on baking sheet. Bake at 375° (190° C) for 10 minutes or until puffy and light brown.

Olive-Cheese Empanadas

1 cup pimento-stuffed green olives or black olives, chopped, divided	240 ml
1 cup finely shredded cheddar cheese	240 ml
4 tablespoons mayonnaise	60 ml
1 (15 ounce) package of 2 refrigerated piecrusts	425 g

- Preheat oven to 450° (230° C). Combine olives, cheese and mayonnaise.

- Use 3-inch (8 cm) biscuit cutter to cut each piecrust into 12 rounds. Place 1 teaspoon (5 ml) olive mixture in center of pastry round. Fold side of pastry to other side and press edges together.

- Crimp edge with thumb and forefinger or use tines of fork to seal edges. If pastry begins to dry it will not seal properly. Dip finger in water and lightly brush edges and seal.

- Place on baking sheet and bake for about 10 minutes or until golden brown.

Bacon-Wrapped Water Chestnuts

1 (8 ounce) can whole water chestnuts, drained	227 g
¼ cup soy sauce	60 ml
¼ teaspoon cayenne pepper	1 ml
½ pound bacon, cut in thirds	227 g

- Marinate water chestnuts for 1 hour in soy sauce and cayenne pepper. Wrap bacon around water chestnuts and secure with toothpick. Bake at 375° (190° C) for 20 minutes or until bacon is done. Drain and serve hot.

Olive-Cheese Appetizers

1 cup chopped pimento-stuffed olives	240 ml
2 fresh green onions, finely chopped	
1½ cups shredded Monterey Jack cheese	360 ml
½ cup mayonnaise	120 ml
6 English muffins, cut in half	

- In large bowl, combine olives, onions, cheese and mayonnaise; mix well. Spread on muffins and bake at 375° (190° C) until bubbly.

- Cut muffins into quarters and serve hot.

Artichoke Bites

1½ cups mayonnaise	360 ml
¾ cup freshly grated parmesan cheese	180 ml
1 (4 ounce) can chopped green chilies	114 g
1 (14 ounce) jar artichoke hearts, chopped	396 g

- Combine mayonnaise, parmesan cheese, green chilies and artichoke hearts. (Remove any spikes or tough leaves from artichokes.) Place 1 teaspoon (5 ml) mixture on bite-size toast rounds. Broil until light brown.

Baked Cheese Snacks

1½ cups baking mix	360 ml
2 eggs, slightly beaten	
1 (4 ounce) can chopped green chilies	114 g
1 cup shredded cheddar cheese	240 ml

- Preheat oven to 375° (190° C). Blend together baking mix, eggs and green chilies and stir in cheese. Drop dough by teaspoonfuls about 2 inches (5 cm) apart on sprayed baking sheet. Bake for 12 minutes or until golden brown. Serve warm.

Sausage Cheese Balls

2 pounds sausage, one hot, one regular	1 kg
1½ cups biscuit mix	360 ml
1 (16 ounce) package shredded sharp cheddar cheese	.5 kg
½ cup finely chopped celery and onion	120 ml
½ teaspoon garlic powder, optional	2 ml

• Preheat oven to 375° (190° C). Combine all ingredients and form into 1-inch (2.5 cm) balls. Place balls on ungreased cookie sheet. Bake about 15 minutes. Balls can be made and frozen; then baked at a later time.

Sausage Rounds

1 (8 ounce) package crescent dinner rolls	227 g
½ teaspoon garlic powder	2 ml
½ cup grated cheddar cheese	120 ml
1 pound sausage, uncooked	.5 kg

• Open package of rolls, smooth out dough with rolling pin and seal seams. Sprinkle dough with garlic powder and cheese.

• Break up sausage with hands and spread thin layer sausage over rolls. Roll into a log. Wrap in wax paper and freeze for several hours.

• Slice into ¼-inch (.6 cm) rounds. Place on baking sheet and bake at 350° (176° C) for 20 minutes or until light brown.

Bits of Frank

1 (8 count) package frankfurters	
1 (8 ounce) package cornbread-muffin mix	227 g
½ teaspoon chili powder	2 ml
½ cup milk	120 ml
1 (10 ounce) bottle chili sauce	280 g

• Cut franks into 1-inch (2.5 cm) slices. Combine corn-muffin mix, chili powder and milk. Add frankfurters slices to corn-muffin mix and stir well to coat each piece. Drop one at a time into hot oil in deep fryer. Fry for 2 minutes or until brown; drain. Serve warm with chili sauce for dipping.

Bubbly Franks

1 (10 count) package wieners	
½ cup chili sauce	120 ml
½ cup packed brown sugar	120 ml
½ cup bourbon	120 ml

• Cut wieners into half inch slices. Combine chili sauce, sugar and bourbon in saucepan. Add wieners to sauce and simmer for 30 minutes. Serve in chafing dish.

Need A Snack Fix, Quick

Large tortilla chips	
1 (15 ounce) can refried beans	425 g
1 (8 ounce) package cheddar cheese	227 g
1 (16 ounce) jar chunky salsa	.5 kg

• Spread large tortilla chips on microwave-safe plate. Top each chip with dab of refried beans and sprinkle of cheese. Top with heaping teaspoon (5 ml) of salsa. Microwave on HIGH just until cheese melts.

Make Your Own Cajun Chips

2 teaspoons Cajun seasoning	10 ml
1 teaspoon paprika	5 ml
¼ teaspoon sugar	1 ml
½ teaspoon dried thyme	2 ml
½ teaspoon garlic powder	2 ml
10 (6-inch) flour tortillas	10 (15 cm)

- Preheat oven to 375° (190° C). Combine Cajun seasoning, paprika, sugar, thyme, garlic powder and ½ teaspoon (2 ml) salt. Spread tortillas on 2 baking sheets and coat with cooking spray and sprinkle Cajun seasoning over tortillas. Cut tortillas into wedges. Bake for 6 minutes or until crispy. Cool and store in airtight baggies.

Cheese Drops

2 cups biscuit mix	480 ml
⅓ cup sour cream	80 ml
1 egg	
1 (4 ounce) can chopped green chilies, drained	114 g
1½ cups shredded sharp cheddar cheese	360 ml

- Preheat oven to 375° (190° C). In bowl, combine biscuit mix, sour cream, egg and green chilies and mix until well blended. Stir in cheese, mixture will be thick. Drop by heaping teaspoons onto a greased baking sheet. Bake 10 minutes or until golden brown. Serve warm.

Cucumber Squares

1 (8 ounce) package cream cheese, softened	227 g
½ teaspoon dillweed	2 ml
3 medium cucumbers, peeled, grated	
1 (1 ounce) packet dry ranch-style salad dressing mix	28 g

- In mixing bowl, combine cream cheese and dillweed and beat until creamy. Fold in grated cucumbers and ranch dressing mix. Spread on pumpernickel or rye bread slices.

Deviled Ham Roll-Ups

1 (8 count) package refrigerated crescent dinner rolls	
1 (2 ounce) can deviled ham	57 g
½ cup sour cream	120 ml
1 teaspoon dijon-style mustard	5 ml

- Preheat oven to 350° (176° C). Unroll crescent rolls on sheet of wax paper and form triangles. In bowl, combine deviled ham, sour cream and mustard and spoon heaping teaspoon (5 ml) mixture on each roll.

- Spread filling and leave ½-inch (1.2 cm) at edge. Roll each crescent from wide end to point. Place point-side down on sprayed baking pan and bake 15 minutes or until light brown. Serve warm.

Mexican Fudge

1 (16 ounce) package shredded American cheese, divided	.5 kg
4 eggs, beaten	
⅔ cup jalapeno green sauce	160 ml
1 teaspoon Worcestershire sauce	5 ml

- Spread half cheese in sprayed 9 x 13-inch (23 x 33 cm) baking dish. Combine eggs with green sauce and Worcestershire and pour over cheese in dish. Add remaining cheese.

- Bake at 350° (176° C) for 30 minutes. Cut into squares to serve. May be served hot or room temperature.

English Muffin Pizza

English muffins, halved
Canned or bottled pizza sauce
Sliced salami or pepperoni
Grated mozzarella or cheddar cheese

• Split muffins in half. Spread pizza sauce on muffins. Add salami or pepperoni. Top with grated cheese and place under broiler until cheese melts and begins to bubble.

Puffy Taco Balls

½ pound pork sausage	**.5 kg**
1 (8 ounce) package shredded cheddar cheese	**227 g**
⅓ cup mild taco sauce	**80 ml**
1½ cups biscuit mix	**360 ml**

• Preheat oven to 375° (190° C). In skillet, brown sausage, drain and crumble; allow to cool. In mixing bowl, combine sausage, cheese, taco sauce and biscuit mix, mixing well. Form into 1-inch (2.5 cm) balls and place on baking sheet.

• Bake about 18 minutes or until balls are light brown.

Shrimp-Stuffed Eggs

8 eggs, hard-boiled	
¼ cup mayonnaise	**60 ml**
1 (6 ounce) can tiny shrimp, drained	**168 g**
2 tablespoons sweet pickle relish, drained	**30 ml**

• Cut eggs in half lengthwise and set aside egg whites. In small bowl, mash egg yolks with mayonnaise. Add shrimp and pickle relish and mix well. Refill egg whites and refrigerate.

Spicy Cheese Bites

1 cup flour	240 ml
½ teaspoon cayenne pepper	2 ml
1 (8 ounce) package finely shredded sharp cheddar	
cheese	227 g
½ cup (1 stick) butter, softened	120 ml

- Preheat oven to 375° (190° C). In bowl, combine flour, cayenne pepper, a little salt, cheese and butter. Mixture will be hard to combine, so the easiest way is to work with your hands until dough forms a ball. Place dough on large piece of wax paper and form into log. Roll tightly in paper and chill.

- Slice dough into ¼-inch (.6 cm) rounds and place on baking sheet 1-inch (2.5 cm) apart. Bake about 17 to 18 minutes or until edges are golden. Cool before serving.

Border Queso

2 canned jalapeno peppers with liquid	
1 (16 ounce) package cubed processed cheese	.5 kg
1 (4 ounce) jar pimentos, drained, chopped	114 g
3 green onions with tops, chopped	

- Seed and chop jalapeno peppers. Combine peppers, cheese, pimentos and onions in saucepan. Heat on low and stir constantly, until cheese melts. Stir in 1 tablespoon (15 ml) jalapeno liquid. Serve with tortilla chips.

Spinach Pinwheels

1 (8 ounce) can crescent dinner rolls	227 g
1 (8 ounce) package garlic-herb spreadable cheese, softened	227 g
6 thin slices cooked deli ham	
30 fresh spinach leaves, stems removed	

• Preheat oven to 350° (176° C). Separate crescent dough into 4 rectangles and press perforations to seal. Generously spread rectangles with cheese, leaving ¼-inch (.6 cm) around edge without cheese. Top with ham slices and spinach leaves.

• Starting at short side of dough, roll each rectangle and press edges to seal. Refrigerate rolls for at least 30 minutes and slice each roll into 6 slices. Place slices on ungreased baking sheet and bake about 15 minutes or until lightly brown.

Tuna Melt Appetizer

1 (10 ounce) package frozen spinach, drained	280 g
2 (6 ounce) cans white tuna in water, drained, flaked	2 (168 g)
¾ cup mayonnaise	180 ml
1½ cups shredded mozzarella cheese, divided	360 ml

• Drain spinach well with several paper towels. In large bowl, combine spinach, tuna, mayonnaise and 1 cup (240 ml) cheese and mix well.

• Spoon into buttered, pie plate and bake at 350° (176° C) for 15 minutes. Remove from oven and sprinkle remaining cheese over top. Bake another 5 minutes. Serve with crackers.

Stuffed Jalapenos

12 - 15 medium jalapeno chiles with stems attached	
1 (8 ounce) package cream cheese, softened	227 g
¾ cup finely shredded Monterey Jack cheese	180 ml
3 slices cooked ham, chopped very fine	
1 tablespoon lime juice	15 ml
1 tablespoon garlic powder	15 ml

- Preheat oven to 325° (162° C). Cut (using rubber gloves) each jalapeno lengthwise through stem and remove ribs and seeds.

- In bowl, combine cream cheese, Jack cheese, ham, lime juice and garlic powder, beat until well blended. Fill each jalapeno half with cheese mixture. Place on foil lined baking sheet. Bake 15 minutes. Cool slightly before serving.

Cheese Straws

1 (5 ounce) package piecrust mix	143 g
¾ cup shredded cheddar cheese	180 ml
Cayenne pepper	
¼ teaspoon garlic powder	1 ml

- Prepare piecrust according to package directions. Roll into rectangular shape. Press cheese into dough and sprinkle cayenne pepper and garlic powder over cheese. Fold dough over once to cover cheese. Roll to make ¼-inch (.6 cm) thickness.

- Cut dough into 3 x ½-inch (8 x 1.2 cm) strips and place on lightly sprayed baking sheet. Bake at 350° (176° C) for 12 to 15 minutes.

Turkey Pizza

4 (8-inch) flour tortillas   4 (20 cm)

Topping:

2 cups deli smoked turkey, diced   480 ml
1 (11 ounce) can mexicorn, drained   312 g
1 (15 ounce) can black beans, rinsed, drained   425 g
2 tablespoons lemon juice   30 ml
1 cup Monterey Jack cheese with jalapeno peppers   240 ml

- Preheat oven to 350° (176° C). Place tortillas on greased baking sheet and bake 10 minutes or until edges are light brown. Remove from oven, stack and press down to flatten.

- In skillet with a little oil, combine diced turkey, corn and black beans. Heat, stirring constantly until mixture is thoroughly hot; stir in lime juice.

- Place tortillas on baking sheet and spoon about ¾ cup (180 ml) turkey-corn mixture on each tortilla. Sprinkle cheese on top of each pizza and return to oven for 2 minutes or just until cheese melts.

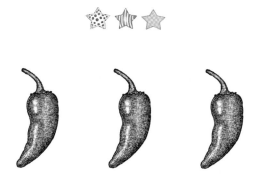

Skillet Nachos

½ (16 ounce) package tortilla chips	½ (.5 kg)
1 (8 ounce) can whole kernel corn, drained	227 g
1 cup chili beans (from 15 ounce can)	240 ml/425 g
½ cup thick-and-chunky salsa, extra salsa for garnish	120 ml
1 (8 ounce) package shredded 4-cheese blend	227 g
1 (4 ounce) can ripe olives, sliced	114 g

- Arrange tortilla chips in single layer in large 12-inch (32 cm) skillet (use a skillet that you can take to the table). In saucepan, combine corn, beans and salsa and heat just until hot and bubbly.

- Spoon salsa mixture over tortilla chips, then sprinkle on about three-fourths cheese. Cover skillet and cook on medium high heat about 5 minutes or until cheese melts. To serve, sprinkle ripe olives and remaining cheese over top. You may want to serve with more salsa.

Cheesy Quick Broccoli Quesadillas

1 (8 ounce) package shredded cheddar cheese	227 g
1 (10 ounce) package frozen chopped broccoli, well drained	280 g
⅓ cup salsa	80 ml
8 (6 inch) flour tortillas	8 (15 cm)

- In bowl, combine cheese, broccoli and salsa and mix well. Spoon about ¼ cup (60 ml) cheese-broccoli mixture onto 1 side of each tortilla and fold tortilla over filling.

- Spray large non-stick skillet with cooking spray and cook 2 quesadillas at a time on medium heat. Cook about 3 minutes on both sides or until tortillas are light brown.

Taste-Tempting Hot Squares

1 cup grated parmesan cheese	240 ml
1 cup mozzarella cheese	240 ml
2 (14 ounce) cans artichoke hearts, drained, chopped	2 (396 g)
1 (8 ounce) carton chive and onion cream cheese	227 g
2 (8 ounce) tubes refrigerated crescent rolls	2 (227 g)

• Preheat oven to 350° (176° C). In mixing bowl, combine both cheeses, chopped artichokes and cream cheese and beat until well blended.

• Unroll both tubes of dough and press into greased 10 x 15-inch (25 x 38 cm) baking pan, making it rectangle shape and sealing seams and perforations. Spread with artichoke mixture. Bake for 20 minutes or until crust is light golden brown. Cut into squares to serve.

Cinnamon Pecans

1 pound pecan halves	.5 kg
1 egg white, slightly beaten	
2 tablespoons cinnamon	30 ml
¾ cup sugar	180 ml

• Combine pecans and egg white and mix well. Sprinkle with mixture of cinnamon and sugar. Stir until all pecans are well coated.

• Spread on baking sheet and bake at 325° (162° C) for about 20 minutes. Cool and store in covered container.

Crispy-Crunchy Treats

2 (10 ounce) packages marshmallows	2 (280 g)
½ cup (1 stick) butter	120 ml
12 cups crisp rice cereal	3 L
1 cup coarsely chopped walnuts, toasted	240 ml

- In large saucepan, combine marshmallows and butter; cook on low-medium heat, stirring several times until marshmallows are melted. Stir in half cereal and walnuts until well combined. Stir in remaining cereal and walnuts

- Transfer mixture to well-buttered 9 x 13-inch (23 x 33 cm) baking dish, spreading evenly with back of large buttered spoon or spatula. Cool completely. Cut into large squares and then into triangles.

Barbecued Walnuts

3 tablespoons butter, melted	45 ml
¼ cup Worcestershire sauce	60 ml
3 dashes hot sauce	
2 tablespoons ketchup	30 ml
5 cups walnut halves	1.3 L

- Preheat oven to 400° (204° C). In bowl, combine butter, Worcestershire sauce, hot sauce ketchup and a little touch of salt, mixing well. Pour over walnut halves and stir until all walnuts are well coated.

- Bake uncovered in a 9 x 13-inch (23 x 33 cm) baking pan, stirring every 5 minutes, for 20 minutes. Remove from oven and pour walnuts out onto 2 layers of paper towels. Cool to room temperature.

Sweet Nibblers

1 (6 ounce) package semi-sweet chocolate chips	168 g
⅓ cup peanut butter	80 ml
1 cup chopped peanuts	240 ml
7 cups Crispix cereal	1.6 L
1½ cups powdered sugar	360 ml

- In heavy saucepan over low heat, melt chocolate, stirring constantly. When melted, stir in peanut butter and peanuts until well mixed. Add cereal, stirring until evenly coated.

- Place powdered sugar in a large baggie and add coated cereal; close bag. Toss cereal gently until cereal is evenly coated. Store in airtight container in refrigerator.

Creamy Strawberry Punch

1 (10 ounce) package frozen strawberries, thawed	280 g
½ gallon strawberry ice cream, softened	2 L
2 (2 liter) bottles ginger ale, chilled	2 L
Fresh strawberries	

- Process frozen strawberries through blender. Combine strawberries, chunks of ice cream and ginger ale in punch bowl.

- Stir and serve immediately with fresh strawberries.

Apple-Party Punch

3 cups sparkling apple cider	710 ml
2 cups apple juice	480 ml
1 cup pineapple juice	240 ml
½ cup brandy	120 ml

- Combine all ingredients and freeze. Remove punch from freezer 30 minutes before serving. Place in small punch bowl and break into chunks. Stir until slushy.

Pina Colada Punch

1 (46 ounce) can pineapple juice, chilled	1.3 kg
1 (20 ounce) can crushed pineapple with juice	567 g
1 (15 ounce) can cream of coconut	425 g
1 (32 ounce) bottle lemon-lime carbonated drink, chilled	1 kg

- Combine all ingredients. Serve over ice cubes.

Perfect Party Punch

1 (12 ounce) can frozen limeade concentrate	340 g
1 (46 ounce) can pineapple juice, chilled	1.3 kg
1 (46 ounce) apricot nectar, chilled	1.3 kg
1 quart ginger ale, chilled	1 L

- Dilute limeade concentrate according to directions on can. Add pineapple juice and apricot nectar and stir well. When ready to serve, add ginger ale.

Cranberry Punch

2 (28 ounce) bottles ginger ale, chilled	2 (794 g)
1 (48 ounce) can pineapple juice, chilled	1.3 kg
1 quart cranberry juice, chilled	1 L
1 quart pineapple sherbet, broken up	1 L

- Pour all ingredients in punch bowl. Serve.

Cranberry-Lemon Punch

2 quarts cranberry juice	2 L
1 (6 ounce) can lemonade concentrate, thawed	168 g
⅔ cup maraschino cherry juice	160 ml
1 (2 liter) lemon-lime soda, chilled	2 L

- Combine all ingredients and mix well.

Best Tropical Punch

1 (46 ounce) can pineapple juice	1.3 kg
1 (46 ounce) can apricot nectar	1.3 kg
3 (6 ounce) cans frozen limeade concentrate, thawed	3 (168 g)
3 quarts ginger ale, chilled	3 L

- Combine all ingredients and stir in ginger ale to serve.

Apricot Punch

1 (12 ounce) can apricot nectar	340 g
1 (6 ounce) can frozen orange juice concentrate, thawed	168 g
2 tablespoons lemon juice	30 ml
1 (2 liter) bottle ginger ale, chilled	2 L

- Combine apricot nectar, orange juice concentrate, lemon juice and 1 cup (240 ml) water. Chill. When ready to serve stir in ginger ale.

Tropical Fruit Smoothie

2 (8 ounce) cartons vanilla yogurt	2 (227 g)
1 cup fresh frozen blueberries	240 ml
1 cup fresh frozen peach slices	240 ml
1 (8 ounce) can pineapple chunks, drained	227 g

- Process all ingredients in blender until smooth.

Banana-Peach Smoothie

3 ripe bananas, sliced	
2 cups frozen (or fresh) peaches	480 ml
1 cup buttermilk	240 ml
¼ cup orange juice	60 ml
2 tablespoons honey	30 ml

- Place all ingredients in blender and process until smooth, stopping to scrape down sides. Serve immediately.

Watermelon Smoothie

About 2 cups watermelon cubes, seeded	480 ml
2 tablespoons honey	30 ml
Dash of cinnamon	
1 (8 ounce) carton lemon yogurt	227 g

- With blender puree watermelon, honey and cinnamon quickly, being careful not to over blend. Pulse in lemon yogurt and serve immediately.

Fruit Smoothies

2 cups apple juice	480 ml
1 cup frozen strawberries and raspberries, thawed	240 ml
1 large banana, sliced	
2 cups raspberry sherbet	240 ml

- In blender, combine apple juice, strawberries, raspberries and banana; process just 1 minute, then add raspberry sherbet and process until well blended. Serve immediately.

Strawberry Smoothie

2 bananas, peeled, sliced	
1 pint fresh strawberries, washed, quartered	.5 kg
1 (8 ounce) container strawberry yogurt	227 g
¼ cup orange juice	60 ml

- Place all ingredients in blender. Process until smooth.

Orange Slush

1 (20 ounce) can crushed pineapple with juice	567 g
½ cup frozen pina colada concentrate	120 ml
1 pint orange sherbet	.5 kg
½ cup orange juice	120 ml

- Combine all ingredients in blender. Cover and blend on high speed until smooth. Serve immediately in sherbet glasses.

Blue Moon Slushes

1 (8 ounce) carton blueberry yogurt	227 g
1 cup chilled grape juice	240 ml
½ cup milk	120 ml

- In blender, combine yogurt, grape juice and milk, cover and blend. Add ice cubes and blend until slushy. Serve immediately.

Peanut Power Shake

2 bananas, cut up	
½ cup frozen orange juice concentrate, thawed	120 ml
¼ cup peanut butter	60 ml
¼ cup milk	60 ml

- Combine all ingredients in blender container. Cover and blend until smooth. Blend 1 cup (240 ml) ice cubes until smooth.

Purple Shakes

1 (6 ounce) can frozen grape juice concentrate,	
thawed	168 g
1 cup milk	240 ml
2½ cups vanilla ice cream	600 ml
2 tablespoons sugar	30 ml

- In blender, combine all ingredients. Cover and blend at high speed for 30 seconds. Serve immediately.

Breakfast Shake

1 banana, cut into 1-inch (2.5 cm) slices	
1 mango, peeled, cubed	
1½ cups pineapple juice or orange juice, chilled	360 ml
1 (8 ounce) container vanilla yogurt	227 g

- Process banana slices, mango, juice and yogurt in blender until smooth. Scrape sides of blender and mix. Serve immediately.

Banana-Strawberry Shake

1 (10 ounce) package frozen strawberries, partially	
thawed	280 g
2 bananas, sliced in 1-inch pieces	2.5 cm
1 cup half-and-half cream	240 ml
½ cup sugar	120 ml
1 quart vanilla ice cream	1 L

- In blender, combine fruit, cream and sugar. Cover and blend at high speed for about 30 seconds. Add ice cream and blend for about 45 seconds. Serve immediately.

Creamy Orange Drink

1¾ cups milk	420 ml
½ pint vanilla ice cream	227 g
⅓ cup frozen orange juice concentrate	80 ml
1 teaspoon non-dairy creamer	5 ml

• In blender, combine all ingredients and blend until smooth.

Strawberry Cooler

1 cup sliced fresh strawberries	240 ml
½ cup milk	120 ml
⅓ cup sugar (or equal of Splenda)	80 ml
1 pint frozen strawberry yogurt	.5 kg

• Place all ingredients in blender. Cover and blend on high speed until smooth, about 30 seconds.

Berry Delight

1 (8 ounce) carton vanilla yogurt	227 g
1 ripe banana, cut in 1-inch pieces	
1 cup fresh or frozen raspberries	240 ml
1 pint raspberry sherbet	.5 kg

• Place all ingredients in blender and process until thick and smooth. Serve immediately.

Banana Split Float

2 ripe bananas, mashed
3 cups milk   710 ml
1 (10 ounce) package frozen sweetened strawberries,
     thawed   280 g
1½ pints chocolate ice cream, divided   .7 kg

- Place bananas in blender and add milk, strawberries and ½ pint (227 g) chocolate ice cream. Beat just until they blend. Pour into tall, chilled glasses and top each with scoop of chocolate ice cream.

Orange Ice Cream Soda

2 large scoop orange sherbet
1 large scoop vanilla ice cream
1 (12 ounce) can orange soda, chilled   340 g
1 can redi-whip whipped topping

- Place sherbet and ice cream in tall 16-inch (40 cm) glass, slowly pour some of orange soda into glass, mixing well with spoon. Top with dash of whipped topping. Serve with straw and long teaspoon.

Party Orange Sipper

2½ cups vodka   600 ml
4 cups orange juice   1 L
2 (12 ounce) cans lemon-lime soft drink   2 (340 g)
⅓ cup maraschino cherry juice   80 ml

- In pitcher, combine vodka, orange juice and lemon-lime soft drink. Fill 8 glasses with crushed ice and pour vodka-orange juice mixture over ice. Spoon about 2 teaspoons (10 ml) cherry juice into each glass, but do not stir. Serve immediately.

Pineapple-Strawberry Cooler

2 cups milk	480 ml
1 (20 ounce) can crushed pineapple, chilled	567 g
½ pint vanilla ice cream	227 g
1 pint strawberry ice cream	.5 kg

- In mixing bowl, combine milk, pineapple and vanilla ice cream until they blend. Pour into tall glasses and top with scoop of strawberry ice cream.

Spiced Coffee

1 cup instant coffee	240 ml
4 teaspoons grated lemon peel	20 ml
4 teaspoons ground cinnamon	20 ml
1 teaspoon ground cloves	5 ml

- In small jar, combine all ingredients and cover tightly.

- For each serving, spoon 2 teaspoons (10 ml) coffee mix into coffee cup and stir in ¾ cup (180 ml) boiling water. Sweeten to taste.

Strawberry Drink

¾ cup milk	180 ml
¾ cup applesauce	180 ml
1 small ripe banana, halved	
¾ cup strawberries	180 ml
8 - 10 ice cubes	

- In blender, combine all ingredients, cover and process until smooth. Serve immediately in chilled glasses.

Sweet Orange Fluff

1¾ cups milk	420 ml
½ pint vanilla ice cream	227 g
⅓ cup frozen orange juice concentrate	80 ml
1 teaspoon non-dairy creamer	5 ml

- In blender, combine all ingredients, and blend until smooth.

Strawberry Lemonade

1 (16 ounce) package frozen strawberries, thawed	.5 kg
1 (10 ounce) jar maraschino cherries (without stems) with juice	280 g
2 cups sugar	480 ml
1 cup lemon juice	240 ml

- Place strawberries, cherries, sugar and lemon juice in blender; blend until smooth, stopping to scrape down sides. Pour mixture through strainer and pour into pitcher, discarding solids.

- Stir in 3 cups (710 ml) cold water, mixing well and serve over chipped ice.

Limeade Cooler

1½ pints lime sherbet	.7 kg
1 (6 ounce) can frozen limeade concentrate	168 g
3 cups milk	710 ml
Lime slices to garnish, optional	

- Beat lime sherbet in mixing bowl and add concentrated limeade and milk. Blend all ingredients. Top each glass with lime sherbet. Serve immediately.

Lemonade Tea

2 family-size tea bags	
½ cup sugar	120 ml
1 (12 ounce) can frozen lemonade	340 g
1 quart ginger ale, chilled	1 L

- Steep tea in 3 quarts (3 L) water and mix with sugar and lemonade. Add ginger ale just before serving.

Spiced Iced Tea

2 quarts tea	2 L
⅔ cup sugar	160 ml
1 (12 ounce) can frozen lemonade concentrate, thawed	340 g
1 (2 liter) ginger ale, chilled	2 L

- Combine tea, sugar and lemonade and chill. Just before serving, add chilled ginger ale.

Alamo Splash

¼ cup tequila	60 ml
¼ cup orange juice	60 ml
¼ cup pineapple juice	60 ml
Splash lemon-lime soda	

- Mix with cracked ice and pour into Collins glass.

White Sangria

4 cups dry white wine	1 L
1 cup silver rum	240 ml
½ cup orange liqueur	120 ml
Thin slices of lemon and limes	
2 cups club soda, chilled	480 ml
Ice cubes	

• In 3-quart (3 L) pitcher, combine wine, rum and orange liqueur and add lemon and lime slices. Cover and chill. When ready to serve, stir in club soda and about 2 cups (480 ml) ice cubes.

Holiday Egg Nog

1 gallon refrigerated egg nog	4 L
1 pint whipping cream	.5 kg
1 quart brandy	1 L
½ gallon vanilla ice cream, softened	2 L

• Mix all ingredients. Serve in individual cups, sprinkle with nutmeg and serve immediately.

Southwest Pina Colada

1 (8 ounce) can crushed pineapple with juice	227 g
1 (7 ounce) can cream of coconut	198 g
1 cup rum	240 ml
Ice cubes	

• Combine all ingredients in blender, except ice and mix. Add enough ice for desired consistency and process until liquid is "slushy".

Chocolate-Mint Fizz

¼ cup creme de menthe	60 ml
¼ cup creme de cocoa	60 ml
1 pint vanilla ice cream	.5 kg
1 pint chocolate ice cream	.5 kg

- Place liqueurs into blender container. Add ice creams gradually and blend until smooth after each addition.

Peach Delight

¾ cup pink lemonade concentrate, thawed	180 ml
¾ cup vodka	180 ml
3 - 4 peaches, pitted, peeled	

- Place all ingredients in blender. Mix well. Add crushed ice and blend until smooth.

Easy Frozen Strawberry Margarita

1 (10 ounce) can frozen strawberries	280 g
1 (6 ounce) can frozen limeade concentrate, thawed	168 g
1 (6 ounce) can tequila	168 g

- Pour all ingredients and ice into blender and process until smooth. Pour into margarita glasses.

Kahlua® Frosty

1 cup coffee liqueur	240 ml
1 pint vanilla ice cream	.5 kg
1 cup half-and-half cream	240 ml
¼ teaspoon almond extract	1 ml

- In blender combine all ingredients and 1 heaping cup (240 ml) ice cubes. Blend until smooth. Serve immediately.

Coffee Liqueur

1 cup instant coffee granules	240 ml
4 cups sugar	1 L
1 quart vodka	1 L
3 tablespoons Mexican vanilla	45 ml

- In large saucepan combine 3 cups (710 ml) hot water and coffee, mix well. Add sugar. Boil 2 minutes, turn off heat and cool. Add vodka and vanilla. Shake in bottle or jar before serving.

Amaretto Cooler

1¼ cups amaretto	300 ml
2 quarts orange juice	2 L
1 (15 ounce) bottle club soda, chilled	425 g
Orange slices	

- Combine all ingredients and stir well. Serve over crushed ice.

Amaretto

3 cups sugar	710 ml
1 pint vodka	.5 kg
3 tablespoons almond extract	45 ml
1 tablespoon vanilla (not the imitation)	15 ml

- Combine sugar and 2¼ cups (540 ml) water in large pan. Bring to a boil. Reduce heat. Simmer for 5 minutes and stir occasionally. Remove from stove. Stir in remaining ingredients. Store in airtight jar.

Mexican Coffee

1 ounce coffee liqueur	28 g
1 cup hot, black coffee	240 ml
Ground cinnamon	
Sweetened whipped cream	

- Pour liqueur and coffee into tall mug. Top with cinnamon and whipped cream.

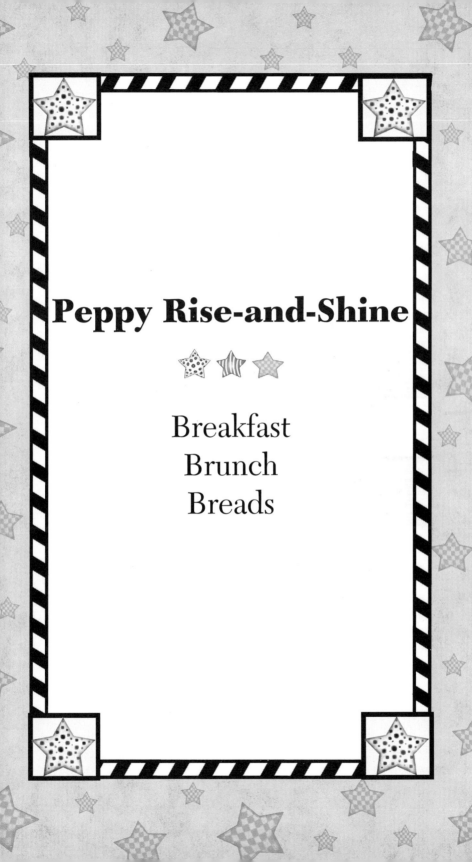

Peppy Rise-and-Shine

Breakfast
Brunch
Breads

Baked Eggs

4 eggs	
4 tablespoons cream, divided	60 ml
4 tablespoons cracker crumbs, divided	60 ml
4 tablespoons shredded cheddar cheese, divided	60 ml

- Grease 4 muffin cups and place 1 egg in each.

- Add 1 tablespoon (15 ml) each of cream, crumbs and cheese for each egg. Sprinkle with a little salt and pepper.

- Bake at 325° (162° C) for 12 to 20 minutes until eggs are set.

Bacon and Egg Burrito

2 slices bacon, cooked, chopped	
2 eggs, scrambled	
¼ cup shredded cheddar cheese	60 ml
1 flour tortilla	

- Sprinkle bacon, eggs and cheese in middle of tortilla. Fold tortilla sides over and place seam-side down on dinner plate. Microwave for 30 seconds or just until mixture heats thoroughly.

A Better Scramble

1 (10 ounce) can cheddar cheese soup	280 g
8 eggs, lightly beaten	
2 tablespoons butter	30 ml
Snipped chives	

- Pour soup into bowl and stir until smooth. Add eggs and a little pepper and mix well.

- In skillet, melt butter. Pour in egg mixture and scramble over low heat until set. Sprinkle with chives.

Easy Omelet

2 tablespoons butter	30 ml
4 - 5 eggs	
⅓ cup shredded cheddar cheese	80 ml

- Melt butter in 10-inch (25 cm) skillet over medium heat. While butter melts, whisk together eggs and ¼ teaspoon (1 ml) salt. Pour eggs into skillet and stir gently until they begin to set.

- Spread eggs evenly in pan and sprinkle with cheese. Reduce heat and cook until omelet just sets. Hold skillet over serving plate, tilt skillet until omelet slides out and almost half touches plate. Immediately turn skillet upside down to make omelet fold over itself. Serve immediately.

Cheesy Scrambled Eggs

2 tablespoons (¼ stick) butter	30 ml
8 eggs	
1 (4 ounce) can chopped green chilies	114 g
½ cup grated cheddar cheese	120 ml

- Melt butter in skillet. Beat remaining ingredients well and add a little salt and pepper and pour into skillet; stirring until set.

Creamy Eggs on Toast

¼ cup (½ stick) butter	60 ml
4 level tablespoons flour	60 ml
2 cups milk	480 ml
6 eggs, hard-boiled, sliced	

- Melt butter in skillet, stir in flour and add milk. Cook over medium heat and stir constantly until sauce thickens.

- Gently fold in egg slices. Serve over 6 slices toasted bread.

Eggs in a Basket

2 (15 ounce) cans corned beef hash   2 (425 g)
6 eggs
¼ cup seasoned breadcrumbs   60 ml
Butter

- Preheat oven to 325° (162° C). Grease 7 x 11-inch (18 x 28 cm) baking dish and spread hash evenly in dish. Press bottom of ½ cup measuring cup into hash to make 6 impressions.

- Break 1 egg into each impression. Sprinkle spoonful of breadcrumbs over each egg and top with dot of butter. Bake 20 to 25 minutes or until eggs are as firm as desired.

Mexican Eggs

4 corn tortillas
4 eggs
1 cup green chile salsa   240 ml
4 ounces grated longhorn cheese   114 g

- Dip tortillas in heated oil in skillet and remove quickly. Set tortillas in baking pan to keep warm.

- In skillet, fry eggs in a little butter until whites set. Place fried egg on each tortilla. Heat salsa and spoon over each egg. Sprinkle grated cheese on top.

- Place baking pan under broiler until cheese melts.

Heavenly Eggs

Bread and Butter
Eggs
Mozzarella cheese slices
Cooked bacon strips

- Preheat oven to 350° (176° C). Butter slice of bread for each person to be served and place butter side down in baking dish. Place cheese slice over bread.

- Separate an egg for each slice of bread; add a pinch of salt to whites and beat until stiff. Pile egg whites on cheese, making a nest in the top. Slip an egg yolk into each nest and bake 20 minutes and serve immediately. Place cooked bacon slice over top of each egg.

Sunrise Tacos

4 eggs, scrambled, divided
½ cup grated cheddar cheese, divided   **120 ml**
½ cup salsa, divided   **120 ml**
2 flour tortillas, divided

- For each taco, spread half scrambled eggs, ¼ cup (60 ml) cheese and ¼ cup (60 ml) salsa on tortilla and roll.

Breakfast Tacos

4 eggs
4 flour tortillas
1 cup chopped, cooked ham   **240 ml**
1 cup grated cheddar cheese   **240 ml**

- Scramble eggs in skillet. Lay tortillas flat and spoon eggs over 4 tortillas. Sprinkle with ham and cheese and roll to enclose filling. Place tacos in microwave-safe dish. Microwave for about 30 seconds or until cheese melts. Serve immediately.

Spicy Oven Omelet

4 eggs	
¼ cup mayonnaise	60 ml
¼ cup milk	60 ml
2 tablespoons flour	30 ml
1 cup shredded cheddar cheese	240 ml
½ cup chopped ham	120 ml

- Preheat oven to 350° (176° C). In blender, combine eggs, mayonnaise, milk and flour and blend 15 seconds. Immediately after blending, pour mixture into sprayed 2-quart (2 L) glass baking dish.

- Stir in cheese and ham and bake 30 minutes or until omelet is firm when you shake the baking dish.

Corned Beef Hash Bake

2 (15 ounce) cans corned beef hash, slightly warmed	2 (425 g)
Butter	
6 - 8 eggs	
⅓ cup half-and-half cream	80 ml

- Spread corned beef hash in greased 9 x 13-inch (23 x 33 cm) pan. Pat down with back of spoon and make 6 to 8 deep hollows in hash large enough for egg to fit.

- Fill hollows with tiny dab of butter. Pour eggs into each hollow and cover with about 1 tablespoon (15 ml) of cream.

- Bake uncovered at 350° (176° C) for 15 to 20 minutes or until eggs set as desired. Divide into squares to serve.

English Muffin Breakfast Sandwich

4 - 6 eggs	
1 (16 ounce) package pre-cooked bacon slices, halved	.5 kg
1 (12 ounce) package English muffins, halved, toasted	340 g
1 (16 ounce) package cheese slices	.5 kg

• Preheat oven to 325° (162° C). Lightly scramble eggs in skillet over medium heat and stir often. Season according to taste. Heat bacon in microwave according to package directions. Spoon egg mixture onto bottom of muffin, add cheese slice, bacon and muffin top. Place on baking sheet and bake about 10 minutes or just until cheese begins to melt.

Sausage Gravy

½ pound pork sausage	227 g
¼ cup flour	60 ml
2½ cups milk	600 ml

• Cook sausage in large skillet over medium heat, stirring until it crumbles. Remove sausage, but reserving about 2 tablespoons (30 ml) drippings in skillet.

• Stir flour into drippings and cook, stirring constantly until flour is slightly brown. Gradually stir in milk and cook, stirring constantly until gravy thickens. Stir in ¾ teaspoon (4 ml) black pepper, a little salt and cooked sausages.

Sausage Bites

¾ - 1 pound bacon slices	340 g
2 (8 ounce) sausage links	2 (227 g)
1 cup brown sugar, divided	240 ml
½ teaspoon cinnamon	2 ml

- Preheat oven to 350° (176° C). Cut each bacon strip in half widthwise and cut each sausage link in half. Wrap piece of bacon around each sausage half and secure with toothpick. Place brown sugar in shallow bowl and mix in cinnamon. Roll sausage rolls in brown sugar (you will have some brown sugar left).

- Place each sausage roll in large, foil-lined baking dish. Cover and refrigerate until ready to bake. Sprinkle brown sugar over each roll and bake 30 minutes, turning once.

Glazed Bacon

1 pound bacon	.5 kg
⅓ cup packed brown sugar	80 ml
1 teaspoon flour	5 ml
½ cup finely chopped pecans	120 ml

- Arrange bacon slices close together, but not overlapping, on wire rack over drip pan. In bowl, combine brown sugar, flour and pecans and sprinkle evenly over bacon. Bake at 350° (176° C) for about 30 minutes. Drain on paper towels.

Easy Way to Cook Bacon

1 pound bacon   .5 kg

- Preheat oven to 400° (204° C). Bake on rack of roasting pan 20 to 30 minutes or until crisp. Remove bacon with tongs and discard bacon drippings.

Hot Tamale-Cheese Fiesta

2 (15 ounce) jars beef tamales with sauce	2 (425 g)
1 (8 ounce) package shredded Mexican 4-cheese blend, divided	227 g
1 (10 ounce) can cream of mushroom soup	280 g
2 teaspoons taco seasoning	10 ml

- Drain sauce from tamales into cup and set aside. Put tamales onto plate and remove paper from tamales.

- Place tamales, side by side, in 9 x 13-inch (23 x 33 cm) baking dish. Sprinkle one-fourth of cheese over top of tamales.

- Combine ½ cup (120 ml) sauce from tamales, mushroom soup and taco seasoning and mix well. Pour sauce mixture over tamales.

- Bake at 350° (176° C) for 5 to 10 minutes. Sprinkle remaining cheese over top and continue to heat until cheese melts.

Bacon-Cheese Stromboli

1 (10 ounce) tube refrigerated pizza dough	280 g
¾ cup shredded cheddar cheese	180 ml
¾ cup shredded mozzarella cheese	180 ml
6 bacon strips, cooked, crumbled	

- On ungreased baking sheet, roll dough into 12-inch (32 cm) circle. On one-half of dough, sprinkle cheeses and bacon to within ½-inch (1.2 cm) of edge.

- Fold dough over filling and pinch edges to seal.

- Bake at 400° (204° C) for about 10 minutes or until golden. Serve with salsa. Cut in pie slices.

Cheese Enchiladas

1 dozen corn tortillas	
1 (8 ounce) package shredded cheddar cheese, divided	227 g
½ cup chopped onion, divided	120 ml
2 (10 ounce) cans enchilada sauce	2 (280 g)

- Wrap tortillas in slightly damp paper towel. Place between 2 salad plates and microwave on high for 45 seconds.

- Sprinkle ⅓ cup (80 ml) cheese and onions on each tortilla and roll. Place seam-side down in 9 x 13-inch (23 x 33 cm) baking dish.

- Pour sauce over enchiladas. Sprinkle with remaining cheese and onions. Cover and microwave on MEDIUM HIGH for 5 to 6 minutes.

Chile Rellenos

2 (7 ounce) cans chopped green chilies, drained	2 (198 g)
1 (16 ounce) package shredded Monterey	
Jack cheese	.5 kg
4 eggs, beaten	
½ cup milk	120 ml

- In 7 x 11-inch (18 x 28 cm) baking dish, layer half green chilies, half cheese, then remaining chilies and cheese.

- Combine eggs, milk and a little salt and pepper in small bowl and mix well. Pour over layers and bake uncovered at 350° (176° C) for 30 minutes or until light brown and set. Cool for 5 minutes before cutting into squares.

Rellenos Quiche

1 (9- inch) frozen pie shell	
(½ of 15 ounce package)	23 cm/425 g
1 (8 ounce) package shredded Monterey Jack cheese	227 g
1 (7 ounce) can chopped green chilies, drained	198 g
4 large eggs, lightly beaten	
1¼ cups half-and-half cream	300 ml

- Preheat oven to 425° (220° C). Bake pie shell for 5 minutes. Remove from oven and reduce heat to 350° (176° C). Sprinkle half cheese and half green chilies over partially baked pie shell. Repeat both layers.

- Combine beaten eggs and cream, adding an ample amount of black pepper and pour over cheese mixture. Bake 30 minutes.

Creamy Grits

3 pints half-and-half cream	1.3 kg
½ teaspoon garlic powder	2 ml
½ teaspoon hot sauce	2 ml
1½ cups uncooked grits	360 ml
2 (3 ounce) packages cream cheese	2 (84 g)

- In large saucepan combine half-and-half, garlic powder, hot sauce and 1 teaspoon (5 ml) salt. Bring to a boil and gradually stir in grits. Reduce heat and simmer 6 minutes or until it thickens, stir occasionally. Stir in cream cheese, stirring until cream cheese melts.

Quick Cheese Grits

1⅔ cups uncooked quick-cooking grits	400 ml
1 (8 ounce) package shredded sharp cheddar cheese	227 g
¾ cup shredded Monterey Jack cheese	180 ml
⅔ cup half-and-half cream	160 ml
2 tablespoons butter	30 ml

- In saucepan on medium-high heat, bring 6 cups (1.5 L) water, adding a little salt, to a boil and gradually add grits. Reduce heat to low-medium and simmer for 10 minutes, stirring occasionally or until mixture has thickened. Stir in both cheeses, cream and butter, mixing until well blended. Serve immediately.

Cherry-Pecan Oatmeal

2 cups of your favorites cooked oatmeal	480 ml
½ cup dried cherries, chopped	120 ml
½ cup packed brown sugar	120 ml
2 tablespoons butter, softened	30 ml
½ teaspoon ground cinnamon	5 ml
½ cup chopped toasted pecans	120 ml

- While oatmeal is cooking, combine cherries, brown sugar, butter and cinnamon. Stir into cooked oatmeal.

- Sprinkle toasted pecans over top of each serving.

Breakfast Ready Oatmeal

1½ cups uncooked oatmeal	360 ml
3½ cups milk	830 ml
½ cup chopped pecans	120 ml
⅓ cups brown sugar	80 ml

- In saucepan over medium heat, combine and cook oats, milk, pecans, brown sugar and a dash of salt. Bring to a boil, lower heat and simmer for 6 minutes, stirring occasionally. Let stand several minutes before serving.

Light and Crispy Waffles

2 cups biscuit mix	480 ml
1 egg	
½ cup oil	120 ml
1⅓ cups club soda	320 ml

- Preheat waffle iron. Combine all ingredients in mixing bowl and stir by hand. Pour just enough batter to cover waffle iron.

Waffle Flash

2 eggs
1 cup milk   240 ml
½ teaspoon vanilla   2 ml
8 slices stale bread

- Heat waffle iron according to directions. Beat eggs, slowly add milk and vanilla and beat well. Remove crust from bread and butter both sides of bread. When waffle iron is ready, dip bread in egg mixture and place in waffle iron. Close lid and grill until light brown.

Pecan Waffles

2 cups self-rising flour   480 ml
½ cup oil   120 ml
½ cup milk   120 ml
⅔ cup finely chopped pecans   160 ml

- Preheat waffle iron. In bowl, combine flour, oil and milk. Beat until they mix well. Stir in chopped pecans.

- Pour approximately ¾ cup (180 ml) batter into hot waffle iron and bake until brown and crispy.

No-Mess Oven Pancakes

⅔ cup flour   160 ml
⅔ cup milk   160 ml
¼ cup sugar   60 ml
5 large eggs, beaten

- Preheat oven to 425° (220° C). Combine flour, milk, sugar and beaten eggs in mixing bowl. Place a little oil on large baking sheet and rub oil to cover whole surface of pan. Place in oven for 5 minutes. Pour pancake mixture onto pan to make several pancakes. Bake about 18 minutes or until puffy and golden.

Croissant French Toast with Strawberry Syrup

4 large day-old croissants	
¾ cup half-and-half cream	180 ml
2 large eggs	
1 teaspoon vanilla	5 ml
¼ cup (½ stick) butter	60 ml

• Slice croissants in half lengthwise. In shallow bowl, whisk together cream, eggs and vanilla. Heat 1 tablespoon (15 ml) butter at a time in large skillet.

• Dip croissant halves into egg mixture and coat well. Cook 4 croissant halves about 2 minutes each time. Turn and cook on both sides until light brown. Repeat with remaining butter and croissant halves.

Strawberry Syrup:

¾ cup sugar	180 ml
1 quart fresh strawberries, slices	1 L
¼ cup orange juice	60 ml

• In saucepan, combine all ingredients and let stand 30 minutes. Cook over low heat, and stir occasionally for 5 to 8 minutes. Serve warm over croissant toast.

French Toast

4 eggs
1 cup whipping cream   240 ml
2 thick slices bread, cut into 3 strips
Powdered sugar

- Place a little oil in skillet. Beat eggs, cream and pinch of salt.
  Dip bread into batter and allow batter to soak in.

- Fry bread in skillet until brown, turn and fry on other side.

- Transfer to baking sheet. Bake at 325° (162° C) for about
  4 minutes or until they puff. Sprinkle with powdered sugar.

Orange-French Toast

1 egg, beaten
½ cup orange juice   120 ml
5 slices raisin bread
1 cup crushed graham crackers   240 ml
2 tablespoons butter, more if needed for frying   30 ml

- Combine egg and orange juice and dip each slice of bread in egg
  mixture and then in graham cracker crumbs. Fry in batches in
  butter until light brown.

Praline Toast

½ cup (1 stick) butter, softened   120 ml
1 cup packed brown sugar   240 ml
½ cup finely chopped pecans   120 ml

- Combine all ingredients. Spread on bread slices. Toast in broiler
  until brown and bubbly.

Cinnamon Toast

⅔ cup sugar 160 ml
1 heaping tablespoon cinnamon 15 ml
Bread
Butter, softened

- Mix sugar with cinnamon. Place in large salt or sugar shaker. Place bread on baking sheet and toast top by broiling in oven until light brown.

- Remove baking sheet and spread soft butter on toasted side. Sprinkle with cinnamon mixture.

- Return to oven and broil until tops are bubbly. Watch closely.

Berry Cream for Waffles

1 (8 ounce) carton whipping cream 227 g
½ cup powdered sugar 120 ml
2 cups sliced strawberries, well drained 480 ml
½ cup blueberries 120 ml

- Whip heavy cream with powdered sugar until very stiff and fold in strawberries and blueberries. This will be enough berry cream to serve over 6 prepared frozen waffles.

Pumpkin and Apple Butter for Toast or Waffles

1 (15 ounce) can pumpkin	425 g
1 (24 ounce) jar applesauce	680 g
1½ cups packed light brown sugar	360 ml
¼ teaspoon ground ginger	60 ml
½ teaspoon ground cinnamon and nutmeg	2 ml

- In large, heavy saucepan, on high heat, combine all ingredients, stirring constantly. Reduce heat to low and simmer, uncovered for about 20 minutes, stirring occasionally or until mixture is very thick. Cool and spoon into pint jars or ½-pint (227 g) jelly jars; cover and refrigerate.

Cherry-Raspberry Syrup for Waffles

2 cups pitted, chopped sweet fresh cherries	480 ml
2 cup raspberries, divided	480 ml
1 cup sugar	240 ml
2 cinnamon sticks	
¼ cup brandy	60 ml

- Place cherries, 1 cup (240 ml) raspberries, sugar and cinnamon sticks in saucepan and bring to a boil, reduce heat and simmer, stirring occasionally, about 20 minutes. Remove from heat and stir in brandy and remaining raspberries.

Nutty Apple Syrup for Pancakes

1 cup sugar	240 ml
1½ cups packed brown sugar	360 ml
½ cup apple jelly	120 ml
¼ cup finely chopped pecans	60 ml
1 teaspoon maple flavoring	5 ml

- In saucepan, combine both sugars and ⅓ cup (80 ml) water. Bring to a boil and cook and stir for 2 minutes. Remove from heat and stir in jelly, pecans and maple flavoring.

Strawberry Butter

1 (10 ounce) package frozen strawberries, with juice	280 g
1 cup (2 sticks) unsalted butter, softened	240 ml
1 cup powdered sugar	240 ml

- Mix all ingredients in food processor or mixer.

Honey Butter

½ cup (1 stick) butter, softened	120 ml
¼ cup honey	60 ml
2 tablespoons lemon juice	30 ml
1 tablespoon brown sugar	15 ml

- With hand mixer, cream butter until fluffy and add honey in fine stream. Add lemon juice and brown sugar and stir until all ingredients blend evenly. Chill until ready to serve.

Orange Butter

⅔ cup butter, room temperature   160 ml
¼ cup frozen orange juice concentrate, thawed   60 ml
1 (16 ounce) box powdered sugar   .5 kg
1 teaspoon dried orange peel   5 ml

- Blend all ingredients in mixer. Store in refrigerator.

Peach Bake

2 (15 ounce) cans peach halves, drained   2 (425 g)
1 cup packed brown sugar   240 ml
1 cup round, buttery cracker crumbs   240 ml
½ cup (1 stick) butter, melted   120 ml

- Butter 2-quart (2 L) casserole and layer peaches, sugar and cracker crumbs until all ingredients are used.

- Pour melted butter over casserole. Bake at 325° (162° C) for 30 minutes or until cracker crumbs are slightly brown. Serve hot or at room temperature.

Mini-Apricot Bake

2 (15 ounce) cans apricot halves, drained   2 (425 g)
¾ cup packed brown sugar   180 ml
1 cup round, buttery cracker crumbs   240 ml
½ cup (1 stick) butter, melted   120 ml

- Butter 2-quart (2 L) casserole and layer apricots, sugar and cracker crumbs until all ingredients are gone.

- Melt butter and pour over casserole.

- Bake at 325° (162° C) for 30 minutes or until cracker crumbs are slightly brown. Serve hot or room temperature.

Melon Boats

2 cantaloupes, chilled
4 cups red and green seedless grapes, chilled   1 L
1 cup mayonnaise   240 ml
⅓ cup frozen concentrated orange juice   80 ml

- Prepare each melon in 6 lengthwise sections and remove seeds and peel. Place on lettuce leaves on separate salad plates.

- Heap grapes over and around cantaloupe slices.

- Combine mayonnaise and juice concentrate and mix well. Ladle over fruit.

Ambrosia Spread

1 (11 ounce) can mandarin orange sections, drained   312 g
1 (8 ounce) container soft cream cheese with
    pineapple, softened   227 g
¼ cup flaked coconut, toasted   60 ml
¼ cup slivered almonds, chopped, toasted   60 ml

- Chop orange sections and set aside.

- Combine cheese, coconut and almonds and blend well. Gently fold in orange sections and chill.

Cheese Bread

1 (16 ounce) package shredded, sharp cheddar cheese .5 kg
1 cup mayonnaise   240 ml
1 (1 ounce) package ranch-style dressing mix   28 g
10 (1-inch) slices French bread   10 (2.5 cm)

- Preheat oven to 300° (148° C).

- Combine cheese, mayonnaise and dressing mix.

- Spread on bread slices and heat in oven until brown.

Bacon-Cheese French Bread

1 (16 ounce) loaf unsliced French bread   .5 kg
5 slices bacon, cooked, crumbled
1 (8 ounce) package shredded mozzarella cheese   227 g
½ cup (1 stick) butter, melted   120 ml

- Slice bread into 1-inch (2.5 cm) slices. Place sliced loaf on large
  piece of foil. Combine bacon and cheese. Sprinkle bacon and
  cheese in between slices of bread.

- Drizzle butter over loaf and let some drip in between slices.
  Wrap loaf tightly in foil. Bake at 350° (176° C) for 20 minutes or
  until thoroughly hot. Serve immediately.

French Cheese Loaf

1 (16 ounce) loaf unsliced French bread	.5 kg
½ cup (1 stick) butter, softened	120 ml
1 teaspoon prepared minced garlic	5 ml
1 (4 ounce) package crumbled blue cheese	114 g

- Preheat oven to 375° (190° C). Slice bread at 1-inch (2.5 cm) intervals, cutting to, but not through, bottom of loaf.

- In bowl, combine softened butter, garlic and blue cheese and spread evenly on both sides of each bread slice. Wrap loaf in foil and place on large baking pan. Bake 10 to 12 minutes or until bread is thoroughly hot.

Poppy Seed-Onion Loaf

2 tablespoons instant minced onions	30 ml
1 tablespoon poppy seeds	15 ml
½ cup (1 stick) butter, melted	120 ml
2 cans refrigerated butter flake biscuits	

- Combine onions and poppy seeds with butter.

- Separate each biscuit into 2 or 3 rolls.

- Dip each piece in butter mixture and turn to coat.

- Place rolls on edge of loaf pan and arrange rolls into 2 rows. Pour any remaining butter mixture over top of loaf.

- Bake at 325° (162° C) for 30 minutes. Serve warm.

Ranch-French Bread

1 loaf unsliced French bread	
½ cup (1 stick) butter, softened	120 ml
1 tablespoon ranch-style dressing mix	15 ml

- Cut loaf in half horizontally. Blend butter and dressing mix.

- Spread butter mixture on bread. Wrap bread in foil. Bake at 350° (176° C) for 15 minutes.

Toasted French Bread

1 unsliced loaf French bread	
½ cup (1 stick) butter, softened	120 ml
¾ cup parmesan cheese	180 ml
1½ teaspoons hot sauce	7 ml

- Slice bread in half lengthwise and quarter. Combine butter, parmesan cheese and hot sauce. Spread entire mixture on top of slices. Place on baking sheet.

- Bake at 325° (162° C) for 25 minutes or until thoroughly hot and brown on top.

Cheese Biscuits

2 cups biscuit mix	480 ml
⅔ cup milk	160 ml
⅔ cup grated sharp cheddar cheese	160 ml
¼ cup (½ stick) butter, melted	60 ml

- Spray baking sheet with non-stick spray. Mix baking mix, milk and cheese. Drop 1 heaping tablespoon (15 ml) dough for each biscuit onto baking sheet. Bake at 400° (204° C) for 10 minutes or until slightly brown. While hot, brush tops of biscuits with melted butter.

Speedy Biscuits

6 tablespoons shortening	90 ml
3 cups flour	710 ml
1 cup milk	240 ml

- Cut shortening into flour with pastry cutter or by hand. Add milk and mix until dough forms a ball. Knead until dough is smooth.

- Place on floured surface and flatten slightly. Cut with floured biscuit cutter, place in well-greased pan and turn to grease both sides of biscuits. Bake at 400° (204° C) for 10 to 12 minutes.

Sausage-Cheese Biscuits

1 (8 ounce) package grated cheddar cheese	227 g
1 pound hot bulk pork sausage	.5 kg
2 cups biscuit mix	480 ml
¾ cup milk	180 ml

- Combine all ingredients. Drop on ungreased baking sheet.

- Bake at 400° (204° C) until light brown.

French-Onion Biscuits

2 cups biscuit mix	480 ml
¼ cup milk	60 ml
1 (8 ounce) container French-onion dip	227 g
2 tablespoons finely minced green onion	30 ml

- Mix all ingredients until soft dough forms. Drop dough onto greased baking sheet. Bake at 400° (204° C) for 10 minutes or until light golden brown.

Quick Sour Cream Biscuits

⅓ cup club soda	80 ml
⅓ cup sour cream	80 ml
½ tablespoon sugar	7 ml
2 cups biscuit mix	480 ml

- In mixing bowl, combine all ingredients with fork just until dry ingredients are moist. Turn bowl out onto lightly floured board and knead gently several times.

- Roll dough into 1-inch (2.5 cm) thickness and cut with biscuit cutter. Place dough in sprayed 9 x 13-inch (23 x 33 cm) baking pan.

- Bake at 400° (204° C) for 12 to 14 minutes or until golden brown.

Maple Syrup Biscuits

2¼ cups baking mix	540 ml
⅔ cup milk	160 ml
1½ cups maple syrup	360 ml

- Combine baking mix and milk. Stir just until moist. On floured surface, roll dough into ½-inch (1.2 cm) thickness. Cut with 2-inch (5 cm) biscuit cutter.

- Pour syrup into 7 x 11-inch (18 x 28 cm) baking dish. Place biscuits on top of syrup.

- Bake at 425° (220° C) for 13 to 15 minutes or until biscuits are golden brown. Serve with butter.

Come and Get 'Em Biscuits

2 cups flour	480 ml
4 tablespoons mayonnaise	60 ml
1 cup milk	240 ml
Butter	

- Mix all ingredients and drop by teaspoonfuls on baking sheet.

- Bake at 425° (220° C) until biscuits are golden brown.

- Serve with plain or flavored butters.

Best Ever Biscuits

5 cups baking mix	1.3 L
¾ cup buttermilk	180 ml
½ cup (1 stick) butter, softened	120 ml
¼ cup club soda	60 ml
1 large egg, beaten	
2 tablespoons sugar	30 ml

- Preheat oven to 425° (220° C). Prepare baking sheet with a little oil. In large bowl, stir together all ingredients and 1 teaspoon (5 ml) salt. Knead dough by hand until smooth.

- With flour on your hands and on wax paper, pat dough flat to ¾-inch (1.8 cm) thickness. Cut out biscuits with 3-inch (8 cm) diameter biscuit cutter. Place biscuits on prepared baking sheet and bake 12 minutes or until golden brown.

Strawberry Topping for Biscuits

3½ cups sugar	830 ml
1 (10 ounce) carton frozen strawberries, thawed	280 g
1 (6 ounce) can frozen orange juice concentrate,	
thawed	168 g
2 tablespoons lemon juice	30 ml

- Combine sugar and strawberries in large saucepan and mix well. Over high heat bring to full rolling boil. Boil 1 minute, stirring constantly.

- Remove from heat and stir in orange juice concentrate and lemon juice. Return to heat and bring to boil for 1 minute, stirring constantly. Skim foam off top. Add red food coloring, if you like. Pour into jelly glasses and seal with hot paraffin.

Parmesan-Bread Deluxe

1 (16 ounce) loaf unsliced Italian bread	.5 kg
½ cup refrigerated creamy Caesar dressing and dip	120 ml
⅓ cup grated parmesan cheese	80 ml
3 tablespoons finely chopped green onions	45 ml

- Cut 24 (½-inch /1.2 cm) thick slices from bread. Reserve remaining bread for other use.

- In small bowl, combine dressing, cheese and onions. Spread 1 teaspoon (5 ml) dressing mixture on each bread slice.

- Place bread on baking sheet. Broil 4 inches (10 cm) from heat until golden brown. Serve warm.

Parmesan Ring

2 (10 ounce) cans refrigerated flaky biscuits	2 (280 g)
¼ cup (½ stick) butter, melted	60 ml
⅔ cup grated parmesan cheese	160 ml
1 tablespoon sesame seeds	15 ml

- Preheat oven to 375° (190° C). Dip each biscuit lightly in melted butter and parmesan cheese; place on greased baking pan in a circle, each biscuit overlapping slightly, making a ring. Sprinkle with sesame seeds and bake 15 minutes or until golden brown.

Garlic Rounds

2 teaspoons minced garlic	10 ml
2 teaspoons dried parsley flakes	10 ml
2 tablespoons olive oil	30 ml
½ teaspoon dries oregano	2 ml
1 (13 ounce) package refrigerated pizza crust	370 g

- Preheat oven to 400° (204° C). In small bowl, combine garlic, parsley flakes, olive oil and oregano.

- On flat surface, unroll pizza dough and brush with garlic-oil mixture and reroll dough. Using a serrated knife, cut into 1-inch (2.5 cm) pieces and place each piece in greased muffin pan. Brush any remaining garlic mixture over top of rounds. Bake 15 minutes or until golden brown.

Cheese Sticks

1 loaf thick-sliced bread	
½ cup (1 stick) butter, melted	120 ml
1 cup grated parmesan cheese	240 ml
1½ teaspoons paprika	7 ml

- Remove crust from bread and slice into sticks. Brush or roll in melted butter. Place on baking sheet. Sprinkle parmesan and paprika. Bake at 325° (162° C) for 20 minutes.

Bread Sticks

1½ cups shredded Monterey Jack cheese	360 ml
¼ cup poppy seeds	60 ml
2 tablespoons dry onion soup mix	30 ml
2 (11 ounce) cans breadstick dough	2 (312 g)

- Spread cheese evenly in 9 x 13-inch (23 x 33 cm) baking dish. Sprinkle poppy seeds and soup mix evenly over cheese. Separate breadstick dough into sticks. Stretch strips slightly. Roll strips 1 at a time in cheese mixture and coat all sides. Cut into 3 or 4-inch (8 cm) strips. Place on cookie sheet and bake at 375° (190° C) for 12 minutes.

Seasoned Breadsticks

1 tube (11 ounce) refrigerated breadsticks	312 g
¼ cup (½ stick) butter, melted	60 ml
2 tablespoons prepared pesto	30 ml
¼ teaspoon garlic powder	1 ml
3 tablespoons grated parmesan cheese	45 ml

- Preheat oven to 375° (190° C). Unroll and separate breadsticks and place on ungreased baking pan. Combine melted butter, pesto and garlic powder and brush over breadsticks. Twist each breadstick 3 times. Sprinkle with parmesan cheese.

- Bake for about 12 minutes or until golden brown.

Texas Cornbread

1 cup yellow cornmeal	240 ml
⅔ cup flour	160 ml
¼ teaspoon baking soda	1 ml
1¼ cups buttermilk	300 ml
1 large egg, beaten	

- Preheat oven to 400° (204° C). Combine cornmeal, flour and baking soda and stir in buttermilk and egg, until moistened.

- Pour into a buttered 7 x 11-inch (18 x 28 cm) baking pan and bake 15 minutes, until golden brown.

Sausage Cornbread

1 (10 ounce) can condensed golden corn soup	280 g
2 eggs	
1 (8 ounce) package corn muffin mix	227 g
⅓ pound pork sausage, crumbled, cooked	150 g

- In medium bowl combine soup, eggs, and ¼ cup (60 ml) water or milk. Stir in corn muffin mix just until it blends. Fold in sausage. Pour mixture into greased 9-inch (23 cm) baking pan.

- Bake at 375° (190° C) for 25 minutes or until golden brown.

Mexican Cornbread

1 (16 ounce) package Mexican cubed cheese	.5 kg
¼ cup milk	60 ml
2 (8 ounce) packages corn muffin mix	2 (227 g)
2 eggs, beaten	

- In saucepan, melt cheese with milk over low heat. Combine corn muffin mix and eggs in bowl. Fold in cheese and mix until moist. Pour into greased 9 x 13-inch (23 x 33 cm) baking pan. Bake at 375° (190° C) for 25 minutes.

Corn Sticks

2 cups biscuit mix	480 ml
2 tablespoons minced green onions	30 ml
1 (8 ounce) can cream-style corn	227 g

- Combine biscuit mix, green onions and cream-style corn. Place dough on floured surface and cut into 3 x 1-inch (8 x 2.5 cm) strips. Roll in melted butter. Bake at 400° (204° C) for 15 to 16 minutes.

Green Chili-Cheese Bread

1 loaf unsliced Italian bread	
½ cup (1 stick) butter, melted	120 ml
1 (4 ounce) can diced green chilies, drained	114 g
¾ cup grated Monterey Jack cheese	180 ml

- Slice bread almost all the way through. Combine melted butter, chilies and cheese. Spread between bread slices.

- Cover loaf with foil. Bake at 350° (176° C) for 25 minutes.

Hot-Water Cornbread

2 cups yellow cornmeal	480 ml
¼ teaspoon baking powder	1 ml
1 teaspoon sugar	5 ml
¼ cup half-and-half cream	60 ml

- In bowl combine cornmeal, baking powder, 1 teaspoon (5 ml) salt and sugar, mixing well. Stir in cream and gradually add about 1 cup (240 ml) boiling water, stirring until batter is consistency of grits. In heavy skillet, pour enough oil for depth of ½-inch (1.2 cm) and heat on medium-high heat. Scoop batter into ¼-inch (.6 cm) measure and drop in hot oil. Fry in batches about 3 minutes on both sides; drain. Serve immediately.

Broccoli-Cheddar Corn Bread

1 (8 ounce) box corn muffin mix	227 g
1 egg	
⅓ cup milk	80 ml
½ cup frozen chopped broccoli, thawed, drained	120 ml
½ cup cheddar cheese	120 ml

- Preheat oven to 375° (190° C). In bowl, combine muffin mix, egg and milk (the egg and milk are ingredients the mix calls for). Gently stir in chopped broccoli and cheese. Batter can be placed in muffin pan (with paper cupcake liners) or in greased 8-inch (20 cm) baking pan. If using muffin pan, bake 18 minutes or 20 to 25 minutes for pan of cornbread.

Filled Muffins

1(16 ounce) box blueberry muffin mix with blueberries	.5 kg
1 egg	
⅓ cup red raspberry jam	80 ml
¼ cup sliced almonds	60 ml

- Rinse blueberries and drain; set aside. In bowl, combine muffin mix, egg and ½ cup (120 ml) water. Stir until moist and break up lumps in mix.

- Place paper liners in 8 muffin cups. Fill cups halfway.

- Combine raspberry jam with blueberries. Spoon mixture on top of batter. Cover with remaining batter and sprinkle almonds over batter.

- Bake at 375° (190° C) for about 18 minutes or until light brown.

Quick Cinnamon Rolls

2½ cups baking mix, plus ¼ cup	600 ml/60 ml
1 egg	
⅓ cup milk	80 ml
¼ cup (½ stick) butter, softened	60 ml
⅔ cup sugar	160 ml
2 teaspoons cinnamon	10 ml

- Preheat oven to 375° (190° C). In bowl, combine 2½ cups (600 ml) baking mix, egg and milk, mixing until soft dough forms. Place dough on wax paper sprinkled with extra ¼ cup (60 ml) baking mix. Shape into ball and knead gently just until smooth.

- Pat dough into 8 x 10-inch (20 x 25 cm) rectangle and spread with softened butter. Mix sugar and cinnamon and sprinkle over dough. Roll tightly and pinch edge of dough into roll to seal. Place sealed side down on ungreased baking sheet. With kitchen scissors, cut roll at 1-inch (2.5 cm) sections almost through to bottom.

- Bake 25 minutes or until light brown. Serve warm and if you like, sprinkle with powdered sugar.

Blueberry-Orange Muffins

1 (16 ounce) package blueberry muffin mix with blueberries	.5 kg
2 egg whites	
½ cup orange juice	120 ml
Orange marmalade	

- Wash blueberries with cold water and drain.

- Stir muffin mix, egg whites and orange juice and break up any lumps.

- Fold blueberries gently into batter.

- Pour into muffin tins (with paper liners) about half full.

- Bake at 375° (190°) for 18 to 20 minutes or until toothpick inserted in center comes out clean.

- Spoon orange marmalade over top of hot muffins.

Banana-Gingerbread Muffins

1 (14 ounce) package gingerbread cookie mix	396 g
1 large ripe bananas, mashed	
2 eggs	
¾ cup oats	180 ml
1(16 ounce) can prepared caramel icing	.5 kg

• Preheat oven to 350° (176° C). Line bottoms of 16 muffin cups with paper liners.

• Combine cookie mix, bananas, eggs and oats in bowl, mix well. Divide batter evenly among muffin cups. Bake 18 minutes and immediately remove from pan. Cool before icing muffins.

Easy Cinnamon Crisps

Flour tortillas
Vegetable oil
Sugar
Ground cinnamon

• Cut tortillas into wedges and carefully place in large skillet with hot oil. Fry until golden brown, remove from skillet and drain on paper towels. Sprinkle both sides of tortilla wedges heavily with sugar and cinnamon.

Honey-Cinnamon Butter

1 cup (2 sticks) butter	240 ml
½ cup honey	120 ml
1 teaspoon ground cinnamon	5 ml
Breakfast breads	

• Combine all ingredients in small mixing bowl and beat until smooth.

Topping for English Muffins

½ pound bacon slices, cooked, crumbled	227 g
¼ (½ stick) butter, softened	60 ml
1 (5 ounce) jar sharp processed cheese spread	143 g
2 fresh green onion, finely minced	

• Preheat oven to 325° (162° C). In bowl, combine all ingredients, mixing well and spread on each half (8) of 4 English muffins.

• Bake for 15 minutes or until each slice is light golden brown.

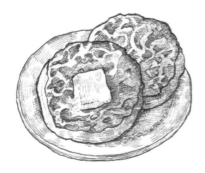

Breakfast Cinnamon Cake

⅔ cup brown sugar	160 ml
1 tablespoon grated orange peel	15 ml
2 (12.4 ounce each) refrigerated cinnamon rolls	2 (340 g)

- Preheat oven to 375° (190° C). Coat 10-inch (25 cm) bundt pan with cooking spray. In small bowl, combine brown sugar and orange peel.

- Open cans of rolls (save icing) and cut each in quarters and coat each quarter with cooking spray. Dip in sugar-orange mixture and arrange evenly in bundt pan; gently pressing down. Bake 30 minutes until light brown and about double in size. Cool slightly in pan.

- Invert serving plate on top of pan and with oven mitts, hold plate and pan together and invert. Remove pan. Spread icing unevenly over top of cake and serve warm.

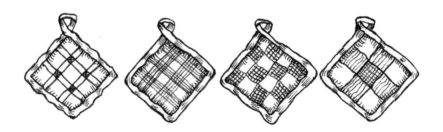

Take-Your-Pick Quick

Soups
Salads
Sandwiches

Easy Gazpacho

2 (28 ounce) cans diced tomatoes	2 (794 g)
1 unpeeled seedless cucumber, cut in chunks	
1 cup red onion, cut in chunks	240 ml
1 cup celery, cut in chunks	240 ml
2 serrano chile peppers, seeded, coarsely chopped	

- Working in batches, combine all ingredients plus a little salt and pepper, in food processor and pulse until mixture is a thick soup. Serve chilled in individual bowls.

Swiss-Vegetable Soup

1 (1 ounce) packet dry vegetable soup mix	28 g
1 cup half-and-half cream	240 ml
1½ cups shredded Swiss cheese	360 ml

- In saucepan, combine soup mix and 3 cups (710 ml) water and boil. Lower heat and simmer about 10 minutes. Add half-and-half cream and cheese and serve hot.

Tomato-French Onion Soup

1 (10 ounce) can tomato-bisque soup	280 g
2 (10 ounce) cans French-onion soup	2 (280 g)
Croutons	
Grated parmesan cheese	

- In saucepan, combine soups and 2 soup cans water. Heat thoroughly.

- Serve in bowls topped with croutons and a sprinkle of cheese.

Tortellini Soup

3 (14 ounce) cans chicken broth	3 (396 g)
2 (9 ounce) packages refrigerated cheese tortellini	2 (255 g)
1 (15 ounce) can cannellini beans, rinsed, drained	425 g
1 (4 ounce) jar chopped pimento	114 g
1 teaspoon dried basil	5 ml
1 tablespoon balsamic vinegar	15 ml

• In large saucepan, bring chicken broth to a boil; add tortellini and cook about 6 minutes or until tender.

• Stir in beans, pimento, basil, vinegar and salt and pepper to taste. Simmer for 8 to 10 minutes.

Zesty Black Bean Soup

2 onions, finely chopped	
1 tablespoon chili powder	15 ml
2 teaspoons cumin	10 ml
3 (15 ounce) cans black beans with liquid	3 (425 g)
2 (14 ounce) cans beef broth	2 (396 g)

• Saute onions in soup pot with a little oil for 5 minutes and stir in chili powder and cumin.

• Puree one can of beans and add to onion mixture. Add remaining beans and beef broth. Bring to a boil; reduce heat and simmer 10 minutes. Garnish with shredded cheese or salsa.

Spinach Soup

2 (10 ounce) packages frozen chopped spinach, cooked	2 (280 g)
2 (10 ounce) can cream of mushroom soup	2 (280 g)
1 cup half-and-half cream	240 ml
1 (15 ounce) can chicken broth	425 g

- Place spinach, mushroom soup and half-and-half in blender; puree until smooth.

- Place spinach mixture and chicken broth in saucepan and heat on medium heat until well heated. Reduce heat to low and simmer for 20 minutes. Serve hot or cold.

Mexican-Style Minestrone Soup

1 (16 ounce) package frozen garlic-seasoned pasta and vegetables	.5 kg
1 (16 ounce) jar thick-and-chunky salsa	.5 kg
1 (15 ounce) can pinto beans with liquid	425 g
1 teaspoon chili powder	5 ml
1 teaspoon cumin	5 ml
1 (8 ounce) package shredded Mexican 4-cheese blend	227 g

- In large saucepan, combine pasta and vegetables, salsa, pinto beans, chili powder, cumin and 1 cup (240 ml) water. Heat to a boil; reduce heat to low-medium and simmer for about 15 minutes, stirring occasionally or until vegetables are tender.

- When ready to serve; top each serving with cheese.

Speedy Taco Soup

1 (12 ounce) can chicken with juice	340 g
1 (14 ounce) can chicken broth	396 g
1 (16 ounce) jar mild thick-and-chunky salsa	.5 kg
1 (15 ounce) can ranch-style beans	425 g

- In large saucepan, combine chicken, broth, salsa and beans.

- Bring to boil, reduce heat and simmer for 15 minutes.

  TIP: A 15-ounce (425 g) can whole kernel corn may also be added.

Home-Made Tomato Soup

3 (15 ounce) cans whole tomatoes with liquid	3 (425 g)
1 (14 ounce) can chicken broth	396 g
1 tablespoon sugar	15 ml
1 tablespoon minced garlic	15 ml
1 tablespoon balsamic vinegar	15 ml
¾ cup heavy cream	180 ml

- With blender, puree tomatoes (in batches) and pour into large
  saucepan. Add chicken broth, sugar, garlic, balsamic vinegar
  and a little salt and bring to a boil. Reduce heat and stir in heavy
  cream, cook stirring constantly for 2 to 3 minutes or until soup is
  thoroughly hot.

Fiesta Vegetable Soup

1 (15 ounce) can Mexican-style stewed tomatoes	425 g
1 (15 ounce) can whole kernel corn	425 g
1 (15 ounce) can pinto beans	425 g
2 (14 ounce) cans chicken broth	2 (396 g)
1 (10 ounce) can fiesta nacho soup	280 g

- In soup pot, on high heat, combine tomatoes, corn, pinto beans, chicken broth and a little salt, mixing well.

- Stir in fiesta nacho soup and heat until hot.

Easy Spinach Soup

2 (10 ounce) packages frozen chopped spinach, cooked	2 (280 g)
2 (10 ounce) cans cream of mushroom soup	2 (280 g)
1 cup half-and-half cream	240 ml
1 (15 ounce) can chicken broth	425 g

- Place spinach, mushroom soup and half-and-half in blender and puree until smooth. Place spinach mixture and chicken broth in saucepan and heat on medium heat until hot.

- Simmer on low for 20 minutes.

Crunchy Peanut Soup

2 (10 ounce) cans cream of chicken soup	2 (280 g)
2 soup cans milk	
1¼ cups crunchy-style peanut butter	300 ml
½ teaspoon celery salt	2 ml

- In saucepan on medium heat, blend soup and milk.

- Stir in peanut butter and celery salt and heat until they blend well.

Easy Potato Soup

1 (20 ounce) package frozen hash brown potatoes with onions and peppers	567 g
1 sweet red bell pepper, seeded, chopped	
2 (14 ounce) cans chicken broth	2 (396 g)
1 (10 ounce) can cream of celery soup	280 g
1 (10 ounce) can cream of chicken soup	280 g
1 (8 ounce) carton whipping cream	227 g
4 fresh green onions, chopped for garnish	

- Combine potatoes, bell pepper, chicken broth and 1 cup (240 ml) water in large saucepan and bring to a boil. Cover, reduce heat and simmer 25 minutes.

- Stir in both soups and whipping cream and stirring well, heat until thoroughly hot. Garnish with green onions.

Avocado-Cream Soup

4 ripe avocados, peeled, diced	
1½ cups whipping cream	360 ml
2 (14 ounce) cans chicken broth	2 (396 g)
¼ cup dry sherry	60 ml

- Blend half avocados and half cream. Repeat with remaining avocados and cream. In saucepan, bring broth to boil, reduce heat and stir in avocado puree. Add 1 teaspoon (5 ml) salt and sherry and chill thoroughly.

At Home Black Bean Soup

2 onions, finely chopped	
3 teaspoons minced garlic	15 ml
3 (15 ounce) cans black beans, rinsed, drained	3 (425 g)
2 (14 ounce) cans beef broth	2 (396 g)
1½ teaspoons dried cumin	7 ml
2 teaspoons chili powder	10 ml

• Saute onions and garlic in soup pot with
  little oil and cook on medium heat for
  5 minutes. Place one can of beans and
  about ½ cup (120 ml) broth in food
  processor and process until beans are
  smooth. Transfer to soup pot and stir in
  remaining beans, remaining broth, cumin, chili powder and salt
  and pepper to taste and bring to a boil, reduce heat and simmer
  15 minutes.

Creamy Broccoli and Rice Soup

1 (6 ounce) package chicken and wild rice mix	168 g
1 (10 ounce) package frozen chopped broccoli	280 g
2 (10 ounce) cans cream of chicken soup	2 (280 g)
1 (12 ounce) can chicken breast chunks	340 g

• In soup pot, combine rice mix, contents of seasoning packet and
  5 cups (1.3 L) water. Bring to a boil, reduce heat and simmer
  15 minutes. Stir in broccoli, chicken soup and chicken; cover and
  simmer for another 5 minutes.

Fiesta-Veggie-Chicken Soup

1 (15 ounce) can Mexican-style stewed tomatoes	425 g
1 (15 ounce) can whole kernel corn	425 g
1 (15 ounce) can pinto beans with liquid	425 g
2 (14 ounce) cans chicken broth	2 (396 g)
1 (10 ounce) can fiesta nacho soup	280 g
1 (12 ounce) can chicken breasts with liquid	340 g

- Combine tomatoes, corn, beans, broth and nacho soup in large soup pot and heat 10 minutes over medium-high heat, mixing well. Stir in chicken and liquid and heat until thoroughly hot.

Cheesy Chicken Soup

1 (10 ounce) can fiesta nacho cheese soup	280 g
1 (10 ounce) can cream of chicken soup	280 g
1 (10 ounce) soup can of milk	2 (280 g)
1 chicken bouillon cube or 1 teaspoon bouillon granules	5 ml

- Mix nacho cheese soup, cream of chicken soup, milk and bouillon cube in saucepan and stir until smooth. Serve hot.

Chicken-Noodle Soup

1 (14 ounce) can chicken broth	396 g
2 tablespoons butter	30 ml
1 (3 ounce) package chicken-flavored ramen noodles, broken	84 g
1 (10 ounce) package frozen green peas, thawed	280 g
1 (4 ounce) jar sliced mushrooms	114 g
3 cups cooked, cubed chicken or deli turkey	710 g

- In large saucepan, boil 2 cups (480 ml) water. Add broth, butter, ramen noodles, contents of seasoning packet and peas.

- Heat to boiling, reduce heat to medium and cook about 5 minutes. Stir in mushrooms and chicken and continue cooking over medium heat until all ingredients are heated thoroughly.

Tasty Turkey Soup

1 (16 ounce) package frozen chopped onions and bell peppers	.5 kg
2 (3 ounce) packages chicken-flavored ramen noodles	2 (84 g)
2 (10 ounce) cans cream of chicken soup	2 (280 g)
1 cup cubed turkey	240 ml

- In soup pot with a little oil, cook onions and peppers just until tender but not brown. Add ramen noodles, seasoning packet and 2 cups (480 ml) water. Cook 5 minutes or until noodles are tender. Stir in chicken soup and cubed turkey. Stir until hot.

Cream of Turkey Soup

1 (10 ounce) can cream of celery soup	280 g
1 (10 ounce) can cream of chicken soup	280 g
2 (10 ounce) cans milk or cream	2 (280 g)
1 cup finely diced turkey	240 ml

- Combine all ingredients in large saucepan. Serve hot.

Hearty 15-Minute Turkey Soup

1 (14 ounce) can chicken broth	396 g
3 (15 ounce) cans navy beans with liquid	3 (425 g)
1 (28 ounce) can stewed tomatoes with liquid	794 g
3 cups small chunk white turkey meat	710 ml
2 teaspoons minced garlic	10 ml
¼ teaspoon cayenne pepper	1 ml
1 (6 ounce) package baby spinach, stems removed	168 g
Freshly grated parmesan cheese for garnish	

• In soup pot, combine broth, beans, stewed tomatoes, turkey chunks, garlic, cayenne pepper and salt and pepper to taste. Bring to a boil; reduce heat and simmer on medium heat for about 10 minutes.

• Stir in baby spinach; bring to a boil and cook, stirring constantly for 5 minutes. When ready to serve, sprinkle each serving with grated parmesan cheese.

Chili-Soup Warmer

1 (10 ounce) can tomato-bisque soup	280 g
1 (10 ounce) can chili	280 g
1 (10 ounce) can fiesta chili-beef soup	280 g
1(15 ounce) can chicken broth	425 g

• In saucepan, combine all soups and broth. Add amount of water to produce desired thickness of soup.

• Heat and serve hot with crackers.

Spaghetti Soup

1 (7 ounce) package spaghetti	198 g
1 (18 ounce) package frozen, cooked meatballs, thawed	510 g
1 (28 ounce) jar spaghetti sauce	794 g
1 (15 ounce) can Mexican stewed tomatoes	425 g

- In soup pot with 3 quarts (3 L) boiling water and a little salt, cook spaghetti about 6 minutes (no need to drain).

- When spaghetti is done, add meatballs, spaghetti sauce and stewed tomatoes and cook until mixture is thoroughly hot.

Bacon-Potato Soup

2 (14 ounce) cans chicken broth seasoned with garlic	2 (396 g)
2 potatoes, peeled, cubed	
1 onion finely chopped	
6 strips bacon, cooked, crumbled	

- In large saucepan, combine broth, potatoes and onion. Bring to boil, reduce heat to medium-high and boil about 10 minutes or until potatoes are tender. Season with a little pepper and sprinkle bacon on servings.

Spicy Tomato Soup

2 (10 ounce) cans tomato soup	2 (280 g)
1 (15 ounce) can Mexican stewed tomatoes	425 g
Sour cream	
½ pound bacon, fried, drained, crumbled	227 g

- Combine soup and stewed tomatoes in saucepan and heat.

- To serve, place dollop of sour cream on top of soup and sprinkle crumbed bacon over sour cream.

Lucky Pea Soup

1 onion, chopped	
1 cup cooked, cubed ham	240 ml
1 (15 ounce) cans black-eyed peas with jalapeno	
peppers with liquid	425 g
1 (14 ounce) can chicken broth	396 g
1 teaspoon minced garlic	5 ml
1 teaspoon rubbed sage	5 ml

- In a large saucepan, saute onion in a little oil. On high heat, add ham, black-eyed peas, broth, garlic and sage. Bring to a boil, reduce heat and simmer, stirring occasionally, for 20 minutes.

Italian Garbanzo Soup

1 (16 ounce) package frozen diced onion and bell	
peppers	.5 kg
1 pound Italian sausages, sliced	.5 kg
1 (14 ounce) can beef broth	396 g
1 (15 ounce) can Italian stewed tomatoes	425 g
2 (15 ounce) cans garbanzo beans, rinsed, drained	2 (425 g)

- Saute onion and bell peppers in soup pot with a little oil. Add Italian sausage and cook until brown. Stir in broth, stewed tomatoes and garbanzo beans.

- Bring mixture to a boil; reduce heat and simmer about 30 minutes.

Easy Meaty Minestrone

2 (20 ounce) cans minestrone soup	2 (567 g)
1 (15 ounce) can pinto beans with juice	425 g
1 (18 ounce) package frozen Italian meatballs, thawed	510 g
1 (5 ounce) package grated parmesan cheese	143 g

- In large saucepan, combine soups, beans, meatballs and ½ cup (120 ml) water. Bring to a boil, reduce heat to low and simmer about 15 minutes. To serve, sprinkle each serving with parmesan cheese.

Italian Vegetable Soup

1 pound bulk Italian sausage	.5 kg
2 onions, chopped	
2 teaspoons minced garlic	10 ml
1 (1 ounce) packet beefy recipe soup mix	28 g
1 (15 ounce) can sliced carrots, drained	425 g
2 (15 ounce) cans Italian stewed tomatoes	2 (425 g)
2 (15 ounce) cans garbanzo beans, drained	2 (425 g)
1 cup uncooked elbow macaroni	240 ml

- In large soup pot, brown sausage, onions and garlic. Pour off fat and add 4 cups (1 L) water, soup mix, carrots, tomatoes, garbanzo beans. Bring to a boil, reduce heat to low-medium and simmer for 15 minutes.

- Add elbow macaroni and continue cooking another 15 minutes or until macaroni is tender.

Potato-Sausage Soup

1 pound pork sausage link	.5 kg
1 cup chopped celery	240 ml
1 cup chopped onion	240 ml
2 (10 ounce) cans potato soup	2 (280 g)
1 (14 ounce) can chicken broth	396 g

• Cut pork sausage in 1-inch (2.5 cm) diagonal slices. In large heavy skillet, brown sausage slices, drain and remove to separate bowl. Leave about 2 tablespoons (30 ml) sausage drippings in skillet and saute celery and onion.

• Add potato soup, ¾ cup (180 ml) water, chicken broth and cooked sausage slices. Bring to a boil, reduce heat and simmer for 20 minutes.

Easy Pork Stew

1 (1 pound) pork tenderloin, cut into small chunks	.5 kg
2 (12 ounce) jars pork gravy	2 (340 g)
½ cup chili sauce	120 ml
1 (16 ounce) package frozen stew vegetables, thawed	.5 kg

• In greased soup pot on medium-high heat, cook pork pieces for 10 minutes, stirring frequently.

• Stir in gravy, chili sauce and stew vegetables and bring to a boil. Reduce heat and simmer for 15 minutes or until vegetables are tender.

Meatball Stew

1 (18 ounce) package frozen, cooked Italian meatballs	510 g
1 (14 ounce) cans beef broth	396 g
2 (15 ounce) cans Italian stewed tomatoes	2 (425 g)
1 (16 ounce) package frozen stew vegetables	.5 kg

- Place meatballs, beef broth and stewed tomatoes in large saucepan. Bring to boiling, reduce heat and simmer for 10 minutes or until meatballs are thoroughly hot.

- Add vegetables and cook on medium heat for 10 minutes. Mixture will be fairly thin. For thicker stew, mix 2 tablespoons (30 ml) cornstarch in ¼ cup (60 ml) water and stir into stew. Bring to a boil and stir constantly until stew thickens.

Southern Turnip Greens Stew

2 (16 ounce) packages frozen chopped turnip greens	2 (.5 kg)
1 (10 ounce) package frozen diced onion and bell peppers	280 g
2 cups chopped, cooked ham	480 ml
2 (15 ounce) cans chicken broth	2 (425 g)

- In soup pot, combine all ingredients and 1 teaspoon (5 ml) black pepper. Bring mixture to a boil, reduce heat, cover and simmer for 30 minutes.

Easy Pork Tenderloin Stew

2 - 3 cups cubed, cooked pork	480 ml
1 (12 ounce) jar pork gravy	340 g
¼ cup chili sauce	60 ml
1 (16 ounce) package frozen stew vegetables	.5 kg

- In soup pot, combine all ingredients and ½ cup (120 ml) water.

- Boil 2 minutes; reduce heat and simmer for 10 minutes. Serve with cornbread or hot biscuits.

Quick Brunswick Stew

1 (15 ounce) can beef stew	425 g
1 (15 ounce) can chicken stew	425 g
1 (15 ounce) can lima beans with liquid	425 g
2 (15 ounce) cans stewed tomatoes with liquid	2 (425 g)
1 (15 ounce) can whole kernel corn	425 g
½ teaspoon hot sauce, optional	2 ml

- In large stew pot, combine beef stew, chicken stew, beans, tomatoes and corn. On medium-high heat, bring stew to boiling, reduce heat and simmer for 20 minutes.

- Brunswick stew needs to be a little spicy, so stir in ¼ teaspoon (1 ml) hot sauce, taste and add more if needed. If you don't want spicy, add 1 tablespoon (15 ml) Worcestershire sauce to stew.

Bean and Chicken Chili

3 (15 ounce) cans navy beans with liquid	3 (425 g)
2 (14 ounce) cans chicken broth	2 (396 g)
¼ cup (½ stick) butter	60 ml
1 large onion, chopped	
3 cups cooked, chopped chicken	710 ml
1 (7 ounce) can chopped green chilies	198 g
2 teaspoons ground cumin	10 ml
½ teaspoon dried oregano	2 ml
Shredded Monterey Jack cheese	

- In large saucepan, combine beans, broth, butter and onion. Bring to a boil; reduce heat and simmer 15 minutes, stirring occasionally.

- With potato masher, mash bean mixture several times so that about half the beans are mashed. Add chicken, green chilies and seasoning. Bring to a boil, reduce heat, cover and simmer another 15 minutes.

- To serve, spoon into soup bowls and top with a heaping tablespoon of cheese.

A Different Chili

2 onions, coarsely chopped	
3 (15 ounce) cans great northern beans, drained	3 (425 g)
2 (14 ounce) cans chicken broth	2 (396 g)
2 tablespoons minced garlic	30 ml
1 (7 ounce) can chopped green chilies	198 g
1 tablespoon ground cumin	15 ml
3 cups cooked, finely chopped chicken breasts	710 ml
1 (8 ounce) package shredded Monterey Jack cheese	227 g

• In large, heavy pot with a little oil, cook onions, about 5 minutes, but do not brown. Place 1 can beans in shallow bowl and mash with fork.

• Add mashed beans, 2 remaining cans of beans, chicken broth, garlic, green chilies and cumin. Bring to a boil, reduce heat, cover and simmer 30 minutes.

• Add chopped chicken (or deli turkey), stirring to blend well and heat until chili is thoroughly hot. When serving, top each bowl with 3 tablespoons (45 ml) of Jack cheese.

Black Bean Stew Supper

1 pound pork sausage ring, thinly sliced	.5 kg
2 onions, chopped	
3 ribs celery, sliced	
3 (15 ounce) cans black beans, drained, rinsed	3 (425 g)
2 (10 ounce) cans diced tomatoes and green chilies	2 (280 g)
2 (14 ounce) cans chicken broth	2 (396 g)

- Place sausage slices, onion and celery in soup pot with a little oil and cook until sausage is slightly brown and onion is soft. Drain fat off. Add beans, tomatoes and green chilies and broth.

- Bring mixture to a boil, reduce heat and simmer for 25 minutes. Take out about 2 cups (480 ml) soup mixture and place in food processor and pulse until almost smooth. Return mixture to soup pot and stir; this will thicken stew. Return heat to high until stew is thoroughly hot.

Supper Gumbo

1 (10 ounce) can condensed pepper pot soup	280 g
1 (10 ounce) can condensed chicken gumbo soup	280 g
1 (6 ounce) can white crabmeat, flaked	168 g
1 (6 ounce) can tiny shrimp	168 g

- In saucepan, combine all ingredients with 1½ soup cans water.

- Cover and simmer for 15 minutes.

Potato and Ham Chowder

1 grated carrot	
2 ribs celery, sliced	
1 onion, chopped	
1 (4.5 ounce) package julienne potato mix	128 g
3 cups milk	710 ml
2 cups cooked, cubed ham	480 ml

- In soup pot, combine 2¾ cups (660 ml) water with carrot, celery, onion and potato mix. Bring to a boil, reduce heat, cover and simmer 20 minutes.

- Stir in milk and packet of sauce mix (from potatoes), mix well and return to boiling. Simmer 2 minutes and stir in ham.

Crab and Corn Chowder

1 (1.8 ounce) package Knorr's® leek soup mix	57 g
2 cups milk	480 ml
1 (8 ounce) can whole kernel corn	227 g
½ (8 ounce) package cubed processed cheese	½ (227 g)
1 (7 ounce) can crabmeat	198 g

- In large saucepan, combine soup mix and milk and cook over medium heat, stirring constantly until soup begins to thicken. While still on medium heat, stir in corn and cheese. Just before serving, add crab and stir until thoroughly hot.

Crunchy Sweet Onion-Jicama Salad

1 supersweet onion, thinly sliced
1 medium jicama, peeled, julienned
Prepared roasted garlic-vinaigrette salad dressing
Red leaf lettuce

- Combine onions and jicama in large bowl, pour enough salad dressing to partially cover. Toss and chill.

- Arrange lettuce leaves on individual salad plates and mound onion-jicama mixture onto lettuce.

Sesame-Romaine Salad

1 large head romaine lettuce	
2 tablespoons sesame seeds, toasted	30 ml
6 strips bacon, fried, crumbled	
½ cup grated Swiss cheese	120 ml
1 (8 ounce) bottle creamy Italian salad dressing	227 g

- Wash and dry lettuce. Tear into bite-size pieces.

- When ready to serve, sprinkle sesame seeds, bacon and cheese over lettuce and toss with about ½ cup (120 ml) salad dressing, adding more if needed.

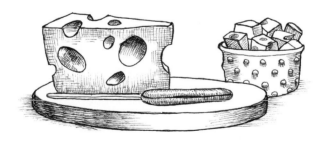

Orange-Almond Salad

1 head green leaf lettuce
4 slices bacon, fried, crumbled
⅓ cup slivered almonds, toasted   80 ml
1 (11 ounce) can mandarin oranges, drained, chilled   312 g

- Combine all ingredients in salad bowl.

- When ready to serve toss with vinaigrette dressing.

Greens and Fruit

1 (10 ounce) package spring salad greens   280 g
1 (11 ounce) can mandarin oranges, drained   312 g
¼ cup sliced almonds   60 ml
1 cup halved green seedless grapes   240 ml
¼ cup precooked bacon bits   60 ml

- In salad bowl, combine salad greens, oranges, almonds and
  grapes. Toss with raspberry vinaigrette salad dressing. Sprinkle
  with bacon bits.

Pear and Goat Cheese Salad

1 (10 ounce) package baby salad greens   280 g
¾ cup crumbled goat cheese   180 ml
2 pears, peeled, sliced
½ cup balsamic vinaigrette   120 ml
½ cup coarsely chopped walnuts   120 ml

- In salad bowl, combine salad greens, cheese and pear slices and
  toss with vinaigrette. Sprinkle walnuts over top of salad to serve.

Harmony Salad

2 heads red leaf lettuce, torn
2 (11 ounce) cans mandarin oranges, drained   (312 g)
2 avocados, peeled, cut into chunks
1 red onion, sliced
¼ cup sunflower kernels   60 ml

Dressing:
3 tablespoons red wine vinegar   45 ml
1 teaspoon ground cumin   5 ml
¼ cup extra-virgin olive oil   60 ml
2 tablespoons honey   30 ml

- In salad bowl, place lettuce, oranges, avocados and onion
  slices. Refrigerate. Using pint jar with lid, combine all dressing
  ingredients and shake well to mix. When ready to serve, shake
  dressing again and drizzle over salad and toss. Sprinkle sunflower
  kernels over top of salad.

Italian Salad

1 (10 ounce) package mixed salad greens   280 g
1 cup shredded mozzarella cheese   240 ml
1 (2 ounce) can sliced ripe black olives   57 g
1 (15 ounce) can cannellini beans, rinsed and drained 425 g

- In salad bowl, combine greens, cheese, olives and well drained
  cannellini beans. Toss with zesty Italian salad dressing.

Swiss Salad

1 large head romaine lettuce
1 bunch fresh green onions with tops, chopped
1 (8 ounce) package shredded Swiss cheese 227 g
½ cup toasted sunflower seeds 120 ml

- Tear lettuce into bite-size pieces. Add onions, cheese, sunflower seeds and toss. Serve with vinaigrette dressing.

Vinaigrette for Swiss Salad:
⅔ cup salad oil 160 ml
⅓ cup red wine vinegar 80 ml

- Mix all ingredients with 1 teaspoon (5 ml) salt and chill.

Crunchy Salad

¼ cup sesame seeds 60 ml
½ cup sunflower seeds 120 ml
½ cup slivered almonds 120 ml
1 head red leaf lettuce

- Toast sesame seeds, sunflower seeds and almonds at 300° (148° C) for about 10 minutes or until light brown.

- Tear lettuce into bite-size pieces and add seed mixture.

- Toss with creamy Italian dressing.

Mandarin Salad

1 head red-tipped lettuce
2 (11 ounce) cans mandarin oranges, drained 2 (312 g)
2 avocados, peeled, diced
1 small red onion, sliced
1 (8 ounce) bottle poppy seed dressing 227 g

- Combine all ingredients. When ready to serve, toss with ½ cup (120 ml) salad dressing, using more if needed.

Berry Delicious Salad

1 (10 ounce) package mixed salad greens	280 g
2 cups fresh blueberries	480 ml
⅔ cup crumbled gorgonzola cheese	160 ml
⅓ cup chopped pecans, toasted	80 ml
1 (8 ounce) bottle raspberry-vinaigrette salad dressing	227 g

- In salad bowl, combine salad greens, blueberries, cheese and pecans. Toss salad with about half the dressing, adding more if needed. Refrigerate.

Luscious Papaya-Chicken Salad

1 (10 ounce) package torn romaine lettuce leaves	280 g
2 ripe papayas, peeled, seeded, cubed	
1 large red bell pepper, seeded, chopped	
2 cups cooked, cubed chicken breast	480 ml
½ cup toasted, chopped pecans	120 ml

Dressing:

¼ cup lime juice	60 ml
⅓ cup honey	80 ml
2 teaspoons minced garlic	10 ml
3 tablespoons extra-virgin olive oil	45 ml

- In large salad bowl, combine lettuce, papayas and bell pepper. In small bowl, whisk together lime juice, honey, garlic and a little salt to taste. Slowly add olive oil in thin stream and whisk dressing until well blended.

- Pour dressing over salad, add cubed chicken and toss. To serve, sprinkle pecans over top of salad.

Raspberry-Orange Tossed Salad

Dressing:

½ cup seedless raspberry preserves	120 ml
¼ cup white wine vinegar	60 ml
¼ cup honey	60 ml
¼ cup oil	60 ml

Salad:

1 (10 ounce) package torn romaine	280 g
1 cup fresh raspberries	240 ml
1 (11 ounce) can mandarin oranges	312 g

• In bowl, combine all dressing ingredients and refrigerate until ready to use. In salad bowl, combine romaine, raspberries and oranges and toss with raspberry dressing.

Grandmother's Wilted Lettuce

6 cups leaf lettuce	1.5 L

Dressing:

3 slices bacon	
½ cup white vinegar	120 ml
1 tablespoon prepared mustard	15 ml
2 hard-boiled egg yolks, mashed, discard whites	

• Place lettuce in salad bowl. Fry bacon until crisp in skillet; remove bacon and drain. Crumble bacon. With bacon dripping remaining in skillet, add vinegar, mustard and egg yolks and cook until hot. While very hot, add crumbed bacon and pour over leaf lettuce and toss until thoroughly mixed. Serve immediately.

Spring Pear Salad Supper

1 (10 ounce) package spring salad mix	280 g
1 pound deli turkey, cut into thin strips	.5 kg
2 pears, cored, sliced	
1 cup Craisins® (dried cranberries)	240 ml
⅔ cup honey roasted slivered almonds	160 ml

Dressing:

1 (8 ounce) bottle wild berry vinaigrette	227 g
2 tablespoons olive oil	30 ml

- In salad bowl, combine salad mix, turkey strips, pears and cranberries and chill. When ready to serve, spoon vinaigrette and olive oil over salad and toss. Sprinkle almonds over top of salad.

Toss the Greens

1 (10 ounce) package mixed salad greens	280 g
1½ cups cherry tomato halves	360 ml
1 sliced cucumber	
1 sliced red onion, separated into rings	
1 pound seasoned, cooked chicken breasts, cut into strips	.5 kg

Dressing:

1 (8 ounce) bottle Italian salad dressing	227 g
¼ teaspoon cayenne pepper	1 ml

- In large salad bowl, combine greens, tomatoes, cucumber and onion rings and toss.

- When ready to serve, toss with salad dressing. Arrange salad on individual salad plates and top with strips of chicken and sprinkle with seasoned black pepper and cayenne pepper.

Green-Rice Salad

1 (10 ounce) package mixed baby salad greens	280 g
2 cups cooked rice, chilled	480 ml
2 (11 ounce) cans mandarin oranges, well drained, chilled	2 (312 g)
½ cup thinly sliced scallions, chilled	120 ml

Dressing:

1 (8 ounce) bottle Italian salad dressing	227 g
1 teaspoon ground cumin	5 ml
1 avocado, peeled and well mashed	

- In salad bowl, combine salad greens, rice, oranges and scallions.

- In jar with lid, combine salad dressing, cumin, avocado, ½ teaspoon (2 ml) each of salt and pepper. Pour about half dressing over salad and toss; adding more as needed.

Colorful Salad Toss

2 (8 ounce) packages baby spinach, stems removed	2 (227 g)
1 small head cauliflower, cut into small florets	
1 red bell pepper, seeded, chopped	
¾ cup whole walnut, halves	180 ml
½ cup roasted sunflower seeds	120 ml
1 (8 ounce) bottle wild berry vinaigrette salad dressing	227 g

- In large salad bowl, combine spinach, cauliflower, bell pepper strips, walnuts, sunflower seeds and a generous amount of salt and chill. Pour about half salad dressing over salad and toss. Add more dressing if needed.

Wilted Spinach-Walnut Salad

2 (8 ounce) packages baby spinach, stems removed	2 (227 g)
1 teaspoon minced garlic	5 ml
2 tablespoons olive oil	30 ml
½ cup whole walnuts, toasted	120 ml

- In skillet, saute spinach and garlic in hot oil on medium-high heat for about 5 minutes or until spinach is wilted. Sprinkle a little salt over spinach and mix. Toss with whole toasted walnuts.

Wilted Spinach Salad

1 (10 ounce) package fresh baby spinach	280 g
1 (15 ounce) can cannellini beans, rinsed, drained	425 g
¾ cup zesty Italian salad dressing	180 ml
¾ cup shredded Monterey Jack cheese	180 ml

- Remove large stems from spinach and place in salad bowl and add cannellini beans, toss. In saucepan, heat Italian salad dressing to boiling and pour over spinach-bean mixture and toss. Sprinkle cheese over salad and serve immediately.

Strawberry-Spinach Salad

1 (10 ounce) package fresh spinach, washed, stemmed	280 g
1 small jicama, peeled, julienne	
1 pint fresh strawberries, stemmed, halved	.5 kg
2½ cups fresh bean sprouts	600 ml
1 (8 ounce) bottle poppy seed dressing	227 g

- Combine spinach, jicama, strawberries and bean sprouts in large bowl. Toss with half the dressing, using more if needed.

Spinach and Apple Salad

1 (10 ounce) package fresh spinach	280 g
⅓ cup frozen orange juice concentrate, thawed	80 ml
¼ cup mayonnaise	60 ml
1 red apple, unpeeled, diced	
5 slices bacon, fried, crumbled	

• Tear spinach into small pieces. Mix orange juice and mayonnaise.
  Mix spinach and apple (cut apple at the last minute); pour
  dressing over salad and top with bacon.

Spinach-Orange Salad

1 (10 ounce) package spinach, stems removed	280 g
2 (10 ounce) cans mandarin oranges, drained	2 (280 g)
⅓ small jicama, peeled, julienned	
⅓ cup slivered almonds, toasted	80 ml

• Combine all ingredients in bowl. Toss with vinaigrette dressing.

Special Spinach Salad

1 (10 ounce) package fresh spinach	280 g
1 (16 ounce) can bean sprouts, drained	.5 kg
8 slices bacon, cooked crisp	
1 (11 ounce) can water chestnuts, chopped	312 g

• Combine spinach and bean sprouts.

• When ready to serve, add crumbled bacon and water chestnuts.
  Toss with vinaigrette salad dressing made from 3 parts olive oil
  and 1 part red wine vinegar.

Spinach Pecan Salad

1 (10 ounce) package baby spinach	280 g
2 eggs, hard-boiled, sliced	
½ cup toasted pecans	120 ml
1 (6 ounce) package cooked, crumbled bacon	168 g
¼ cup crumbled blue cheese	60 ml
Italian salad dressing	

- In salad bowl, combine spinach, sliced eggs, pecans, bacon and blue cheese; toss. Drizzle with a prepared Italian salad dressing.

Spinach and Chicken Salad

1 (10 ounce) package baby spinach	280 g
1 seedless cucumber, sliced	
1 red delicious apple, unpeeled, thinly sliced	
1 bunch fresh green onions, sliced	
3 cups coarsely shredded rotisserie chicken meat	710 ml

Dressing:
⅓ cup red wine vinegar	80 ml
3 tablespoons olive oil	710 ml
1 tablespoon dijon-style mustard	15 ml
½ teaspoon dried thyme	2 ml
1 tablespoon sugar	15 ml

- In salad bowl, combine spinach, cucumber, apple slices, green onions and chicken; toss to mix well.

- In saucepan, combine all dressing ingredients and heat just until thoroughly hot. Pour over salad and toss until salad is evenly coated. Serve immediately.

Spinach and Turkey Salad Supper

2 (8 ounce) packages baby spinach, stems removed	2 (227 g)
½ cup whole walnuts	120 ml
½ cup Craisins® (dried cranberries)	120 ml
2 red delicious apples, unpeeled, sliced	
1 pound deli smoked turkey, julienned	.5 kg
½ (15 ounce) bottle refrigerated honey-mustard dressing	½ (425 g)

- In large salad bowl, combine spinach, walnuts, cranberries, apples and turkey. Toss salad with half honey-mustard dressing and add more if needed.

Spinach Salad

1 (10 ounce) bag baby spinach	280 g
1 cup fresh sliced strawberries	240 ml
1 (3 ounce) package silvered almonds, toasted	84 g
½ cup crumbled feta cheese	120 ml

- In salad bowl, combine all ingredients and toss with poppy seed vinaigrette dressing.

Poppy Seed Vinaigrette Dressing:

½ cup sugar	120 ml
¼ cup white wine vinegar	60 ml
⅓ cup olive oil	80 ml
2 teaspoons poppy seeds	10 ml

- Combine all ingredients and toss with spinach mixture.

Salad Surprise

1 (10 ounce) bag fresh spinach, washed, stemmed	280 g
1 pint fresh strawberries, stemmed, halved	.5 kg
1 large banana, sliced	
⅔ cup chopped walnuts	160 ml
Poppy seed dressing	

- In large bowl, combine all salad ingredients.

- When ready to serve, toss with prepared poppy seed dressing.

Spinach Salad Oriental

1 (10 ounce) package fresh spinach	280 g
2 eggs, hard-boiled, sliced	
1 (14 ounce) can bean sprouts, drained	396 g
1 (8 ounce) can water chestnuts, chopped	227 g

- Combine all 4 ingredients. Top with dressing.

Dressing for Spinach Salad Oriental:

¾ cup olive oil	180 ml
⅓ cup sugar	80 ml
¼ cup ketchup	60 ml
3 tablespoons red wine vinegar	45 ml

- Combine all ingredients and mix well. Use desired amount of dressing and refrigerate remaining salad dressing.

Warm Spinach Salad

1 (10 ounce) package fresh spinach, stems removed	280 g
1 (15 ounce) can cannellini beans, rinsed, drained	425 g
1 (11 ounce) can mexicorn, drained	312 g
1 cup shredded Monterey Jack cheese	240 ml

Dressing:
1 (8 ounce) bottle zesty Italian salad dressing	227 g
1 sweet red bell pepper, seeded and chopped	

- In salad bowl combine spinach, cannellini beans and corn.

- In saucepan, combine salad dressing and chopped bell pepper. On high heat, bring to boiling, reduce heat to low and cook 2 minutes. Pour hot dressing over spinach-corn mixture and toss. Sprinkle with cheese and serve warm.

Spinach-Feta Cheese Salad

1 (10 ounce) bag baby spinach	280 g
1 cup fresh sliced strawberries	240 ml
1 (3 ounce) package slivered almonds, toasted	84 g
½ cup crumbled feta cheese	120 ml

Dressing:
½ cup sugar	120 ml
¼ cup white wine vinegar	60 ml
⅓ cup olive oil	80 ml
2 teaspoons poppy seeds	10 ml

- Combine spinach, strawberries, almonds and feta cheese in salad bowl.

- Combine all dressing ingredients and toss with spinach mixture.

Tossed Zucchini Salad

¾ cup unpeeled, grated zucchini	180 ml
1 (6 ounce) package shredded lettuce	168 g
½ cup sliced ripe olives	120 ml
1 carrot, grated	
⅓ cup shredded mozzarella cheese	80 ml
Zesty Italian salad dressing	

- In salad bowl, toss zucchini, lettuce, olives and grated carrot. Add cheese and toss with salad dressing.

Green Salad with Candied Pecans

Candied pecans:

1⅓ cups pecan halves	320 ml
¼ cup honey	60 ml
3 tablespoon light corn syrup	45 ml

Salad:

1 (10 ounce) package baby spinach	280 g
4 cups young salad greens	1 L
1 tart apple, thinly sliced	
1 cup crumbled blue cheese	240 ml
1 (8 ounce) bottle zesty Italian salad dressing	227 g

- Preheat oven to 350° (176° C). Combine pecans, honey and corn syrup in bowl and stir until all pecans are well coated. Spread out to rimmed baking sheet and bake 12 minutes. Remove to piece of foil, separating clumps with fork; cool.

- In salad bowl, combine spinach, greens, apple slices and bleu cheese; toss with about half bottle of salad dressing.

Red and Green Salad

3 small zucchini, thinly sliced	
2 red delicious apples with peel, chopped	
2 cups fresh broccoli florets	480 ml
¾ cup coarsely chopped walnuts	180 ml
1 (8 ounce) bottle creamy Italian salad dressing	227 g

• In salad bowl, combine zucchini, apples, broccoli and walnuts and toss.

• Pour about ¾ bottle of salad dressing over salad and toss. Use more dressing if needed. Serve immediately.

Summer Cucumbers

2 seedless cucumbers, peeled, sliced	
1 (8 ounce) bottle zesty Italian salad dressing	227 g
1 (8 ounce) carton sour cream	227 g
1 tablespoon chopped chives	15 ml

• Place cucumbers in bowl and pour salad dressing over cucumbers and marinate about 30 minutes, tossing once to distribute marinade. To serve, drain marinade from cucumbers and stir in sour cream and chives.

Sunshine Carrots

3 cups shredded carrots	710 ml
1 (15 ounce) can crushed pineapple, drained	425 g
½ cup mayonnaise	120 ml
½ cup sliced almonds and sunflower seeds	120 ml

• In bowl, combine carrots and pineapple and stir in mayonnaise. Refrigerate until ready to serve. To serve, stir in almonds and sunflower seeds and toss to coat almonds and sunflower seeds.

Special Stuffed Celery

1 bunch celery	
1 (8 ounce) package cream cheese	227 g
¼ cup finely chopped pecans	60 ml
¼ cup finely chopped bell pepper	60 ml
1 (4 ounce) jar chopped pimento	114 g

- Cut celery into pieces convenient for handling.

- With mixer, beat cream cheese until creamy and stir in pecans, bell pepper, pimentos and a little salt. Fill celery hollows and serve with a relish plate.

Marinated Cucumbers

⅓ cup vinegar	80 ml
2 tablespoons sugar	30 ml
1 teaspoon dried dillweed	5 ml
3 cucumbers, peeled, sliced	

- Combine vinegar, sugar, 1 teaspoon (5 ml) salt, dill weed and ¼ teaspoon (1 ml) pepper. Pour over cucumbers. Chill.

Carrot Salad

3 cups finely grated carrots	710 ml
1 (8 ounce) can crushed pineapple, drained	227 g
4 tablespoons flaked coconut	60 ml
1 tablespoon sugar	15 ml
⅓ cup mayonnaise	80 ml

- Combine all ingredients. Toss with mayonnaise and mix well. Chill.

Sweet Corn Salad

2 (10 ounce) packages frozen whole kernel corn	2 (280 g)
2 ribs celery, sliced	
⅓ cup sweet pickle relish, drained	80 ml
¾ cup diced apples	180 ml
3 tablespoons lemon juice	45 ml

Dressing:

⅓ cup mayonnaise	80 ml
1½ tablespoons mustard	22 ml
2 tablespoons sugar	30 ml
1 teaspoon dried parsley	5 ml

- Cook corn as directed on package. Toss with celery, pickle relish and apples that have been covered with lemon juice.

- In small bowl, combine mayonnaise, mustard, sugar and parsley, mixing well. Spoon over corn mixture and toss; chill.

Cucumber-Onion Salad

2 - 3 seedless cucumbers, sliced	
2 onions, sliced	
1 tablespoon white vinegar	15 ml
½ cup sour cream	120 ml

- In mixing bowl, sprinkle ½ teaspoon (2 ml) salt over cucumbers and let stand 20 minutes; drain. Add onions and vinegar, toss. Chill. When ready to serve, stir in sour cream.

Veggie Salad

1 (5.6 ounce) box toasted pine nut couscous	155 g
1 (15 ounce) can mixed vegetables, well drained	425 g
1 sweet red bell pepper, diced	
⅔ cup crumbled feta cheese	160 ml

Dressing:

⅓ cup olive oil	80 ml
2 tablespoons lemon juice	30 ml
2 teaspoons sugar	30 ml
1 teaspoon lemon pepper	5 ml

- Cook couscous as directed on box and cool. In bowl, combine couscous, mixed vegetables, bell pepper and cheese, mixing well.

- In jar with lid, combine oil, lemon juice, sugar and lemon pepper; shake well to blend ingredients. Pour over salad and toss. Serve on bed of lettuce and garnish with cherry tomatoes.

Green and White Salad

1 (16 ounce) package frozen green peas, thawed	.5 kg
1 head cauliflower, cut into bite-size pieces	
1 (8 ounce) carton sour cream	227 g
1 (1 ounce) package dry ranch-style salad dressing	28 g

- In large bowl, combine peas and cauliflower.

- Combine sour cream and salad dressing. Toss with vegetables and chill.

Warm Bean Salad

1 small onion, diced
2 large ribs celery, diced
1 sweet red bell pepper, diced
2 (15 ounce) cans cannellini beans, washed, drained   2 (425 g)

Dressing:

¼ cup olive oil	60 ml
2 teaspoons prepared minced garlic	10 ml
⅓ cup lemon juice	80 ml
1 teaspoon sugar	5 ml

- In skillet with a little oil, cook onion and celery for 5 minutes or until onion is slightly brown and celery is tender-crisp. Add bell pepper and beans and toss.

- Combine dressing ingredients and 1 teaspoon (5 ml) salt, mixing well. Pour over bean mixture and toss. Serve warm.

Colorful English Pea Salad

2 (16 ounce) packages frozen green peas, thawed, drained	2 (.5 kg)
1 (12 ounce) package cubed mozzarella cheese	340 g
1 red and 1 orange bell pepper, chopped	
1 onion, chopped	
1¼ cups mayonnaise	300 ml

- In large salad bowl, combine peas (uncooked), cubed cheese, bell peppers and onion; toss to mix. Stir in mayonnaise, 1 teaspoon (5 ml) each of salt and pepper. Chill.

Colorful Veggie Salad

4 cups fresh broccoli florets	1 L
4 cups cauliflower florets	1 L
1 red onion, sliced	
1 (4 ounce) can sliced ripe olives	114 g
3 small zucchini, sliced	

Dressing:

1 packet zesty Italian dry dressing mix	
1½ cups bottled zesty Italian salad dressing	360 ml
2 tablespoons extra-virgin olive oil	30 ml

- In large bowl, combine broccoli, cauliflower, onion, olives and zucchini and toss together.

- In small bowl, combine dry dressing mix, bottled dressing and olive oil, mixing well. Pour over vegetables and toss to coat. Chill.

Cashew-Pea Salad

1 (16 ounce) package frozen green peas, thawed	.5 kg
¼ cup diced celery	60 ml
1 bunch fresh green onions with tops, chopped	
1 cup cashew pieces	240 ml
½ cup mayonnaise	120 ml

- Combine peas, celery, onions and cashews.

- Toss with mayonnaise and seasoned with ½ teaspoon (2 ml) each of salt and pepper.

Cherry Tomato Salad

Dressing:
2 tablespoons red-wine vinegar	30 ml
2 tablespoons olive oil	30 ml

Salad:
2 pints cherry tomatoes, halved	1 kg
1 bunch fresh green onions, chopped	
1 small cucumber, peeled, chopped	

- Combine all dressing ingredients and 1 teaspoon (5 ml) salt and ½ teaspoon (2 ml) pepper, mixing well.

- In salad bowl, combine tomato halves, green onion and cucumber and toss with dressing. Refrigerate.

Black Bean and Mandarin Salad

1 (15 ounce) can beans, rinsed, drained	425 g
1 (11 ounce) can mandarin oranges, well drained	312 g
1 cup diced jicama	240 ml
¼ cup finely diced red onion	60 ml
¼ cup finely diced jalapeno	60 ml
½ (8 ounce) bottle zesty Italian dressing	½ (227 g)

- In large bowl, combine all ingredients and chill until ready to serve, tossing occasionally.

Carrot and Apple Salad

1 (16 ounce) package shredded carrots	.5 kg
1 green apple, unpeeled, chopped	
1 red apple, unpeeled, chopped	
½ cup golden raisins	120 ml
1 tablespoon mayonnaise	15 ml
1 tablespoon lemon juice	15 ml

- In bowl, combine shredded carrots, apples and raisins. Add mayonnaise and lemon juice and toss. Refrigerate.

Festive Green and Yellow Veggie Salad

3 - 4 cups small broccoli florets	710 ml
3 small yellow squash, seeded, cubed	
3 - 4 cups small cauliflower florets	710 ml
1 cup chopped celery	240 ml
1 cup chopped red bell pepper	240 ml

Dressing:

½ cup mayonnaise	120 ml
2 tablespoons white vinegar	30 ml
3 tablespoons sugar	45 ml

- In large salad bowl (with lid) combine broccoli, squash, cauliflower florets, celery and bell pepper and mix.

- Combine all dressing ingredients with 1 teaspoon (5 ml) salt and mix well. Spoon over veggie ingredients and toss. Refrigerate 30 minutes before serving.

Four Bean Salad and Extra

2 (15 ounce) cans garbanzo beans, rinsed, drained	2 (425 g)
1 (15 ounce) can cut green beans, drained	425 g
1 (15 ounce) can great northern, drained	425 g
1 (15 ounce) can black beans, drained	425 g
2 ribs celery, sliced	
1 red onion, thinly sliced	

Dressing:

⅓ cup red wine vinegar	80 ml
¼ cup extra-virgin olive oil	60 ml
2 teaspoons dijon-style mustard	10 ml
1 tablespoon sugar	15 ml

- In large bowl, combine the 5 cans of beans, celery and onion slices, mixing well.

- In pint jar with lid combine vinegar, olive oil, mustard, sugar and about 1 teaspoon (5 ml) of salt. Shake jar vigorously until all ingredients are mixed well. Pour over bean mixture, stirring well. Chill.

Broccoli Salad

5 cups stemmed broccoli florets	1.3 L
1 red bell pepper, julienned	
1 cup chopped celery	240 ml
8 - 12 ounces Monterey Jack cheese, cubed	227 g

- Combine all ingredients and mix well.

- Toss with dressing. Chill.

Creamy Vegetable Salad

1 (10 ounce) package frozen green peas, thawed	280 g
1 cup chopped celery	240 ml
1 cup diced carrots	240 ml
1 (15 ounce) can Italian green beans, drained	425 g
1 cucumber, peeled and sliced	

Dressing:

1 (8 ounce) bottle French dressing	227 g
½ cup mayonnaise	120 ml
1 teaspoon minced garlic	5 ml

• In bowl (with lid) combine peas, celery, carrots, green beans and cucumber. Combine French dressing, mayonnaise and garlic, mixing well and pour over vegetables; toss. Refrigerate 30 minutes before serving.

Cheesy Vegetable Salad

2 seedless cucumbers coarsely chopped	
1 sweet red bell pepper, julienned	
1 sweet (Vidalia) onion, coarsely chopped	
1 cup crumbled feta cheese	240 ml
⅔ cup vinaigrette salad dressing	160 ml

• In salad bowl, combine cucumbers, bell pepper, onion and feta cheese and toss with salad dressing.

Asparagus With Citrus Dressing

2 bunches fresh asparagus, ends trimmed

Citrus Dressing:

3 tablespoons extra-virgin olive oil	45 ml
⅔ cup fresh orange juice	160 ml
1 teaspoon orange zest	5 ml

- Place about 2 cups (480 ml) water and ½ teaspoon (2 ml) salt in large skillet (large enough to lay asparagus flat in skillet) and bring to a boil. Add asparagus and cook until tender, about 7 or 8 minutes. Drain asparagus on cloth towel and scatter some ice cubes over asparagus to cool.

- For dressing, combine oil, orange juice, orange zest and ½ teaspoon (2 ml) black pepper in small bowl, mix well. Refrigerate, but bring to room temperature before using. When serving, spoon dressing over asparagus and serve immediately.

Avocado-Corn Salad

2 ripe avocados, peeled, diced	
2 tablespoons fresh lime juice	30 ml
3 cups grape tomatoes, halved	710 ml
2 (11 ounce) cans mexicorn, drained	2 (312 g)
1 (8 ounce) bottle zesty Italian salad dressing	227 g

- Place avocados in salad bowl and spoon lime juice and a little salt over avocados. Add tomatoes and corn.

- Spoon about ½ cup (120 ml) of dressing over salad.

Green Beans With Tomatoes

2 pounds frozen, cut green beans	1 kg
4 tomatoes, chopped, drained	
1 bunch green onions, chopped	
1 cup Italian salad dressing	240 ml

- Place beans in saucepan, cover with water and bring to boil.

- Cook uncovered for 8 to 10 minutes or until tender crisp, drain and chill.

- Add tomatoes, green onions and salad dressing and toss to coat.

Cabbage-Carrot Slaw

1 (10 ounce) package slaw mix	280 g
1 (16 ounce) package shredded carrots	.5 kg
2 delicious apples, diced	
1 cup Craisins® (dried cranberries)	240 ml
⅔ cup chopped walnuts	160 ml
1 (8 ounce) bottle poppy seed salad dressing	227 g

- In salad bowl, combine slaw mix, carrots, apples, cranberries and walnuts. Toss with poppy seed dressing and chill.

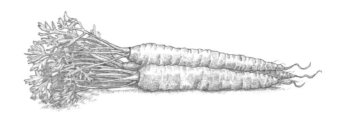

Jicama-Zucchini Slaw

Dressing:
½ cup olive oil	120 ml
⅓ cup red wine vinegar	80 ml
1 teaspoon dijon-style mustard	5 ml
2 tablespoon mayonnaise	30 ml

Slaw:
1½ pounds jicama	.7 kg
3 small zucchini	
½ sweet red bell pepper, died	

- Combine all dressing ingredients in bowl. Toss with jicama, zucchini and bell pepper. Chill.

Red Cabbage Slaw

1 large head red cabbage	
2 onions, chopped	
½ cup coleslaw dressing	120 ml
½ cup French salad dressing	120 ml

- Slice cabbage and combine with onions.

- Combine dressings and toss with cabbage and onions and chill.

Nutty Slaw

1 (16 ounce) package shredded carrots	.5 kg
3 cups shredded cabbage	710 ml
2 red delicious apples, diced	
¾ cup raisins	180 ml
¾ cup chopped walnuts	180 ml
1 (8 ounce) bottle coleslaw dressing	227 g

- In plastic bowl with lid, combine shredded carrots, shredded cabbage, apples, raisins and walnuts.

- Pour about three-fourths bottle of slaw dressing over mixture and increase dressing as needed. Cover and refrigerate.

Broccoli Slaw

1 (16 ounce) package broccoli slaw (broccoli rabe)	.5 kg
1 cup very small fresh broccoli florets	240 ml
¾ cup Craisins® (dried cranberries)	180 ml
1 Granny Smith apples, unpeeled, diced	
1 (11 ounce) can mandarin oranges, well drained	312 g
1 (8 ounce) bottle poppy seed dressing	227 g
½ cup toasted, slivered almonds	120 ml

- In salad bowl, combine broccoli slaw, broccoli florets, cranberries, apple and oranges. Toss with poppy seed dressing. Sprinkle almonds on top of salad. Refrigerate 20 minutes before serving.

Coleslaw with Buttermilk Dressing

Slaw:
2 (10 ounce) packages finely shredded cabbage   2 (280 g)
1 carrot, shredded

Dressing:
½ cup mayonnaise   120 ml
½ cup sugar   120 ml
½ cup buttermilk   120 ml
3 tablespoons lemon juice   45 ml

• Place cabbage and carrot in salad bowl.

• In small bowl, combine mayonnaise, sugar, buttermilk, lemon juice and 1 teaspoon (5 ml) salt. Pour over cabbage and carrot and toss. Cover and chill at least 25 minutes.

Color-Coded Salad

1 (16 ounce) package tri-colored macaroni, cooked,
   drained   .5 kg
1 red bell pepper, julienne
1 cup chopped zucchini   240 ml
1 cup broccoli florets   240 ml
1 (8 ounce) bottle Caesar salad dressing   227 g

• Combine all ingredients. Toss with salad dressing. Chill.

Sesame-Broccoli Salad

¼ cup sesame seeds	60 ml
1 (16 ounce) package broccoli rabe slaw	.5 kg
1 sweet red bell pepper, seeded, chopped	
2 (9 ounce) packages fresh tortellini, cooked	2 (255 g)

Dressing:

1 (8 ounce) bottle vinaigrette salad dressing	227 g
2 tablespoons olive oil	30 ml

- In skillet, toast sesame seeds over low to medium heat in just a little oil and set aside. In salad bowl, combine broccoli rabe, bell pepper and cooked tortellini. Drizzle salad dressing and olive oil over salad and toss. Chill and just before serving, sprinkle sesame seeds over salad.

Tri-Color Pasta Salad

3 cups tricolor spiral pasta	710 ml
1 tablespoon olive oil	15 ml
1 (8 ounce) package cubed cheddar cheese	227 g
1 large bunch broccoli, cut into small florets	
1 cup celery, cubed	240 ml
1 cup cucumber, peeled, cubed	240 ml
Ranch salad dressing	

- Cook pasta according to package directions, drain well and add olive oil to keep pasta from sticking together. Transfer to large salad bowl and add cheese cubes, broccoli, celery, cucumber and ample amount of salt and pepper. Toss with salad dressing.

Pronto Pasta Lunch

1 pound refrigerated fettuccine	.5 kg
1 cup diced zucchini	240 ml
1 cup diced yellow squash	240 ml
1 (10 ounce) package frozen peas and carrots, thawed	280 g
¼ cup pine nuts, toasted	60 ml

Dressing:
½ cup ricotta cheese	120 ml
1 cup chicken broth	240 ml
2 tablespoons butter	30 ml

- Cook fettuccine according to package directions, drain.

- While fettuccine is cooking, place all dressing ingredients with ½ teaspoon (2 ml) each of salt and pepper in saucepan and heat, mixing well. Add vegetables and cook about 3 minutes or until vegetables are tender-crisp.

- Stir into cooked fettuccine and add pine nuts; toss to serve. If you like, parmesan cheese can be sprinkled over tossed vegetables and pasta.

Special Macaroni Salad

1 (16 ounce) carton deli macaroni salad	.5 kg
1 (8 ounce) can whole kernel corn, drained	227 g
2 small zucchini, diced	
⅔ cup chunky salsa	160 ml

- In salad bowl with lid, combine macaroni salad, corn, zucchini and salsa, mixing well. Cover and chill until ready to serve.

Quick Salad Supper

1 (12 ounce) package frozen precooked salad tortellini, thawed	340 g
1 (16 ounce) package frozen cooked salad shrimp	.5 kg
1 (4 ounce) can sliced ripe olives, drained	114 g
⅓ cup finely chopped red onion	80 ml

Dressing:

1 (8 ounce) bottle zesty Italian salad dressing	227 g
½ teaspoon paprika	

- In salad bowl, combine tortellini, shrimp, olives and onion and toss with about ½ cup (120 ml) of salad dressing. Before serving, sprinkle with ½ teaspoon (2 ml) pepper and paprika.

Pasta Salad Bowl

1 (16 ounce) package bow-tie pasta	.5 kg
1 (16 ounce) package frozen green peas	.5 kg
½ cup sliced scallions	120 ml
1 seedless cucumber, thinly sliced	
2 cups deli (or leftover) ham, cut in strips	480 ml

Dressing:

⅔ cup mayonnaise	160 ml
¼ cup cider vinegar	60 ml
2 tablespoons sugar	30 ml
2 teaspoons dried dill	10 ml

- Cook pasta according to package directions; drain and cool under cold running water and drain again. Transfer to serving bowl and add peas, scallions, cucumber slices and ham strips.

- In small bowl, combine all dressing ingredients and spoon over salad; toss to mix and coat well. Chill.

Pasta Plus Salad

1 (16 ounce) package bow-tie pasta	.5 kg
1 (10 ounce) package frozen green peas, thawed	280 g
1 red bell pepper, seeded, cut in strips	
1 (8 ounce) package cubed Swiss cheese	227 g
1 small yellow summer squash, sliced	

Dressing:

¾ cup mayonnaise	180 ml
2 tablespoons lemon juice	30 ml
1 tablespoon sugar	15 ml
½ cup heavy cream	120 ml

- Cook pasta according to package directions and add peas last 2 minutes of cooking time. Drain pasta and peas; rinse in cold water and drain again. Transfer to large salad bowl. Add bell pepper, cheese and squash.

- Combine dressing ingredients and mix well. Spoon over salad with a little salt and pepper to taste. Toss salad and refrigerate.

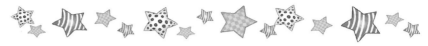

Nutty Rice Salad

1 (6 ounce) package long-grain and wild rice mix	168 g
1 (6 ounce) jar marinated artichoke hearts, drained,	
chopped	168 g
1 cup golden raisins	240 ml
4 fresh green onions, chopped with tops	
¾ cup toasted pecan halves	180 ml

Dressing:

⅓ cup orange juice	80 ml
¼ cup olive oil	60 ml
1 tablespoon lemon juice	15 ml
1 tablespoon sugar	15 ml

- Prepare rice mix according to package directions, drain and cool. Place in salad bowl and add artichoke hearts, raisins and green onions.

- For dressing, combine orange juice, oil, lemon juice, and sugar. Stir dressing until well blended and spoon over salad; toss. Cover and chill at least 30 minutes; top with pecans before serving.

TIP: Pecans can be toasted in 300° (148° C) oven for 10 minutes.

Skillet Rice Salad

Dressing and Topping:

8 slices bacon	
Bacon drippings	
1 tablespoon flour	**15 ml**
1 tablespoon sugar	**15 ml**
¼ cup white vinegar	**60 ml**

Salad:

1 (6 ounce) box long-grain, wild rice	**168 g**
1 cup chopped celery	**240 ml**
1 cup chopped cucumbers	**240 ml**
1 small onion, sliced, separated into rings	
3 cups romaine, broken into bite-size pieces	**710 ml**

- In large skillet, fry bacon until crisp. Break into small chunks; set aside. With bacon drippings still in skillet, stir in flour, sugar, vinegar, a little salt and stir in ¾ cup (180 ml) water. Cook over low-medium heat, stirring constantly until dressing is smooth.

- In saucepan, cook rice as directed on box; drain. While rice is still hot, add celery, cucumbers, onion rings and romaine to skillet and toss with dressing until all ingredients are well coated. Serve right from skillet with bacon pieces sprinkled over top.

Cool Couscous and Spinach Salad

1 (10 ounce) package chicken-flavored couscous	280 g
1 (8 ounce) package fresh baby spinach, torn	227 g
1 bunch fresh green onions, sliced	
1 (5 ounce) package grated parmesan cheese	143 g

Dressing:

⅓ cup olive oil	80 ml
¼ cup lemon juice	60 ml
2 tablespoons snipped fresh dill	30 ml
2 tablespoons sugar	30 ml

- Cook couscous according to package directions and let stand 5 minutes, then fluff with fork. Cool. Stir in torn spinach and green onions. In small bowl, combine all dressing ingredients, mixing well.

- When ready to serve, place couscous, spinach and green onions in salad bowl and toss with dressing. Sprinkle with parmesan cheese and toss lightly.

Couscous Salad

1 (5.6 ounce) box parmesan couscous	155 g
¾ cup chopped fresh mushrooms	180 ml
1 (4 ounce) can sliced ripe olives, drained	114 g
½ cup green bell pepper	120 ml
½ cup red bell pepper	120 ml
½ cup Italian salad dressing	120 ml

- Cook couscous according to package directions. Cover and let stand 5 minutes, then fluff with fork. In salad bowl, combine couscous, mushrooms, olives and bell peppers. Stir in salad dressing, cover and chill before serving.

Gourmet Couscous Salad

1 (10 ounce) box chicken-flavored couscous	280 g
2 tomatoes, coarsely chopped	
2 zucchini, coarsely chopped	
4 fresh green onions, sliced	
1 cup feta cheese, crumbled	240 ml

Dressing:
1 tablespoon lemon juice	15 ml
¼ cup olive oil	60 ml
½ teaspoon dried basil	2 ml
½ teaspoon seasoned black pepper	2 ml

- Cook couscous according to package directions, leaving out butter. In salad bowl combine tomatoes, zucchini, green onions and couscous. Combine dressing ingredients in pint jar with lid and shake until well blended. When ready to serve, add feta cheese to salad, pour dressing over salad and toss.

Cracker Salad

1 sleeve saltine crackers	
1 tomato	
1 egg, hard-boiled, finely chopped	
½ green bell pepper, chopped	
4 green onions, chopped	
1½ cups mayonnaise	360 ml

- This salad must be made just before serving!

- In salad bowl, coarsely crush crackers with your hands (in large pieces). Add remaining ingredients, adding a little salt and pepper, if you like. Serve immediately; it will not keep.

Dilled Potato Salad

2 pounds small new (red) potatoes	1 kg
1 sweet red bell pepper, chopped	
1 bunch fresh green onions, sliced	
¾ cup crumbled feta cheese	180 ml

Dressing:

½ cup olive oil	120 ml
⅓ cup red wine vinegar	80 ml
1 tablespoon dried dill	15 ml
1 teaspoon sugar	5 ml

- In saucepan, bring potatoes and about 2 cups (480 ml) water to a boil and cook about 25 minutes or until potatoes are tender; drain and bring to room temperature. Cut potatoes in quarters. Place in bowl and add bell pepper and green onions.

- For dressing, combine oil, vinegar, dill, sugar, 1 teaspoon (5 ml) pepper and liberal amount of salt. Pour over warm potatoes, bell pepper and onions and toss. Sprinkle cheese over top and gently stir to toss.

A Crunchy Potato Salad

10 - 12 small new (red) potatoes, cut in wedges	
1 (10 ounce) package red-tip lettuce	280 g
6 ounces feta cheese, crumbled	168 g
½ cup whole pecans	120 ml
3 eggs, hard-boiled, cut in wedges	

Dressing:

⅓ cup very finely chopped shallots	80 ml
⅓ cup honey	80 ml
¼ cup lemon juice	60 ml
½ cup olive oil	120 ml

- In saucepan, cook potatoes in salted water about 15 minutes or until tender; drain and set aside to cool. In salad bowl, combine lettuce, feta cheese and pecans.

- For dressing, combine shallots, honey, lemon juice, olive oil and an ample amount of salt and pepper in pint jar with lid. Shake vigorously until well blended.

- When ready to serve, add potatoes to salad bowl mixture and toss. Shake dressing again and pour over salad and toss. Garnish with egg wedges.

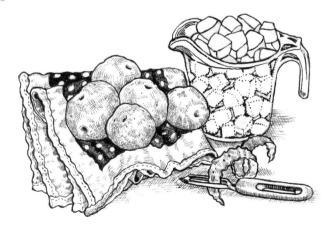

Super Orzo-Veggie Salad

1 (8 ounce) package uncooked orzo pasta	227 g
1 (10 ounce) package frozen broccoli florets	280 g
1 (10 ounce) package frozen green peas	280 g
1 (12 ounce) jar baby corn nuggets, drained	340 g
3 cups cooked (deli or leftover) cubed ham	710 ml

Dressing:

1 (8 ounce) jar sweet-and-sour sauce	227 g
2 tablespoon olive oil	30 ml

- In large saucepan, cook orzo according to package directions. Five minutes before orzo is done, stir in broccoli and peas; bring back to boiling and cook 5 minutes. Drain well.

- Transfer pasta and vegetables to salad bowl and add corn and ham. Sprinkle salad with 1 teaspoon (5 ml) salt and add sweet-and-sour sauce and olive oil. Toss and serve immediately.

Sour Cream Potato Salad

12 medium red potatoes, unpeeled	
1¼ cups mayonnaise	300 ml
1 cup sour cream	240 ml
1 cup fresh green onions with tops, chopped	240 ml

- Boil red potatoes until tender about 20 minutes. Slice potatoes.

- Combine mayonnaise, sour cream and 1 teaspoon (5 ml) salt.

- When potatoes are cool toss with sour cream mixture. Add green onions.

Quick Potato Salad

3 - 4 baking potatoes	
½ cup diced dill or sweet pickles	120 ml
3 eggs, hard-boiled, chopped	
¾ - 1 cup mayonnaise	180 ml

- Cook potatoes (potatoes can be cooked the night before using) in microwave and when cooled, peel and cut into 1-inch (2.5 cm) cubes. Place in large bowl. Add pickles (or pickle relish), chopped eggs and ample amount of salt and pepper. Stir in mayonnaise.

Potato Salad-German Style

2 pounds new (red) potatoes, cut in thin slices	1 kg
½ pound bacon, cooked and crumbled	
(save drippings)	227 g
1 small onion, chopped	
¼ cup chopped fresh parsley	60 ml
1 red and 1 green bell pepper, chopped	

Dressing:

½ cup cider vinegar	120 ml
¼ cup sugar	60 ml
Bacon drippings from cooked bacon	

- Steam potatoes, covered 10 to 12 minutes or until tender and transfer to bowl with lid. Add onion, parsley and bell peppers.

- For dressing, combine vinegar, sugar and 1 teaspoon (5 ml) each of salt and pepper, mix well and stir in bacon drippings. Spoon over potato-onion mixture and toss. Serve at room temperature.

Deviled Eggs

6 eggs, hard-boiled
2 tablespoons sweet pickle relish   30 ml
3 tablespoons mayonnaise   45 ml
½ teaspoon mustard   2 ml

• Peel eggs and cut in half lengthwise. Take yolks and mash with
  fork. Add relish, mayonnaise and mustard to yolks. Place this
  yolk mixture back into egg white halves.

Chunky Egg Salad

12 eggs, hard-boiled, quartered
⅓ cup sun-dried tomato gourmayo   80 ml
2 ribs celery, sliced
½ cup sliced, stuffed green olives   120 ml

• Place all ingredients in salad bowl and add salt and pepper to
  taste.

• Gently toss and serve over bed of lettuce leaves with crackers.

A Different Deviled Egg

10 large eggs, hard-boiled, peeled
⅔ cup creamy dijon gourmayo   160 ml
2 tablespoons fresh snipped parsley   30 ml
2 teaspoons dried dill weed and chives   10 ml

• Cut off tops (about ⅓-inch/.8 cm) of each egg and scoop out yolks
  and place in mixing bowl. Cut thin slice from bottom of egg so
  egg will sit up.

• Mash yolks with fork and add gourmayo, parsley, dill weed, chives
  and salt and pepper to taste. Carefully stuff each egg with yolk
  mixture and place on serving plate sitting up.

Basic Deviled Eggs

8 large eggs	
3 - 4 tablespoons mayonnaise	**45 ml**
1 tablespoon prepared mustard	**15 ml**
3 tablespoons sweet pickle relish, drained	**45 ml**

- In large saucepan place eggs adding water to cover. Bring to boil and cook 2 minutes. Cover and let stand about 15 minutes. Cool.

- Peel eggs under cold water and slice eggs in half lengthwise, carefully removing yolks. Mash yolks with mayonnaise, mustard, pickle relish and a little salt and pepper.

- Spoon yolk mixture into egg whites and chill before serving.

Savory Chicken Salad

4 boneless skinless chicken breast halves, cooked	
1 cup chopped celery	**240 ml**
1 red bell pepper, seeded, chopped	
⅔ cup slivered almonds, toasted	**160 ml**
½ cup mayonnaise	**120 ml**
1 tablespoon lime juice	**15 ml**

- Slice chicken breasts into long thin strips.

- Combine chicken, celery, bell pepper and almonds.

- Combine mayonnaise and lemon juice, stir into salad and toss.

Strawberry-Chicken Salad

1 pound boneless, skinless chicken breast halves	.5 kg
1 (10 ounce) package spring greens mix	280 g
1 pint fresh strawberries, sliced	5 kg
½ cup chopped walnuts	120 ml

Dressing:
¾ cup honey	180 ml
⅔ cup red wine vinegar	160 ml
1 tablespoon soy sauce	15 ml
½ teaspoon ground ginger	2 ml

• Cut chicken into strips and place in large skillet with a little oil. Cook on medium-high heat for about 10 minutes and stir occasionally.

• While chicken cooks, combine all dressing ingredients and mix well. After chicken strips cook for 10 minutes, pour ½ cup (120 ml) dressing into skillet with chicken and cook 2 minutes longer or until liquid evaporates. In salad bowl, combine spring greens mix, strawberries and walnuts, pour on remaining dressing and toss. Top with chicken strips.

Broccoli-Chicken Salad

3 - 4 boneless skinless chicken breast halves, cooked, cubed	
2 cups fresh broccoli florets	480 ml
1 red bell pepper, seeded, chopped	
1 cup chopped celery	240 ml
1 (16 ounce) jar refrigerated honey-mustard salad dressing	.5 kg

• Combine chicken, broccoli, bell pepper and celery. Toss with about half the dressing, using more if needed and refrigerate.

Tarragon-Chicken Salad

1 cup chopped, toasted pecans	240 ml
3 - 4 boneless skinless chicken breast halves	
cooked, cubed	
1 cup chopped celery	240 ml
¾ cup peeled, chopped cucumbers	180 ml

- Place pecans in shallow pan and toast at 300° (148° C) for 10 minutes. Combine chicken, celery and cucumbers.

Dressing:

⅔ cup mayonnaise	160 ml
1 tablespoon lemon juice	15 ml
2 tablespoons tarragon vinegar	30 ml
1¼ teaspoons crumbled, dried tarragon	6 ml

- Mix all dressing ingredients. When ready to serve, toss with chicken mixture and add pecans.

Chicken Caesar Salad

4 boneless, skinless chicken breast halves, grilled	
1 (10 ounce) package romaine salad greens	280 g
½ cup shredded parmesan cheese	120 ml
1 cup seasoned croutons	240 ml
1 (8 ounce) bottle Caesar salad dressing	227 g

- Cut chicken breasts into strips.

- Combine chicken, salad greens, cheese and croutons in large bowl. When ready to serve, toss with salad dressing.

Bridge Club Luncheon

1 rotisserie-cooked chicken	
1 cup red grapes, halved	240 ml
1 cup green grapes, halved	240 ml
2 cups chopped celery	480 ml
⅔ cup whole walnuts	160 ml
1 orange bell pepper, seeded, chopped	

Dressing:

½ cup mayonnaise	120 ml
1 tablespoon orange juice	15 ml
2 tablespoons red wine vinegar	30 ml
1 tablespoon honey	15 ml
1 teaspoon paprika	5 ml

- Skin chicken and cut chicken breast in thin strips (reserve dark meat for another use) and place in bowl with lid. Add red and green grapes, celery, walnuts and bell pepper.

- Combine all dressing ingredients, adding salt and pepper to taste; mix well. Spoon over salad mixture and toss. Chill.

Chicken-Artichoke Salad

4 cups cooked, chopped chicken breasts	1 L
1 (14 ounce) can artichoke hearts, drained, chopped	396 g
½ cup chopped walnuts	120 ml
1 cup chopped red bell pepper	240 ml
⅔ cup mayonnaise	160 ml

- In bowl, combine all ingredients, adding salt and pepper to taste. Cover and refrigerate until ready to serve.

Derby Chicken Salad

3 - 4 boneless skinless chicken breast halves, cooked, cubed
¼ pound bacon, cooked, crumbled   114 g
2 avocados, peeled, diced
2 tomatoes, diced, drained
1 (8 ounce) bottle Italian salad dressing   227 g

- Combine all ingredients. When ready to serve, pour dressing over salad and toss. Chill.

Chicken Waldorf Salad

1 pound boneless, skinless chicken breasts   .5 kg
1 red and 1 green apple, unpeeled and sliced
1 cup sliced celery   240 ml
½ cup chopped walnuts   120 ml
1 (6 ounce) carton orange yogurt   168 g
½ cup mayonnaise   120 ml
1 (6 ounce) package shredded lettuce   168 g

- Place chicken in large saucepan and cover with water. On high heat, cook about 15 minutes; drain and cool. Cut into 1-inch (2.5 cm) chunks and season with salt and pepper; place in large salad bowl.

- Add sliced apples, celery and walnuts. Stir in yogurt and mayonnaise; toss to mix well (may be served room temperature or chilled several hours). Serve over shredded lettuce.

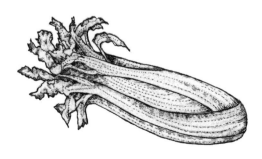

Hawaiian Chicken Salad

3 cups cooked, diced chicken breasts	710 ml
1 (20 ounce) can pineapple tidbits, well drained	567 g
1 cup halved red grapes	240 ml
3 ribs celery, sliced	
1 large ripe banana, sliced	

Dressing:

½ cup mayonnaise	120 ml
¾ cup poppy seed dressing	180 ml
½ cup salted peanuts	120 ml

- In bowl, combine diced chicken, pineapple, grapes and celery and toss. Cover and chill. Combine mayonnaise, poppy seed dressing and a sprinkle of salt. When ready to serve, add bananas and top with mayonnaise-poppy seed dressing, toss and sprinkle peanuts over top.

Chicken-Grapefruit Salad Supper

1 (10 ounce) package romaine salad mix	280 g
1 (24 ounce) jar grapefruit sections, well drained	680 g
1 rotisserie chicken, boned, cubed	
½ red onion, sliced	

Dressing:

2 tablespoons orange juice	30 ml
2 tablespoons white wine vinegar	30 ml
2 tablespoons extra-virgin olive oil	30 ml

- Combine salad mix, well-drained grapefruit sections, chicken and onion in salad bowl.

- In small bowl combine all dressing ingredients with 1 teaspoon (5 ml) each of salt and pepper, pour over salad and toss.

Great Chicken 'N Greens Salad

2 cups skinned, diced rotisserie chicken	480 ml
1 (10 ounce) package mixed salad greens	280 g
½ cup chopped sun-dried tomatoes	120 ml
1 red bell pepper, seeded, chopped	
3 tablespoons toasted sunflower seeds	45 ml

Dressing:

½ (8 ounce) bottle vinaigrette salad dressing	½ (227 g)
2 tablespoons refrigerated honey-mustard salad dressing	30 ml

- In salad bowl, combine diced chicken, greens, tomatoes and bell pepper and toss.

- Combine vinaigrette dressing and honey-mustard dressing and pour over salad (using more vinaigrette dressing if needed) and toss. Sprinkle sunflower seeds over salad and serve.

Brown Rice Chicken Salad

1 (8.8 ounce) package whole-grain brown ready rice	255 g
1 (12 ounce) can premium chunk chicken breasts, drained	340 g
⅔ cup sun-dried tomatoes, chopped	160 ml
2 ripe avocados, peeled, diced	
¾ cup dijon-style mustard vinaigrette dressing	180 ml

- Prepare rice according to package directions (microwave in package). Combine rice, chicken, tomatoes, avocados and salt and pepper to taste. Spoon dressing over salad and gently toss to mix well. Served chilled.

Fruited Chicken Salad

1 (10 ounce) package spring salad mix	280 g
1 (6 ounce) package frozen, ready-to serve chicken strips, thawed	168 g
½ cup fresh strawberries and raspberries	120 ml
1 (8 ounce) bottle raspberry salad dressing	227 g
Shredded lettuce	

- In salad bowl, combine salad mix, chicken strips and berries.

- Toss with just enough salad dressing to coat salad, adding more if needed. Serve on a bed of shredded lettuce with crackers.

Herbed Chicken Salad

1 rotisserie-cooked chicken	
¼ cup chopped fresh chives	60 ml
½ cup chopped pecans	120 ml
1 cup chopped celery	240 ml
1 cup chopped sweet pickles	240 ml

Dressing:

2 tablespoons honey	30 ml
¼ cup extra-virgin olive oil	60 ml
3 tablespoons white wine vinegar	45 ml
1 teaspoon chopped fresh thyme	5 ml

- Skin chicken and cut meat from bones. Slice chicken pieces in thin strips and place in bowl. Add fresh chives, pecans, celery and sweet pickles, mixing well. In bowl, whisk together honey, olive oil, vinegar, thyme and salt and pepper to taste. Spoon over chicken salad and toss. Chill.

Tri-Color Pasta-Turkey Salad Supper

1 (12 ounce) package tri-color spiral pasta	340 g
1 (4 ounce) can sliced ripe olives, drained	114 g
1 cup fresh broccoli florets	240 ml
1 cup cauliflower florets	240 ml
2 small yellow squash, sliced	
1 cup halved cherry tomatoes	240 ml
1 (8 ounce) bottle cheddar and parmesan ranch dressing	227 g
Slices from a 1½ pound hickory smoked cracked pepper turkey breast	.7 kg

• Cook pasta according to package directions; drain and rinse in cold water. Place in large salad bowl and add olives, broccoli, cauliflower, squash and tomatoes. Toss with dressing.

• Place thin slices of the turkey breast, arranged in a row, over salad. Serve immediately.

Noodle-Turkey Salad

1 (3 ounce) package oriental-flavor ramen noodle soup mix	84 g
1 (16 ounce) package finely shredded coleslaw mix	.5 kg
¾ pound deli smoked turkey, cut into strips	340 g
½ cup purchased vinaigrette salad dressing	120 ml

• Coarsely crush noodles and place in bowl with lid. Add coleslaw mix and turkey strips. In small bowl, combine vinaigrette salad dressing and seasoning packet from noodle mix and pour over noodle-turkey mixture and toss to coat mixture well. Chill.

Asian Turkey Salad

¾ pound deli turkey breasts, julienned	340 g
1 (9 ounce) package coleslaw mix	255 g
¼ cup chopped fresh cilantro	60 ml
1 sweet red bell pepper, seeded, julienned	
1 bunch fresh green onions, sliced in 1-inch slices	2.5 cm

Dressing:

¼ cup olive oil	60 ml
2 tablespoons lime juice	30 ml
1 tablespoon sugar	15 ml
1 tablespoon peanut butter	15 ml
1 tablespoon soy sauce	15 ml

- In salad bowl, combine salad ingredients.

- In jar with lid, combine dressing ingredients. Seal jar and shake dressing until well blended. Spoon over salad and toss. Serve immediately.

Fiesta Holiday Salad

1 (10 ounce) package torn romaine lettuce	280 g
3 cups diced smoked turkey	710 ml
1 (15 ounce) can black beans, rinsed, drained	425 g
2 tomatoes, quartered, drained	

Dressing:

⅔ cup mayonnaise	160 ml
¾ cup prepared salsa	180 ml

- Combine salad ingredients in large salad bowl. Combine mayonnaise and salsa.

- When ready to serve, spoon dressing over salad and toss.

Friday After Thanksgiving Salad

2 (10 ounce) packages prepared romaine lettuce	2 (280 g)
3 cups cooked, sliced turkey	710 ml
1 (8 ounce) jar baby corn, cut in fourths	227 g
2 tomatoes, chopped	
1 (8 ounce) package shredded Colby cheese	227 g

Dressing:

⅔ cup mayonnaise	160 ml
⅔ cup prepared salsa	160 ml
¼ cup cider vinegar	60 ml
2 tablespoons sugar	30 ml

- Combine salad ingredients in large bowl. Combine all dressing ingredients in separate bowl. When ready to serve, sprinkle on a little salt and pepper and then spoon dressing over salad and toss to coat well.

After Thanksgiving Day Salad

1 (10 ounce) package torn romaine lettuce	280 g
1 (15 ounce) can black beans, rinsed, drained	425 g
1 (8 ounce) package cubed cheddar cheese	227 g
2 - 3 cups cooked, leftover, diced turkey	480 ml
⅓ cup precooked, crumbled bacon	80 ml

Dressing:

½ cup mayonnaise	120 ml
¾ cup salsa	180 ml

- In salad bowl, combine lettuce, black beans, cheese and turkey (deli turkey can be used), mixing well.

- Combine mayonnaise, salsa and ¾ teaspoon (4 ml) pepper; spoon over salad and toss. Sprinkle crumbled bacon over top.

Beefy Green Salad

⅓ pound cooked deli roast beef	150 g
1 (15 ounce) can 3-bean salad, chilled, drained	425 g
½ pound mozzarella cheese, cubed	227 g
1 (8 ounce) bag mixed salad greens	227 g
1 (8 ounce) bottle Italian dressing	227 g

• Cut beef in thin strips. In large salad bowl, lightly toss beef, 3-bean salad, cheese and greens. Pour in just enough salad dressing to moisten greens.

Supper Ready Beef and Bean Salad

¾ pound deli roast beef, cut in strips	340 g
2 (15 ounce) can kidney beans, rinsed, drained	2 (425 g)
1 cup chopped onion and celery	240 ml
3 eggs, hard-boiled, chopped	

Dressing:

⅓ cup mayonnaise	80 ml
⅓ cup chipotle chili gourmayo	80 ml
¼ cup ketchup	60 ml
¼ cup sweet pickle relish	60 ml
2 tablespoons olive oil	30 ml

• Combine salad ingredients in salad bowl. In small bowl, combine dressing ingredients, mixing well. Spoon over beef-bean mixture and toss. Chill.

Warm Cannellini Salad

4 slices prosciutto
1 (19 ounce) can cannellini beans, rinsed, drained   538 g
3 fresh green onions, chopped
1 tablespoon dried parsley   15 ml
½ red bell pepper, finely chopped
1 (10 ounce) package fresh arugula   280 g

Dressing:

¼ cup olive oil   60 ml
2 teaspoons minced garlic   10 ml
2 tablespoons lemon juice   15 ml
2 teaspoons snipped fresh sage   10 ml

- Preheat oven to 350° (176° C). Arrange prosciutto in single layer on large baking sheet and bake 25 minutes. Set aside.

- Prepare dressing by heating oil in small saucepan and cook garlic until it begins to brown. Remove from heat and stir in lemon juice, sage and salt and pepper to taste.

- Combine beans, green onions, parsley and bell pepper in bowl. Arrange arugula, bean mixture and prosciutto on individual plates. Drizzle with warm dressing and serve immediately.

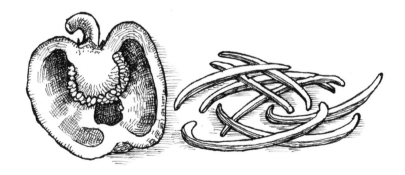

Cauliflower-Bacon Salad

1 large head cauliflower, cut into florets	
1 red and 1 green bell pepper, chopped	
1½ cups cubed mozzarella cheese	360 ml
1 (6 ounce) package cooked, crumbled bacon	168 g
1 bunch fresh green onions, sliced	

Dressing:

1 cup mayonnaise	240 ml
1 tablespoon sugar	15 ml
1 tablespoon lemon juice	15 ml

- In plastic bowl with lid, combine cauliflower, bell peppers, cheese, crumbled bacon and green onions.

- In small bowl, combine mayonnaise, sugar, lemon juice and 1 teaspoon (5 ml) salt, stirring to blend well. Spoon dressing over salad and toss to coat. Cover and chill 20 minutes before serving.

Hot Bean Salad

6 slices bacon	
½ cup mild taco sauce	120 ml
2 (15 ounce) cans cut green beans, drained	2 (425 g)
2 (15 ounce) cans pinto beans with jalapenos, drained	2 (425 g)

- In skillet fry bacon until crisp; remove from skillet, reserving drippings. Crumble bacon and set aside. In saucepan, combine remaining ingredients and reserved bacon drippings. Heat until thoroughly hot, stirring occasionally. Place in serving bowl and sprinkle crumbled bacon on top.

Tuna-Tortellini Salad

1 (7 ounce) package cut spaghetti	198 g
¼ cup (½ stick) butter	60 ml
1 (12 ounce) can tuna, drained	340 g
1 (4 ounce) can sliced ripe olives	114 g

Dressing:
¾ cup whipping cream	180 ml
1 teaspoon dried basil leaves	5 ml
2 tablespoons parmesan cheese	15 ml

• Cook spaghetti according to package directions and drain. Add butter and stir until butter melts. Add tuna and olives.

• Combine whipping cream, basil, cheese and 1 teaspoon (5 ml) salt for dressing. Pour over spaghetti-tuna mixture and toss.

Supper Ready Shrimp Salad

1 (14 ounce) package frozen, cooked tortellini, thawed	396 g
1 (16 ounce) package frozen salad shrimp, thawed	.5 kg
½ cup sliced ripe olives	120 ml
½ cup chopped celery	120 ml
1 (8 ounce) bottle zesty Italian salad dressing, divided	227 g

• In salad bowl, combine tortellini, shrimp, olives and celery. Pour about half salad dressing over salad and toss.

Fruit and Pork Salad Lunch

1 (10 ounce) package fresh green salad mix	280 g
2 cups halved seedless green grapes	480 ml
1 cup fresh strawberries, halved	240 ml
1 cup refrigerated red grapefruit sections, drained, save liquid	240 ml
6 (leftover) slices cooked pork tenderloin, cut in strips	

Dressing:

¼ cup reserved grapefruit juice	60 ml
2 tablespoons red wine vinegar	30 ml
2 tablespoons olive oil	30 ml
2 tablespoons honey	30 ml
1 tablespoon poppy seeds	15 ml

- In salad bowl, toss together salad mix, green grapes, strawberries and grapefruit sections. Arrange salad on individual plates and place tenderloin slices over top.

- Combine all dressing ingredients in jar with lid. Seal jar and shake ingredients until well blended. Pour dressing over top of individual salad plates.

Stained-Glass Fruit Salad

2 (20 ounce) cans peach pie filling, chilled	2 (567 g)
3 bananas, sliced, chilled	
1 (16 ounce) package frozen unsweetened strawberries, drained	.5 kg
1 (20 ounce) can pineapple tidbits, drained, chilled	567 g

- Mix fruits, place in crystal bowl and chill.

Creamy Fruit Salad

2 (20 ounce) cans pineapple chunks 2 (567 g)
1 (3 ounce) package cook-and-serve coconut pudding 84 g
2 apples, sliced
2 bananas, sliced
¾ cup chopped pecans 180 ml

- Drain pineapple and place juice in saucepan. Add pudding and cook over low-medium heat until it thickens, stirring constantly. Chill.

- Combine pineapple chunks, sliced apples, bananas and pecans. Stir in cooled pudding and refrigerate until ready to serve.

Zesty Fruit Salad

1 (24 ounce) jar refrigerated mixed fruit salad,
   drained 680 g
1 (24 ounce) jar refrigerated red grapefruit, drained 680 g
1 red delicious apple, with peel, thinly sliced
¼ cup slivered almonds, toasted 60 ml

Dressing:
⅔ cup honey 160 ml
¼ cup frozen limeade concentrate, thawed 60 ml
2 teaspoons poppy seeds 10 ml

- In salad bowl, combine all fruits.

- In small bowl, combine honey, limeade concentrate and poppy seeds and toss with fruit. Sprinkle with almonds.

Sunday Special Apple Salad

Sauce:

1 (20 ounce) can crushed pineapple, reserve juice	567 g
⅔ cup sugar	160 ml
1 tablespoon flour	15 ml
1 tablespoon white vinegar	15 ml

Salad Ingredients:

1 (12 ounce) carton whipped topping	340 g
3 red delicious apples, with peel, diced	
1 (10 ounce) package miniature marshmallows	280 g
½ cup roasted peanuts	120 ml

- Drain pineapple, reserving juice and set pineapple aside. In saucepan, combine sugar, flour, vinegar and reserved pineapple juice, mixing well. Place on medium heat and cook, stirring constantly, until mixture thickens. Set aside to cool.

- In large salad bowl, and first mixture is completely cooled, fold in whipped topping. Fold in reserved pineapple, diced apples and marshmallows and chill. When ready to serve, sprinkle peanuts over top of salad.

Snickers® Salad

6 large delicious apples, with peels, chopped	
6 (2 ounce) Snickers® candy bars, chopped	6 (57 g)
½ cup chopped pecans	120 ml
1 (12 ounce) carton whipped topping	340 g

- In large bowl, combine apples, candy bars and pecans and mix well. Fold in whipped topping and chill.

Citrus-Banana Salad

Dressing:

1 (6 ounce) carton plain yogurt	168 g
1 ripe banana, mashed	
¼ cup sugar	60 ml
1 tablespoon lemon juice	15 ml

Salad:

1 (6 ounce) package shredded lettuce	168 g
1 (24 ounce) jar grapefruit sections, well drained	680 g
2 (11 ounce) cans mandarin oranges, well drained	2 (312 g)

- Whisk together yogurt, banana, sugar and lemon juice, mixing well. Chill.

- Place shredded lettuce on 4 to 6 individual salad plates and arrange grapefruit sections and oranges on top. Drizzle dressing.

Nutty Grape-Pineapple Salad

1 pound seedless green grapes, halved	.5 kg
½ cup chopped pecans	120 ml
⅔ cup shredded cheddar cheese	160 ml
1 (15 ounce) can pineapple tidbits, drained	425 g

- Combine grapes, pecans, cheese and pineapple. Fold in ½ cup (120 ml) mayonnaise. Serve on lettuce leaves.

Pear Mousse

2 (15 ounce) cans sliced pears with juice	2 (425 g)
1 (6 ounce) package lemon gelatin	168 g
1 (8 ounce) package cream cheese, softened	227 g
1 (8 ounce) carton whipped topping	227 g

- Drain pears and reserve juice. Heat juice and add enough water to equal ¾ cup (180 ml). Heat juice to boiling point. Add gelatin. Mix well and cool.

- Place pears and cream cheese in blender and process until smooth. Place into large bowl and fold in cooled but not congealed gelatin mixture and whipped topping. Mix until smooth. Pour into individual dessert dishes. Cover with piece of plastic wrap and chill.

Watergate Salad

1 (20 ounce) can crushed pineapple with juice	567 g
2 (3 ounce) packages pistachio instant pudding mix	2 (84 g)
¾ cup chopped pecans	180 ml
1 (12 ounce) carton whipped topping	340 g

- Mix pineapple with instant pudding mix until it thickens slightly. Add pecans. Mix well and fold in whipped topping.

- Pour into crystal bowl and chill.

Mandarin Fluff

2 (11 ounce) cans mandarin oranges, well drained	2 (312 g)
1 cup miniature marshmallows	240 ml
1 (8 ounce) carton whipped topping	227 g
½ cup chopped pecans	120 ml

- Place oranges in bowl and stir in marshmallows (making sure marshmallows are not stuck together). Fold in whipped topping and pecans and chill. Serve in individual sherbet glasses.

Crunchy Fruit Salad

2 red apples with peels, chopped	
⅓ cup sunflower seeds	80 ml
½ cup green grapes	120 ml
⅓ cup vanilla yogurt	80 ml

- In bowl, combine apples, sunflower seeds, grapes and yogurt. Stir to coat salad. Chill before serving.

Grapefruit-Avocado Salad

2 (15 ounce) cans grapefruit sections, drained	2 (425 g)
2 ripe avocados, peeled, sliced	
½ cup chopped slivered almonds	120 ml
Prepared poppy seed salad dressing	

- Combine grapefruit, avocados and almonds.

- Toss with poppy seed dressing. Serve on bed of lettuce.

Ginger Dressing for Fruit Salad

1 cup vanilla yogurt	240 ml
2 tablespoons honey	30 ml
1 teaspoon sugar	5 ml
2 tablespoons finely minced, crystallized ginger	30 ml

• Combine all ingredients and mix well. Cover and refrigerate.

Classic Apple-Cranberry Salad

Dressing:

¼ cup mayonnaise	60 ml
2 tablespoons peanut butter	30 ml
1 teaspoon lemon juice	5 ml
1 teaspoon sugar	5 ml
2 Gala apples, with peel, chopped	
2 celery ribs, chopped	
⅓ cup cherry-flavored Craisins® (dried cranberries)	80 ml
1 cup shredded lettuce	240 ml
¼ cup chopped pecans	60 ml

• In salad bowl, whisk together mayonnaise, peanut butter, lemon juice and sugar. Stir in apples, celery and cranberries tossing to coat well. Cover and chill.

• Arrange lettuce on 3 to 4 individual salad plates and top with chilled apple mixture and sprinkle evenly with pecans.

Spiced Cranberries

2 (16 ounce) cans whole cranberry sauce, chilled	2 (.5 kg)
⅓ cup orange marmalade, chilled	80 ml
1 cup golden raisins	240 ml
2 teaspoons pumpkin pie spice	10 ml

• Combine all ingredients in bowl and mix well. Chill 30 minutes.

Chilled Cranberry Salad

1 (14 ounce) can sweetened condensed milk	396 g
⅓ cup lemon juice	80 ml
1 (20 ounce) can crushed pineapple, drained	567 g
1 (16 ounce) can whole cranberry sauce	.5 kg
3 cups miniature marshmallows	710 ml
1 (8 ounce) carton whipped topping	227 g

• In large bowl, combine sweetened condensed milk and lemon
  juice and mix well. Add pineapple, cranberry sauce and
  marshmallows and stir until they blend well. Fold in whipped
  topping and spoon into 9 x 13-inch (23 x 33 cm) baking dish.
  Place in freezer until hard, but not frozen through.

Cranberry Waldorf Salad

3 red delicious apples, unpeeled and cubed	
⅔ cup coarsely chopped pecans	160 ml
¾ cup sweetened dried cranberries (Craisins)	180 ml
⅓ cup shredded cheddar cheese	80 ml

Dressing:

⅓ cup mayonnaise	80 ml
2 tablespoons sugar	30 ml

• In salad bowl, combine cubed apples, pecans and cranberries.
  In small bowl, combine mayonnaise and sugar. Toss with salad
  mixture. Chill. When ready to serve, sprinkle cheese over top of
  salad.

Fruited Chicken Salad

1 (10 ounce) package spring salad mix	280 g
1 (6 ounce) package frozen, ready-to-serve	
chicken strips, thawed	168 g
½ cup fresh strawberries and raspberries	120 ml
½ fresh peach, sliced	
1 (8 ounce) bottle raspberry salad dressing	227 g

- In salad bowl, combine salad mix, chicken strips, berries and peach. Toss with salad dressing.

Sunday Night Chicken Sandwiches

1 (10 ounce) package frozen breaded chicken breast	
patties	280 g
1 (8 ounce) carton prepared guacamole dip	227 g
4 whole wheat hamburger buns, split	
⅓ cup thick-and-chunky salsa	80 ml
½ (9 ounce) package shredded lettuce	½ (255 g)

- In skillet with very little oil, cook breaded chicken breast patties as directed on package.

- Spread thin layer of guacamole dip on bottom of each bun and top each with chicken patty; spread salsa on top of patty. Place 3 to 4 tablespoons (45 ml) shredded lettuce over salsa.

- Spread another thin layer of guacamole on top bun.

Chicken-Bacon Sandwiches

1 (12 ounce) can chicken breast meat, drained	340 g
⅓ cup mayonnaise	80 ml
1 tablespoon dijon-style mustard	15 ml
1 celery rib, finely chopped	
¼ cup prepared, cooked, crumbled bacon	60 ml
Sandwich bread	
Shredded lettuce	

- In medium bowl, combine chicken chunks, mayonnaise, mustard, celery, bacon and salt and pepper to taste.

- Spread chicken mixture on 1 slice of whole wheat or white bread; top with shredded lettuce and another slice of bread.

Chicken-Bacon Salad Sandwiches

1 (12 ounce) can chicken breast meat, drained, crumbled	340 g
½ cup mayonnaise	120 ml
1 tablespoon dijon-style mustard	15 ml
1 celery rib, finely chopped	
¼ cup ready-to-serve real bacon bits	60 ml
4 medium size croissants	
Shredded lettuce	

- In medium bowl, combine crumbled chicken, mayonnaise, mustard, celery, bacon, salt and pepper to taste.

- Slice croissants in half horizontally and place salad mixture on bottom half of croissants. Sprinkle shredded lettuce on top and place top half on sandwich.

Wrap-That-Turkey Burger

1 pound ground turkey	.5 kg
⅓ cup shredded 4-cheese blend	80 ml
¼ cup finely grated onion, drained	60 ml
1 teaspoon Creole spicy seasoning	5 ml

Wrap:
4 fajita-size flour tortillas, warmed	
2 cups shredded lettuce	480 ml
⅔ cup prepared guacamole	160 ml

- Combine ground turkey, shredded cheese, grated onion and spicy seasoning in bowl. Shape into 4 patties (make patties a little longer than round) and refrigerate about 30 minutes before cooking. Grill patties about 5 inches (13 cm) from heat for about 8 minutes or until thermometer reads 165° (75° C).

- Place tortillas on flat surface and arrange one-fourth lettuce on each tortilla. Place 1 patty on each tortilla and spread with guacamole. Fold tortilla in half to cover filling.

Wrap Up The Turkey

4 (8-inch) whole wheat tortillas	4 (20 cm)
Sun dried tomato gourmayo	
1 pound thinly sliced deli roasted turkey	.5 kg
½ cup finely chopped lettuce	120 ml
2 tablespoons fresh, chopped cilantro	30 ml

- Place tortillas on flat surface and spread thin layer of gourmayo. Layer each tortilla with 4 slices of turkey. Sprinkle with lots of lettuce and cilantro. Roll tightly and serve whole or cut on diagonal to serve smaller slices.

Apple-Club Sandwich

Dressing:

⅓ cup mayonnaise	80 ml
¼ teaspoon dried tarragon	60 ml
¼ teaspoon dill weed	60 ml
1 teaspoon mustard	5 ml
1 teaspoon lemon juice	5 ml

Sandwich with 4 slices of rye bread:
4 thin slices deli turkey
4 thin slices deli ham
4 thin slices Monterey Jack cheese
Thin slices of tart apple
Lettuce leaves

• In small bowl, combine dressing ingredients and spread on
  4 slices rye bread. On 2 slices of bread, layer turkey, ham and
  cheese; repeat layers and top with apple slices and lettuce leaf
  and remaining 2 slices of bread.

Chicken Sandwich Ole

1 (10 ounce) package frozen breaded chicken breast patties	280 g
½ cup prepared black bean dip	120 ml
⅓ cup thick and chunky hot salsa	80 ml

• Preheat oven to 325° (162° C). Heat chicken breast patties in
  oven as directed on package, adding 4 hoagie buns (or hamburger
  buns) the last 3 minutes of cooking time. Spread bottom of
  each hoagie bun liberally with bean dip and salsa. Top each
  with chicken patty and shredded lettuce and tomatoes. Serve
  immediately.

Reubens on a Bun

1 (1 pound) package smoked frankfurters	.5 kg
8 hot dog buns	
1 (8 ounce) can sauerkraut, drained	227 g
Caraway seeds	
Thousand island dressing	

• Pierce each frankfurter and place into split buns. Arrange 2 tablespoons (30 ml) sauerkraut over each frank. Sprinkle with caraway seed. Place in 9 x 13-inch (23 x 33 cm) shallow pan and drizzle with dressing. Heat until hot dogs are thoroughly hot.

Rueben Sandwiches

12 slices dark rye bread	
6 slices Swiss cheese	
12 thin deli slices corned beef	
4 cups deli coleslaw, drained	1 L

• On 6 slices of rye bread, layer cheese, 2 slices corned beef and lots of coleslaw.

Southwest Burgers

2 pounds lean ground beef   1 kg
1 packet taco seasoning mix
1 cup salsa, divided   240 ml
1 (8 count) package kaiser buns
8 slices hot pepper Jack cheese

- Combine beef, taco seasoning and ¼ cup (60 ml) salsa in large mixing bowl. Shape mixture into 8 patties.

- If you are grilling, cook patties about 12 minutes, turning once. To broil in oven, place patties on broiler pan 4 to 5 inches (10 cm) from heat and broil until they cook thoroughly. Turn once during cooking.

- When patties are almost done, place buns cut side down on grill and heat 1 or 2 minutes. Place 8 patties on bottom half of buns, top with cheese and cook an additional minute or until cheese melts. Top with heaping tablespoon salsa and top half of bun.

Ranch Cheeseburgers

1 (1 ounce) envelope dry ranch-style salad
    dressing mix   28 g
1 pound lean ground beef   .5 kg
1 cup shredded cheddar cheese   240 ml
4 large hamburger buns, toasted

- Combine dressing mix with beef and cheese. Shape into 4 patties. Cook on charcoal grill.

Jack's Firecrackers

1¼ pounds lean ground beef	567 g
2 ounce chunk Monterey Jack cheese with jalapeno peppers	57 g

- Preheat grill or broiler to high. Evenly divide ground beef into 8 large flat patties. Cut cheese into 4 cubes.

- Place one piece of cheese on top of 4 patties. Top each with remaining patties and press edges lightly to seal. Season with salt and pepper.

- Place burgers in broiler pan and broil or grill 8 to 10 minutes on each side. Serve on hamburger buns with lettuce and tomatoes.

Pizza Burger

1 pound lean ground beef	.5 kg
½ cup pizza sauce	120 ml
4 slices mozzarella cheese	

- Combine beef, ½ teaspoon (2 ml) salt and half pizza sauce.

- Mold into 4 patties and pan-fry over medium heat for 5 to 6 minutes on each side. Just before burgers are done, top each with 1 spoonful pizza sauce and 1 slice cheese. Serve on hamburger bun.

No Ordinary Sandwich

3 tablespoons crumbled blue cheese	45 ml
¼ cup mayonnaise	60 ml
2 hamburger buns	
6 thin slices deli roast beef	

- Combine crumbled blue cheese and mayonnaise and spread on cut side of both buns. Place 3 roast beef slices on each bottom bun and top with shredded lettuce and sliced tomatoes.

Hot Roast Beef Sandwich

1 (16 ounce) loaf French bread	.5 kg
¼ cup creamy dijon-style mustard	60 ml
¾ pound sliced deli roast beef	340 g
8 slices American cheese	

- Preheat oven to 325° (162° C). Split French bread and spread mustard on bottom slice. Line slices of beef over mustard and cheese slices over beef with cheese on top.

- Cut loaf in quarters and place on baking sheet. Heat for about 5 minutes or until cheese just partially melts.

Cream Cheese Sandwich Spread

2 (8 ounce) packages cream cheese, softened	2 (227 g)
1 (2 ounce) jar dried beef, finely chopped	57 g
1 bunch fresh green onions with tops, chopped	
¾ cup mayonnaise	180 ml

- Combine all ingredients and 1 teaspoon (5 ml) salt until mixture spreads smoothly. Trim crust of whole wheat bread and spread cream cheese mixture on bread.

- Top with another slice of bread and slice into 3 strips or 4 quarters.

Meatball Heros

Any bread like club rolls, hot dog buns or French rolls will work.

1 (16 ounce) container marinara sauce	.5 kg
1 (16 ounce) package frozen bell peppers, thawed	.5 kg
½ onion, minced	
1 (12 ounce) package cooked Italian meatballs	340 g

- Combine marinara sauce, bell peppers and onion and cook in large saucepan on medium heat for 5 minutes.

- Add meatballs, cover and gently boil for about 5 minutes or until meatballs are hot. Spoon into split club rolls and serve hot.

Philly Meatball Sandwiches

1 tablespoon oil	15 ml
1 (16 ounce) package frozen chopped onions and bell peppers	.5 kg
½ (18 ounce) package frozen, cooked meatballs	½ (510 g)
6 toasted hoagie rolls	
1 (8 ounce) package shredded cheddar cheese	227 g

- In skillet with the oil on medium heat, cook and stir onions and bell peppers for 5 minutes. Add meatballs, cover and cook, stirring occasionally, about 12 minutes or until meatballs are thoroughly hot. Spoon mixture into toasted rolls and sprinkle cheese over meatballs. Serve hot.

Burgers Italian Style

1½ pounds lean ground beef	.7 kg
½ cup spaghetti sauce, plus extra to spoon on burgers	120 ml
¼ cup prepared Italian breadcrumbs	60 ml
1 egg	
10 slices provolone cheese	
10 thick slices Italian bread	

- In bowl, combine ground beef, spaghetti sauce, breadcrumbs and egg, mix well. Shape into 5 patties. Broil patties on rack with tops about 3 inches (8 cm) from heat. Broil about 6 minutes on each side.

- On a baking sheet, lightly toast each bread slice. Place 1 slice cheese on 5 slices, top with patty and a second slice of cheese. Place another slice of bread on top and place baking sheet in oven. Leave in oven about 5 minutes or until cheese is slightly melted. Serve with additional spaghetti sauce.

Easy Dog Wraps

8 wieners	
8 slices cheese	
1 (8 ounce) package refrigerated crescent rolls	227 g
Mustard	

- Split wieners lengthwise and fill with folded cheese slice.
- Wrap in crescent dough roll and bake at 375° (190° C) for about 12 minutes. Serve with mustard.

Barking Dogs

10 wieners
5 slices cheese
10 corn tortillas

- Slice wieners lengthwise and halfway through. Cut each cheese slice in half and place inside each wiener. Wrap tortillas around wiener and secure with toothpick. Heat several inches of oil in frying pan. Fry dogs in oil until tortilla is crisp. Serve hot.

Cheese Doggies

Bacon slices
Sliced frankfurters
Cheddar cheese slices
Hot dog buns

- Use 1 bacon slice for each frankfurter. Place bacon on paper towel or paper plate, cover with paper towel and microwave for 45 seconds or until almost crisp. Cut lengthwise pocket in frankfurter and stuff with 1 strip cheese. Wrap bacon around doggie and secure with toothpick.

- Place in split hot dog bun and microwave for about 30 seconds or until hot dog is warm.

Cucumber Sauce for a Different Burger

1 seedless cucumber, peeled, coarsely grated, drained
½ cup plain yogurt   **120 ml**
¼ cup finely grated onion, drained   **60 ml**
2 teaspoons dill weed   **10 ml**

- In bowl, combine cucumber, yogurt, grated onion, 2 teaspoons (10 ml) salt and dill weed. Use cucumber sauce for grilled hamburgers instead mayonnaise or mustard.

Couples Night Sandwich

1 (9 inch) round loaf focaccia bread	23 cm
6 deli ham slices	
6 slices Swiss cheese	
½ cup chopped, roasted red bell peppers, drained	120 ml
1 (6 ounce) package baby spinach	168 g

Dressing:

⅓ cup romano basil vinaigrette dressing	80 ml
2 tablespoons mayonnaise	30 ml

- Preheat oven to 325° (162° C). Place bread on cutting board and slice horizontally. Place layer of ham and cheese on top with red bell peppers and heavy layer of spinach.

- In small bowl, combine vinaigrette dressing and mayonnaise and drizzle mixture over spinach layer. Place top of loaf over spinach layer and wrap in foil. Bake 15 minutes. Cut focaccia into 4 or 6 wedges and serve immediately.

Apple-Ham Open-Face Sandwiches

4 kaiser bakery rolls (or buns)
Mayonnaise and mustard
16 slices American cheese
8 thin slices deli, boiled ham
1 red delicious apple, finely chopped

- Spread a little mayonnaise and mustard on top and bottom of 4 kaiser rolls and place on baking sheet. Top each with 1 slice of cheese, then slice of ham and about 2 tablespoons (30 ml) chopped apple. Top with remaining slices of cheese.

- Broil 4 to 5 inches (10 cm) from broiler heat just until top slice of cheese melts. Serve immediately.

"Honey Do" Open-Face Sandwich

⅓ cup prepared honey-mustard dressing   80 ml
4 kaiser rolls, split
8 thin slices deli honey ham
8 slices Swiss cheese

- Preheat oven to 400° (204° C). Spread honey-mustard on each split roll. Top each with ham and cheese slices.

- Place on baking sheet and bake 4 to 5 minutes or until cheese melts.

Ham Sandwiches

Kaiser rolls
16 slices American cheese
8 thin slices deli, boiled ham

- Spread a little mayonnaise and mustard on top and bottom of 4 kaiser rolls and place on baking sheet. Top each with 1 slice of cheese and slice ham. Top with remaining slices of cheese.

- Broil 4 to 5 inches (10 cm) from heat just until top slice of cheese melts. Serve immediately.

Grilled Open-Face Sandwich

2 cups cooked, ground ham (leftover or deli ham)   480 ml
½ cup drained pickle relish   120 ml
2 eggs, hard-boiled, chopped
⅓ cup gourmayo, a dijon flavored mayonnaise   80 ml

- In bowl, combine ground ham, pickle relish, eggs and gourmayo. Toast 5 slices of favorite bread and spread butter on untoasted side. Spread ham mixture on untoasted side of bread and broil until mixture browns slightly. Serve piping hot.

Guacamole Ham Salad Wrap

¾ cup prepared guacamole	180 ml
4 (8 inch) spinach tortillas	4 (20 cm)
¾ cup salsa	180 ml
1 cup shredded 4-cheese blend	240 ml
¾ pound deli ham, cut in thin strips	180 ml
Shredded lettuce	

• Spread guacamole over half of each tortilla and layer salsa, cheese, ham strips and lettuce to within 2 inches (5 cm) of edges. Roll tightly.

Wrap It Up NOW!

4 burrito-size flour tortillas	
⅓ cup sweet-honey Catalina dressing	80 ml
4 thin slices deli ham	
4 slices Swiss cheese	
1½ cups deli coleslaw	360 ml

• Spread tortillas with dressing and add 1 slice ham and 1 slice cheese on each tortilla. Spoon one-fourth coleslaw on top.

• Roll and wrap each in wax paper. Place in microwave and heat just until cheese begins to melt. Cut wraps in half to serve.

Party Sandwiches

1 cup bacon, cooked, crumbled	.5 kg
½ cup ripe olives, coarsely chopped	120 ml
½ cup chopped pecans	120 ml
1¼ cups mayonnaise	300 ml

• Mix all ingredients. Spread on thin sliced white bread.

• Cut sandwiches into 3 strips.

Italian Sausage Sandwiches

1 pound sweet Italian sausage, cooked, 　　casing removed	.5 kg
1 red bell pepper, chopped	
1 onion, chopped	
1⅔ cups Italian-style spaghetti sauce	400 ml

- In skillet over medium heat, cook sausage, bell pepper and onion until sausage browns and is no longer pink.

- Stir in spaghetti sauce and heat until boiling. Simmer for 5 minutes; stir constantly. Pour mixture over split hoagie rolls.

B L T Wraps

Flour tortillas, spread with mayonnaise
Sliced turkey (2 per wrap)
Cooked bacon (2 per wrap)
Shredded lettuce and chopped tomatoes

- Top each tortilla with 2 slices turkey, 2 slices bacon and shredded lettuce and tomatoes. Fold edges over to enclose filling. Serve immediately or wrap in wax paper and refrigerate.

Wow 'Em Tenderloin Sandwich

Soft light cream cheese, softened
Orange marmalade
Thin slices (leftover) cooked pork tenderloin
Sliced red onion and lettuce

- Spread thin layer of cream cheese on 2 slices of your favorite bread; then on bottom layer, spread orange marmalade. Top with thin slices of pork tenderloin, red onion slice and lettuce leaf. Place second piece of bread on top.

Hot Cornbread Sandwich

2 (8 ounce) packages corn muffin mix   2 (227 g)
2 eggs, beaten
⅔ cup milk   160 ml
12 slices American cheese
6 slices deli ham slices

• Preheat oven to 400° (204° C). In bowl, combine muffin mix, eggs and milk, mixing well. Pour half of mixture into 7 x 11-inch (18 x 28 cm) greased baking dish. Carefully place 6 slices of cheese, then ham slices over cheese and remaining cheese slices on top of ham. Spoon remaining cornbread batter over top of cheese.

• Bake for 25 minutes or until cornbread is golden brown. Cut into squares and serve hot.

A Family Sandwich

1 (16 ounce) loaf French bread, cut in
  half horizontally   .5 kg
Creamy dijon gourmayo (from 11 ounce bottle)   312 g
8 sliced Swiss cheese
8 slices deli-sliced honey ham
8 sandwich-sliced dill pickles

• Preheat oven to 375° (190° C). Spread dijon gourmayo over cut sides of bread. Arrange half of cheese and half of ham on bottom slice and top with pickle slices. Spread remaining cheese and ham on top of pickles. Cover with top of bread and press down on sandwich; cut into quarters. Place on cookie sheet and bake 5 minutes and serve immediately.

A Special Grilled Cheese Sandwich

Softened butter
1 loaf 7-grain bread

Filling for 1 sandwich:
2 tablespoons gourmayo with chipotle	**30 ml**
2 slices sharp cheddar cheese	
2 tablespoons real crumbled bacon	**30 ml**
¼ of an avocado, thinly sliced	

- For each sandwich, spread softened butter on 2 thick slices of 7-grain bread and place one slice, butter side down in heavy skillet. Spread with 1 tablespoon (15 ml) of gourmayo and one slice of cheese.

- Sprinkle with 2 tablespoons (30 ml) crumbled bacon and avocado slices. Top with second slice of cheese and remaining slice of bread spread with other tablespoon of gourmayo. Heat skillet on medium-high and cook about 2 minutes or until light brown and cheese is melting.

- Turn sandwich over and cook another 2 minutes or until cheese is completely melted.

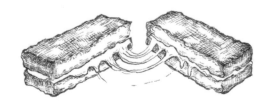

Barbecue Burger On A Muffin

1½ pounds ground pork	.7 kg
1 teaspoon minced garlic	5 ml
¼ teaspoon cayenne pepper	1 ml

Muffin:

6 English muffins	
2 teaspoons dijon-style mustard	10 ml
½ cup favorite prepared barbecue sauce	120 ml
1 cup refrigerated creamy coleslaw	240 ml

- In bowl, combine ground pork, garlic, 1 teaspoon (5 ml) salt and cayenne pepper and shape into 6 patties about ¾-inch (1.8 cm) thick. Using back of spoon press an indentation in center for even grilling. Grill patties about 5 minutes on each side or until thermometer reaches 165° (73° C).

- Lightly toast each side of English muffins and spread with mustard and a little barbecue sauce. Place patties on bottoms of muffins and top with coleslaw and top muffin. Serve extra barbecue sauce on the side, if you like.

Open Face Jumbo

8 slices bacon
1 (8 ounce) package cream cheese, softened   227 g
¼ cup (½ stick) butter, softened   60 ml
2 teaspoons lemon juice   10 ml
1 teaspoon Worcestershire sauce   5 ml
4 English muffins
8 turkey slices
8 ham slices
8 slices Swiss cheese

• Fry bacon until crisp, drain and set aside. In medium size
  bowl, beat together cream cheese, butter, lemon juice and
  Worcestershire sauce; mix well.

• Spread on muffins. Top with turkey, ham and cheese slices. Broil
  on bottom rack of oven for 10 to 12 minutes. Top with bacon.

Crab-Avocado Burgers

4 frozen crab cakes, thawed
1 ripe avocado
¼ cup mayonnaise   60 ml
1 tablespoon lemon juice   15 ml
1 (4 ounce) can green chilies, drained
4 hamburger buns

• Microwave crab cakes as directed on package. Mash avocado
  (with fork) together with mayonnaise, lemon juice and
  ½ teaspoon (2 ml) salt. Stir in green chilies.

• Place crab cakes on buns and spread with avocado-mayonnaise
  mixture. Serve as is or top with lettuce and sliced tomatoes.

Salmon Burgers

1 (15 ounce) can salmon with 2 tablespoons liquid	425 g/30 ml
1 egg, slightly beaten	
¼ cup lemon juice	60 ml
⅔ cup seasoned breadcrumbs	160 ml
Hamburger buns	
Mayonnaise	
Shredded lettuce	
Sliced tomatoes	

• In bowl, combine salmon, 2 tablespoons (30 ml) salmon liquid, egg, lemon juice, breadcrumbs and a little salt and pepper. Form into patties and with a little oil, fry on both sides until golden.

• Serve hot on buns with mayonnaise, lettuce and sliced tomatoes.

Crab Salad Croissants

1 (8 ounce) package imitation crabmeat, flaked	227 g
1 sweet red bell pepper, finely chopped	
3 fresh green onions, minced	
2 tablespoons sunflower kernels	30 ml
½ to ⅔ cup mayonnaise	120 ml
Shredded lettuce	
6 croissants, split	

• In bowl, combine crabmeat, bell pepper, onions, sunflower kernels, 1 teaspoon (5 ml) seasoned salt and a little black pepper. Add mayonnaise and toss to blend well; add more mayonnaise if needed.

• Line croissants with shredded lettuce and top with crab salad.

Seafood Tortilla Wraps

2 (9-inch) garden spinach tortillas	2 (23 cm)
Mayonnaise	
1 cup shredded American cheese	240 ml
1 (9 ounce) package spring salad mix	255 g
1 cup diced, drained tomatoes	240 ml
4 finely chopped green onions	
1 (4 ounce) package albacore steak with lemon	
and cracked pepper, crumbled	114 g

- Heat broiler, place tortillas on baking sheet and broil very briefly on each side. Remover from oven and spread mayonnaise on side of tortilla. Sprinkle cheese over tortillas and return to oven just until cheese melts.

- Combine salad mix, tomatoes and green onions and sprinkle on tortillas. Place as much crumbled albacore on tortilla as needed. Roll or fold over to eat.

Fish and Chips Sandwiches

1 (12 ounce) box frozen breaded fish fillets, thawed	340 g
1 (8 ounce) loaf Italian bread	227 g
1 cup prepared deli coleslaw	240 ml
1 cup potato chips	240 ml

- Heat fish fillets according to package directions. Remove from oven and preheat broiler. Slice bread in half lengthwise and broil, cut side up.

- Layer coleslaw, fish fillets and potato chips and cover with bread tops. To serve, cut into 4 quarters and serve immediately.

Chicken Pizza

4 (8-inch) flour tortillas	4 (20 cm)
2 cups deli chicken breast, diced	480 ml
1 (11 ounce) can mexicorn, drained	312 g
1 (15 ounce) can black beans, rinsed, drained	425 g
2 tablespoons lemon juice	30 ml
1½ cups Monterey Jack cheese with jalapeno peppers	360 ml

- Preheat oven to 350° (176° C). Place tortillas on greased baking sheet and bake 10 minutes or until edges are light brown. Remove from oven, stack and press down to flatten.

- In skillet with a little oil, combine diced chicken, corn and black beans. Heat, stirring constantly until mixture is thoroughly hot and stir in lemon juice.

- Place tortillas on baking sheet and spoon about ¾ cup (180 ml) chicken-corn mixture on each tortilla. Sprinkle cheese on top of each pizza and return to oven for 2 minutes or just until cheese melts.

Caesar Salad Pizza

1 (12-inch) Italian pizza crust	32 cm
2 cups shredded mozzarella cheese	480 ml
1 (6 ounce) package cooked chicken breast strips	168 g
2 cups shredded lettuce	480 ml
3 fresh green onions, sliced	
¾ cup shredded cheddar and colby cheese	180 ml
½ (8 ounce) bottle Caesar dressing	½ (227 g)

- Preheat oven to 400° (204° C). Top pizza crust with mozzarella cheese and bake 8 minutes or until cheese melts. In bowl, combine chicken strips, lettuce, onions and remaining cheese with dressing and toss. Top hot pizza with salad and cut into wedges.

Deep-Dish Pizza

2 (13 ounce) packages refrigerated pizza dough	2 (370 g)
1 cup chopped red onion	240 ml
¼ cup olive oil	60 ml
1 (10 ounce) package frozen chopped spinach, thawed, drained	280 g
1 cup ricotta cheese	240 ml
1 cup shredded mozzarella cheese, divided	240 ml
3 roma tomatoes, sliced	

- Preheat oven to 400° (204° C). Unroll 1 package of pizza dough and gently pull into 12-inch (32 cm) circle. Place dough on greased baking sheet and bake 5 minutes.

- Cook onion in 2 tablespoons (30 ml) oil and add well drained spinach with salt and pepper to taste. Cook 2 minutes and spread over bottom of partially baked crust.

- In small bowl combine ricotta cheese and ¼ cup (60 ml) pizza cheese. Spoon mixture over spinach layer.

- Spread ricotta mixture over spinach layer and top with tomato slices. Sprinkle remaining pizza cheese over top. Unroll remaining pizza dough and place on top tomato slices. Pinch together edges of dough and bake 20 minutes or until top is golden. Cut in wedges to serve.

Green Chile Grilled Cheese

4 slices cheddar cheese
4 slices bread
1 (4 ounce) can chopped green chilies, drained   114 g
3 tablespoons butter, softened   45 ml

- Place 1 slice cheese on 2 slices bread. Sprinkle with green chilies.
  Top with 2 remaining slices cheese and remaining 2 slices bread.

- Butter outside of sandwiches. In large skillet over medium heat,
  brown sandwiches on both sides until golden brown and cheese
  melts.

Watercress Tea Sandwiches

1 small bunch watercress
5 eggs, hard-boiled, peeled
6 tablespoons mayonnaise   90 ml
1 tablespoon dijon-style mustard   15 ml

- Trim half watercress stems. Save rest for garnish. In food
  processor, coarsely chop eggs and add mayonnaise, mustard and a
  little salt. Process until smooth. Fold in chopped watercress and
  chill. Trim crusts and add mixture on thinly sliced white bread.
  Cut into finger sandwiches.

Cream Cheese Tea Sandwiches

1 (8 ounce) package cream cheese, softened	227 g
½ pound bacon, fried, finely chopped	227 g
12 - 14 slices whole wheat bread	
1 (12 ounce) package bean sprouts	340 g
Mayonnaise	

- Using mixer, beat cream cheese until smooth. Add finely chopped bacon or chop cream cheese and bacon together in food processor.

- On 6 to 8 slices bread, spread bacon-cream cheese mixture. Add layer of bean sprouts. On other 6 to 8 slices bread, spread either mayonnaise or butter and place on top of bean sprouts to make 6 or 8 sandwiches. With sharp knife remove crust and cut each sandwich in 3 pieces. Chill.

Cream Cheese Sandwiches

2 (8 ounce) packages cream cheese, softened	2 (227 g)
1 (4 ounce) can black olives, chopped	114 g
¾ cups finely chopped pecans	180 ml
Pumpernickel rye bread	

- Beat cream cheese until creamy. Fold in olives and pecans. Trim crusts on bread. Spread cream cheese on bread.

- Slice sandwich into 3 finger strips.

Confetti Sandwiches

1 tablespoon lemon juice	15 ml
1 (8 ounce) package cream cheese, softened	227 g
½ cup grated carrots	120 ml
¼ cup each grated cucumber, purple onion and bell pepper	60 ml

- Combine lemon juice with cream cheese and add enough mayonnaise to make cheese into spreading consistency. Fold in grated vegetables and spread on bread for sandwiches. Chill.

Luncheon Sandwiches

1 loaf thinly sliced, sandwich bread	
1 cup (2 sticks) butter, softened	240 ml
1 (5 ounce) jar cheese spread, softened	143 g
½ teaspoon Worcestershire sauce	2 ml

- Trim crust on bread. With mixer, beat butter and cheese spread until smooth and creamy and add Worcestershire sauce. Spread mixture on 3 slices bread to make triple-decker sandwich. Place fourth slice bread on top. Cut into finger sandwiches.

Marshmallow Sandwiches

Bread	
1 (7 ounce) jar marshmallow cream	198 g
Chunky peanut butter	
Vanilla wafers	

- On 1 slice bread, spread marshmallow cream. On second slice bread, spread peanut butter. Put marshmallow and peanut butter sides together. Use vanilla wafer to make sandwiches too.

Grandkid's Special

Peanut butter
Grape or plum jelly
4 slices white bread, crusts trimmed
2 eggs, well beaten
Butter
Powdered sugar

- Spread peanut butter and jelly on 2 slices of bread. Top with remaining 2 slices of bread. Beat eggs with 2 tablespoons (30 ml) water in shallow bowl. Dip each sandwich in egg.

- Melt about 2 tablespoons (30 ml) butter in skillet and cook each sandwich on both sides until light brown. Take out of skillet and sprinkle lightly with powdered sugar.

Avocado Butter Spread

2 large ripe avocados	
⅓ cup lime juice	80 ml
⅓ cup extra-virgin olive oil	80 ml
A pinch dried tarragon	
½ teaspoon sugar	2 ml

- Slice avocados and place in food processor or blender. Add remaining ingredients and salt to taste. Pulse until smooth and buttery.

Snap-Your-Fingers

Side Dishes
Vegetables

Potatoes Italian Style

1 (22 ounce) package frozen mashed potatoes, thawed	624 g
1 pint half-and-half cream	.5 kg
1 cup grated parmesan cheese, divided	240 ml
⅔ cup prepared basil pesto (from 8 ounce jar of pesto)	160 ml/227 g

- Place mashed potatoes, cream and an ample amount of salt and pepper in microwavable bowl. Microwave on HIGH for about 10 minutes, stirring once and cooking until potatoes are hot. Stir in half cheese, mixing well.

- Spread half potato-cheese mixture into 7 x 11-inch (18 x 28 cm) greased baking dish and top, spreading out, with basil pesto.

- Spoon remaining potato mixture on top of pesto. Sprinkle remaining parmesan cheese over top and return to microwave for another 2 minutes.

Potato Souffle

2⅔ cups instant mashed potatoes	640 ml
2 eggs, beaten	
1 cup shredded cheddar cheese	240 ml
1 (3 ounce) can french-fried onion rings	84 g

- Prepare mashed potatoes according to package directions. Stir in eggs, cheese and stir until they blend. Spoon mixture into lightly greased 2-quart (2 L) dish. Sprinkle with onion rings. Bake uncovered at 325° (162° C) for 25 minutes.

Philly Potatoes

4½ cups instant mashed potatoes, prepared, hot	1.1 L
2 tablespoons freeze-dried chives	30 ml
1 (8 ounce) package cream cheese, softened	227 g
1 egg, slightly beaten	

- Mix all ingredients and blend well. Place in greased 3-quart (3 L) casserole. Bake covered at 350° (176° C) for 20 minutes. Uncover and bake for 15 minutes more.

Creamy Ranch Potatoes

4 medium russet potatoes, peeled, quartered	
¼ cup (½ stick) butter	60 ml
⅓ cup ranch salad dressing	80 ml
2 tablespoons, cooked, crumbled bacon	30 ml

- In saucepan, boil potatoes in water about 15 minutes or until tender. Drain and beat potatoes with electric mixer until smooth. Add butter, ½ teaspoon (2 ml) salt and a little black pepper and beat until butter melts. Gradually add salad dressing and beat until smooth. Spoon into serving bowl and top with crumbled bacon.

Cheddar Potatoes

1 (10 ounce) can cheddar cheese soup	280 g
⅓ cup sour cream	80 ml
2 fresh green onions, chopped	
3 cups instant seasoned mashed potatoes, prepared	710 ml

- In saucepan, heat soup and add sour cream, onion and little pepper. Stir in potatoes until they blend well. Pour into buttered 2-quart (2 L) casserole. Cook at 350° (176° C) for 25 minutes.

Creamy Potato Bake

6 - 8 baked potatoes	
1 (8 ounce) carton sour cream	**227 g**
1 (8 ounce) package cream cheese, softened	**227 g**
1½ cups shredded cheddar cheese	**360 ml**

- Cut potatoes in half lengthwise. Scoop meat out of potatoes, reserving skins and place in mixing bowl.

- Add salt to taste, sour cream and cream cheese and whip until all mix well. Spoon mashed potatoes back into potato skins and place in hot oven until potatoes are hot. Sprinkle cheddar cheese on top of potatoes.

Dinner-Bell Mashed Potatoes

8 medium to large potatoes	
1 (8 ounce) carton sour cream	**227 g**
1 (8 ounce) package cream cheese, softened	**227 g**
Butter	

- Preheat oven to 325° (162° C). Peel, cut up and boil potatoes until tender and drain.

- Whip hot potatoes and add sour cream, cream cheese, 1 teaspoon (5 ml) salt and ½ teaspoon (2 ml) pepper. Continue whipping until cream cheese melts. Pour in sprayed 3-quart (3 L) baking dish. Dot generously with butter.

- Cover with foil and bake for about 20 minutes.

- Bake 10 minutes longer if reheating.

Broccoli-Topped Potatoes

4 hot baked potatoes, halved
1 cup diced cooked ham   **240 ml**
1 (10 ounce) can cream of broccoli soup   **280 g**
½ cup shredded cheddar cheese   **120 ml**

- Place hot baked potatoes on microwave-safe plate. Carefully fluff up potatoes with fork. Top each potato with ham.

- Stir soup in can until smooth. Spoon soup over potatoes and top with cheese. Microwave on HIGH for 4 minutes.

Creamy Mashed Potatoes

2 pound baking potatoes
1 (8 ounce) package cream cheese, softened   **227 g**
1 teaspoon sugar   **5 ml**
¼ cup (½ stick) butter, softened   **60 ml**

- Preheat oven to 325° (162° C). Peel and quarter potatoes and place in saucepan and cover with water. Cook about 25 minutes or until tender. Drain and place potatoes in mixing bowl. Add cream cheese, sugar, 1 teaspoon (5 ml) salt and butter and beat until fluffy. Place in a greased 7 x 11-inch (18 x 28 cm) baking dish. Bake 25 minutes or until thoroughly hot.

Loaded-Baked Potatoes

6 medium to large potatoes
1 (1 pound) package hot sausage   **.5 kg**
1 (16 ounce) package cubed processed cheese   **.5 kg**
1 (10 ounce) can tomatoes and green chilies, drained **280 g**

- Cook potatoes in microwave. Brown sausage and drain. Add cheese to sausage and heat until cheese melts. Add tomatoes and green chilies. Serve sausage-cheese mixture over baked potatoes.

Ham-Baked Potatoes

4 potatoes, baked	
1 cup diced cooked ham	240 ml
1(10 ounce) can cream of mushroom soup	280 g
1 cup shredded cheddar cheese	240 ml

- Place hot potatoes in microwave-safe plate. Cut in half lengthwise. Fluff up potatoes with fork. Top each potato with one-fourth ham.

- In saucepan, heat soup with ¼ cup (60 ml) water and heat just until spreadable. Spoon soup over potatoes and top with cheese.

- Microwave on HIGH for 4 minutes or until hot.

Loaded Potatoes

6 large baking potatoes, washed	
2 cups cubed ham	480 ml
1 (8 ounce) package cubed processed cheese	227 g
1 (11 ounce) can Mexican corn, drained	312 g

- Cook potatoes in microwave until done. Combine ham, cheese and corn and stir well. With knife, cut potatoes down center and fluff insides with fork.

- Spoon generous amounts of ham-cheese mixture on each potato and reheat in microwave 2 to 3 minutes if necessary.

Baked Potato Toppers

1 cup grated cheddar cheese	240 ml
½ cup sour cream	120 ml
¼ cup (½ stick) butter, softened	60 ml
4 tablespoons chopped green onions	60 ml

- Mix all ingredients and serve on baked potato.

A Better Potato-Latkes

1 large egg	
2 tablespoons chopped chives and grated onion	30 ml
2 tablespoons flour	30 ml
1 tablespoon lemon juice	15 ml
2 pounds medium size potatoes, peeled	1 kg
½ cup oil	120 ml

- Combine egg, chives, onion, flour, lemon juice and 1 teaspoon (5 ml) salt in large bowl. In food processor with shredding disk, shred potatoes and place in colander in sink; squeeze out liquid. Stir into egg mixture.

- In large skillet, place oil and heat until very hot. Drop ¼ cup (60 ml) potato mixture into hot oil (about 6 at a time) and flatten each latke into rounds. Cook about 8 minutes on both sides or until light brown. Transfer to large baking sheet that has been lined with paper towels. Keep warm.

- Repeat this process, stirring mixture each time before frying (you may need to add more oil after each batch).

Grilled New Potatoes

1 pound new potatoes	.5 kg
3 tablespoons orange marmalade	45 ml
1 teaspoon brown sugar	5 ml
2 tablespoons butter, melted	30 ml

- Cook new potatoes covered in boiling water until crisp-tender.

- Drain and cut in half. Thread on skewers. Combine marmalade, brown sugar and butter and brush mixture over potatoes.

- Grill over medium hot coals until potatoes are brown, about 5 minutes each side. Salt and pepper to taste. Baste frequently.

Potato Pancakes

2 pounds white potatoes, peeled, grated   1.3 kg
1 onion, finely minced
3 eggs, beaten
½ cup seasoned dry breadcrumbs   120 ml

- In large bowl, combine potatoes, onions, eggs, a little salt and pepper and breadcrumbs and mix well.

- In skillet, drop by spoonfuls in hot oil and brown on both sides.

Rosemary New Potatoes

2 pounds small red (new) potatoes, halved   1 kg
¼ cup olive oil   60 ml
1 teaspoon dried rosemary   5 ml

- Place potatoes in saucepan with about 1-inch (2.5 cm) of water and a little salt. Cover and cook on medium heat, turning occasionally until tender (about 15 minutes). Drain and toss with olive oil, rosemary, 1 teaspoon (2 ml) salt and an ample amount of black pepper. Cover again to keep warm.

Baked New Potatoes

1 pound new potatoes with peels   .5 kg
1 large onion, coarsely chopped
1 clove garlic, minced
½ cup (1 stick) butter   120 ml

- Par-boil new potatoes. Drain and quarter. In large skillet, saute onion and garlic with butter until onions are translucent. Add potatoes and toss to coat. Place in large baking dish. Add 1 teaspoon (5 ml) salt. Bake at 350° (176° C), basting occasionally, for 25 to 30 minutes until potatoes are fork tender.

Cheesy Potatoes

10 - 12 new potatoes with peels	
1 (8 ounce) carton sour cream	227 g
¼ cup (½ stick) butter, melted	60 ml
1 (16 ounce) package processed cheese, sliced	.5 kg

- Rinse and scrub potatoes. Cut into ¼-inch (.6 cm) slices, place in large saucepan and cover with water. Cook for 25 minutes until slightly tender and drain.

- Place half potatoes in 9 x 13-inch (23 x 33 cm) baking dish. Sprinkle with a little salt and pepper.

- Spread half sour cream and half melted butter over top of potatoes. Place half sliced cheese on top.

- Repeat layer. Bake at 400° (204° C) about 20 minutes or until bubbly.

Maple-Pecan Sweet Potatoes

½ cup chopped, toasted pecans	120 ml
1 (29 ounce) can sweet potatoes, drained	805 g
¼ cup (½ stick) butter, melted	60 ml
½ cup pure maple syrup	120 ml

- Preheat oven to 350° (176° C). Toast pecans in oven about 10 minutes. In bowl, mash sweet potatoes with fork (leaving some small chunks) and add melted butter and maple syrup; mixing well. Transfer to greased 7 x 11-inch (18 x 28 cm) baking dish.

- Sprinkle pecans over sweet potato mixture and bake uncovered for 25 minutes.

Sweet Potatoes and Pecans

2 (15 ounce) cans sweet potatoes, drained, divided	2 (425 g)
1½ cups packed brown sugar	360 ml
¼ cup (½ stick) butter, melted	60 ml
1 cup chopped pecans	240 ml

- Slice half of the sweet potatoes and place in buttered, 2-quart (2 L) baking dish. Mix brown sugar, butter and pecans and sprinkle half mixture over sweet potatoes. Repeat layer. Bake uncovered at 350° (176° C) for 30 minutes.

Sweet Potato Casserole

1 (28 ounce) can sweet potatoes	794 g
½ cup chopped pecans	120 ml
1½ cups packed light brown sugar	360 ml
½ cup (1 stick) butter	120 ml

- Slice sweet potatoes into 2-quart (2 L) casserole dish. Sprinkle pecans over sweet potatoes. Make syrup of brown sugar and butter with just enough water to make it thin enough to pour. Bring to boil and pour syrup over sweet potatoes.

- Bake at 350° (176° C) for 30 minutes or until potatoes brown.

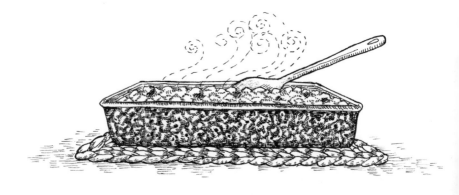

Skillet Candied Sweet Potatoes

⅓ cup (¾ stick) butter	60 ml
2 (15 ounce) cans sweet potatoes, drained	2 (425 g)
1½ cups packed brown sugar	360 ml
1 teaspoon cinnamon	5 ml

• In large skillet, melt butter and stir in sweet potatoes, brown sugar, cinnamon and a little salt. Cook on high heat just until mixture is hot; reduce heat, cover and simmer for 20 minutes.

Whipped Sweet Potatoes

2 (15 ounce) can sweet potatoes	2 (425 g)
¼ cup (½ stick) butter, melted	60 ml
¼ cup orange juice	60 ml
1 cup miniature marshmallows	240 ml

• Combine sweet potatoes, butter, orange juice and ½ teaspoon (2 ml) salt in mixing bowl.

• Beat until fluffy. Fold in marshmallows.

• Spoon into buttered 2-quart (2 L) casserole.

• Bake uncovered at 350° (176° C) for 25 minutes.

Penne Pasta in Creamy Pesto

1 (16 ounce) package penne regate pasta	.5 kg
1 (8 ounce) package Neufchatel cheese, softened	227 g
2 tablespoons butter	30 ml
1 (6 ounce) carton basil pesto	168 g

• Cook pasta according to package directions. Drain, leaving a little pasta water (about ½ cup/120 ml) in pan. While pasta is still hot, cut cheese into chunks and stir cheese and butter into pasta, stirring until both have melted.

• Gently stir in basil pesto, adding a tablespoon or two of water if mixture is too stiff. Serve hot.

Creamy Pasta

1 (8 ounce) jar roasted red peppers, drained	227 g
1 (15 ounce) can chicken broth	425 g
1 (3 ounce) package cream cheese	84 g
8 ounces pasta, cooked	227 g

• Combine red peppers and broth in blender and mix well.

• Pour into saucepan and heat to boiling.

• Turn heat down and whisk in cream cheese. Serve over your favorite pasta.

Ranch Spaghetti

1 (12 ounce) package spaghetti	340 g
¼ cup (½ stick) butter, cut in 3 pieces	60 ml
¾ cup sour cream	180 ml
¾ cup ranch dressing	180 ml
½ cup grated parmesan cheese	120 ml

• Cook spaghetti according to package directions; drain and return
  to saucepan. Stir in butter, sour cream and ranch dressing and
  toss. Spoon into serving bowl and sprinkle with grated parmesan
  cheese. Serve immediately.

Wonderful Alfredo Fettuccine

1 (16 ounce) package uncooked fettuccine	.5 kg
2 tablespoons butter	30 ml
¾ cup grated fresh parmesan cheese	180 ml
1¼ cups heavy cream	300 ml

• Cook fettuccine according to package directions.

• In large saucepan over medium heat, melt butter and stir in
  parmesan cheese, heavy cream and black pepper to taste. Cook
  1 minute, stirring constantly. Reduce heat and pour in fettuccine,
  tossing gently to coat fettuccine.

Creamy Fettuccine

1 (8 ounce) package fettuccine	227 g
1 pound Italian sausage	.5 kg
1 (10 ounce) can cream of mushroom soup	280 g
1 (16 ounce) carton sour cream	.5 kg

• Cook fettuccine and drain. Cut sausage into 1-inch (2.5 cm)
  pieces, brown over medium heat and cook for about 8 minutes.
  Drain. Mix all ingredients and place in 2-quart (2 L) greased
  baking dish. Bake at 325° (162° C) for 30 minutes.

Spinach Fettuccine

1 (6 ounce) can tomato paste	168 g
1 (5 ounce) can evaporated milk	143 g
½ cup (1 stick) butter	120 ml
1 (12 ounce) package spinach fettuccine	340 g

• In saucepan, combine tomato paste, milk and butter and cook until butter melts. Season with a little salt and pepper. Cook fettuccine according to package directions. Serve sauce over fettuccine.

Pesto Sauce For Linguine or Angel Hair Pasta

½ cup extra-virgin olive oil	120 ml
2 teaspoons prepared minced garlic	10 ml
⅓ cup finely minced Italian parsley	80 ml
½ teaspoon cayenne pepper	2 ml

• Combine all ingredients in jar with lid; shake well to blend. This sauce, plus a little salt and pepper, will season 1 pound (.5 kg) of pasta.

Artichoke Fettuccine

1 (12 ounce) package fettuccine	340 g
1 (14 ounce) can water-packed artichoke hearts, drained, chopped	396 g
1 (10 ounce) box frozen green peas, thawed	280 g
1 (16 ounce) jar alfredo sauce	.5 kg
2 heaping tablespoons crumbled blue cheese	30 ml

• Cook fettuccine according to package directions. Drain and place in serving bowl to keep warm. In large saucepan, heat artichoke hearts, peas and alfredo sauce and stir well. Spoon into bowl with fettuccine and toss. Sprinkle with blue cheese and serve hot.

Special Macaroni and Cheese

1 (8 ounce) package small macaroni shells	227 g
1 (15 ounce) can stewed tomatoes	425 g
1 (8 ounce) package cubed processed cheese	227 g
3 tablespoons butter, melted	45 ml

- Cook shells according to package directions and drain.

- In large bowl, combine shells, tomatoes, cheese cubes and butter. Pour into 2-quart (2 L) buttered baking dish.

- Bake covered at 350° (176° C) for 30 minutes.

Spice Up The Macaroni

1 cup uncooked spiral pasta	240 ml
⅓ cup (5½ tablespoons) butter	80 ml
1 (8 ounce) package shredded Mexican processed cheese	227 g
1 (10 ounce) can tomatoes and green chilies with liquid	280 g
½ yellow onion, very finely diced	
1 (8 ounce) carton sour cream	227 g

- Cook macaroni according to package directions, drain and add butter, stirring until butter melts. Set aside covered, keeping warm.

- Preheat oven to 325° (162° C). In large saucepan, combine processed cheese, tomatoes and green chilies and diced onion. Stir in macaroni and heat on low heat for 5 minutes, stirring occasionally. Fold in sour cream and pour into 2-quart (2 L) baking dish. Cover and bake for 20 minutes.

Macaroni and Cheese

1 cup uncooked macaroni	240 ml
1½ cups small curd cottage cheese	360 ml
1½ cups shredded cheddar or American cheese	360 ml
4 tablespoons grated parmesan cheese	60 ml

- Cook macaroni according to package directions and drain.
  Combine cottage cheese and both cheeses. Combine macaroni
  with cheese mixture. Spoon into greased 2-quart (2 L) baking
  dish. Bake covered at 350° (176° C) for 30 minutes.

Mom's Mac and Cheese

1 (10 ounce) package your favorite shape of macaroni	280 g
¼ cup (½ stick) butter	60 ml
5 tablespoons flour	75 ml
2¾ cups whole milk, divided	660 ml
1 (8 ounce) package shredded cheddar cheese, divided	227 g

- In saucepan cook macaroni according to package directions.
  Drain but do not rinse, then transfer to large mixing bowl.

- In heavy saucepan, melt butter and add flour; whisk to form
  smooth mixture. Slowly stir in about ¾ cup (180 ml) milk,
  whisking to avoid lumps. On medium heat, add remaining milk,
  bring to a boil, reduce heat to a gentle simmer, whisking until
  sauce is thick and smooth. Stir in three-fourths of cheese, stirring
  until cheese melts.

- Pour half sauce over drained macaroni, mixing well. Add
  remaining sauce, stirring well. Transfer to serving bowl and
  garnish with remaining cheese.

Skillet Ravioli and Broccoli

1 (16 ounce) package refrigerated cheese ravioli	.5 kg
1 (16 ounce) package frozen broccoli florets, thawed	.5 kg
1 (16 ounce) carton marinara sauce	.5 kg
¾ cup shredded mozzarella cheese	180 ml

- In large saucepan with boiling water, cook ravioli 8 minutes or until tender. Drain ravioli and return to saucepan.

- Cook broccoli according to package directions and drain. Stirring gently, add broccoli and marinara sauce to ravioli in skillet. Cook on medium heat, stirring often, just until mixture is thoroughly hot. Sprinkle with cheese, cover and cook 1 minute until cheese melts.

Colorful Bacon-Rice

¾ pound bacon	340 g
2½ cups cooked rice	600 ml
1 (15 ounce) can sliced carrots, drained	425 g
1 (10 ounce) package frozen green peas, thawed	280 g

- In large skillet, fry bacon until crisp. Drain bacon on paper towels, leaving about ½ cup (120 ml) bacon drippings in skillet. Crumble bacon and set aside.

- Add rice, carrots and peas to skillet and cook, stirring occasionally until mixture is thoroughly hot. Stir in bacon and serve hot.

Tasty Rice

¼ cup (½ stick) butter	60 ml
1 cup instant white rice	240 ml
1 (15 ounce) cans beef broth	425 g
¼ cup parmesan cheese	60 ml

• Melt butter in 3-quart (3 L) casserole dish. Add rice and pour beef broth over rice. Sprinkle with parmesan cheese.

• Cover and bake at 350° (176° C) for 20 minutes.

Spanish Rice

6 tablespoons (¾ stick) butter, melted	90 ml
1 onion, chopped	
2 cups cooked rice	480 ml
1 (10 ounce) can tomatoes and green chilies	280 g

• In large bowl, combine butter, onion, rice, tomatoes and green chilies and salt to taste. Spoon mixture into buttered 3-quart (3 L) baking dish. Cover and bake at 350° (176° C) for 30 minutes.

Mushroom Rice

1 (6 ounce) package chicken Rice-a-Roni®	168 g
1 (4 ounce) can sliced mushrooms, drained	114 g
⅓ cup slivered almonds	80 ml
1 (8 ounce) carton sour cream	227 g

• Prepare rice according to package directions. Fold in mushrooms, almonds and sour cream. Place in 3-quart (3 L) greased casserole. Bake covered at 350° (176° C) for 25 minutes.

Baked Rice

2 cups uncooked instant rice	480 ml
½ cup (1 stick) butter, melted	120 ml
1 (10 ounce) can cream of celery soup	280 g
1 (10 ounce) can cream of onion soup	280 g

- Combine rice, butter, soups and 1½ cups (360 ml) water.

- Pour into buttered 3-quart (3 L) baking dish.

- Cover and bake at 350° (176° C) for 25 minutes.

Chile-Rice Bake

1 cup instant rice	240 ml
1 pint sour cream	.5 kg
1 (7 ounce) can chopped green chilies	198 g
1 (8 ounce) package shredded Monterey Jack cheese	227 g

- Cook rice according to package directions. Add remaining
  ingredients plus ½ teaspoon (2 ml) salt. Place mixture in buttered
  baking dish. Bake covered at 325° (162° C) for 15 to 20 minutes
  or until hot.

Dinner Rice

2 cups cooked instant white rice	480 ml
1 onion, chopped	
¼ cup (½ stick) butter, melted	60 ml
1 (8 ounce) package shredded Mexican processed cheese	227 g

- Combine all ingredients; mix well. Spoon mixture into buttered
  2-quart (2 L) baking dish. Bake covered at 325° (162° C) for
  30 minutes.

Brown Rice

1 cup uncooked instant rice	240 ml
1 (10 ounce) can French onion soup	280 g
1 (15 ounce) can beef broth	425 g
3 tablespoons butter, melted	45 ml

- Put rice in bottom baking dish. Pour soups and butter on top. Bake covered at 350° (176° C) for 20 minutes.

Easy Rice

1 onion, finely chopped	
2 tablespoons (¼ stick) butter	30 ml
1 cup uncooked instant white rice	240 ml
2 (14 ounce) cans chicken broth	2 (396 g)

- In skillet, saute onion in butter until transparent. In 2-quart (2 L) baking dish combine onion, rice and broth. Cover and bake at 350° (176° C) for 30 minutes.

Skillet Beans and Rice

6 slices bacon	
1 (15 ounce) can Mexican stewed tomatoes	425 g
1 cup uncooked instant rice	240 ml
2 (15 ounce) cans chili beans with juice	2 (425 g)

- In skillet fry bacon until crisp and drain, reserving 2 tablespoons (30 ml) drippings. Cut bacon in 1-inch (2.5 cm) pieces and set aside.

- Dry skillet with paper towels and stir in stewed tomatoes, rice, reserved drippings and ⅓ cup (80 ml) water. Bring to boiling, reduce heat and simmer 3 minutes or until rice is tender and most of liquid has evaporated   Add chili beans and cook until mixture is thoroughly hot. Serve right from skillet or spoon into serving bowl and top with bacon pieces.

Broccoli and Wild Rice

2 (10 ounce) packages frozen chopped broccoli	2 (280 g)
1 (6 ounce) box long grain and wild rice	168 g
1 (8 ounce) jar processed cheese spread	227 g
1 (10 ounce) can cream of chicken soup	280 g

• Cook broccoli and rice according to package directions.

• Combine all ingredients and pour into buttered 2-quart (2 L) baking dish. Bake at 350° (176° C) for 25 minutes.

Pecan-Mushroom Rice

1½ cups whole pecans	360 ml
1½ cups uncooked instant rice	360 ml
1 (14 ounce) can chicken broth	396 g
¼ cup (½ stick) butter	60 ml
2 (8 ounce) can whole mushrooms, drained	2 (227 g)
2 teaspoons prepared, minced garlic	10 ml
3 cups baby spinach leaves, stems removed	710 ml
½ cup grated parmesan cheese	120 ml

• In large saucepan, cook and stir pecans over medium heat for 5 minutes. Remove from pan and cool slightly.

• Cook rice in chicken broth and butter according to package directions. Gently stir in mushrooms, garlic, spinach, cheese and pecans. Serve immediately.

Chili Rice and Beans

2 (8.8 ounce) packages whole grain brown rice	2 (255 g)
2 (15 ounce) cans hot chili beans with liquid	2 (425 g)
1 (4.3 ounce) package pre-cooked bacon, divided	114 g
1 (8 ounce) package shredded processed cheese	227 g

- Preheat oven to 350° (176° C). Cook rice 90 seconds in microwave and place in bowl. Add chili beans and half of bacon, mix well. Spoon into greased 7 x 11-inch (18 x 28 cm) baking dish, cover and bake 20 minutes.

- Remove from oven and sprinkle cheese and remaining bacon over top. Return to oven for 5 minutes.

Italian-Style Rice and Beans

1 (16 ounce) package frozen chopped onions and bell peppers	.5 kg
2 tablespoons olive oil	30 ml
1 (15 ounce) can Italian stewed tomatoes	425 g
1 (15 ounce) can great northern beans, drained	425 g
1 cup uncooked instant rice	240 ml

- In large saucepan, saute onions and bell peppers in oil. Add stewed tomatoes, beans, ½ cup (120 ml) water and rice and stir well. Over medium-high heat, cover and cook about 3 minutes. Uncover and continue cooking another 3 minutes, stirring once, or until rice is tender.

Instant Beans and Rice

1 (8.8 ounce) package (microwavable) rice	255 g
1 (15 ounce) can pinto beans with liquid	425 g
½ cup hot thick and chunky salsa	120 ml
1 teaspoon cumin	5 ml

• Microwave rice in package for 90 seconds; transfer to saucepan and add beans, salsa, cumin and salt to taste. Heat on medium heat until thoroughly hot.

Supper Frittata

2 cups cooked white rice	480 ml
1 (10 ounce) box frozen green peas, thawed	280 g
1 cup cooked, cubed ham	240 ml
8 large eggs, beaten	
1 cup shredded pepper jack cheese, divided	240 ml
1 teaspoon dried thyme	5 ml

• In large heavy skillet with a little oil, heat rice, peas and ham 3 to 4 minutes or until mixture is thoroughly hot. In separate bowl, whisk eggs, three-fourths of cheese, thyme and salt to taste. Add to mixture in skillet and shake pan gently to distribute evenly. On medium heat, cover and cook, without stirring, until set on bottom and sides (eggs will still be runny in center).

• Sprinkle remaining cheese over top. Double wrap skillet handle with foil, place in oven and broil about 5 minutes or until frittata is firm in center.

Fried Poblano Rings

3 poblano chile peppers
1 cup flour   **240 ml**
1 cup milk or buttermilk   **240 ml**

- Slice poblanos in rings about ¼-inch (.6 cm) wide and remove seeds. Mix flour, salt and pepper to taste in shallow bowl. Dip chile rings into milk and flour mixture. Carefully place in hot oil in deep-fryer or saucepan with about 3 cups (710 ml) oil. (Oil should be almost to smoking stage when chiles start cooking.) Fry until golden brown. Lightly salt.

Baked Bananas

10 bananas
¾ cup (1½ sticks) butter, melted   **180 ml**
¾ cup brown sugar   **180 ml**
1 teaspoon vanilla   **5 ml**

- Preheat oven to 350° (176° C). Peel bananas and arrange pinwheel fashion in large glass pie plate. In saucepan, combine butter and brown sugar and heat just enough to mix well. Stir in vanilla and pour over bananas. Bake for 20 minutes or until bubbly.

Cinnamon Baked Apples

6 Granny Smith apples
¾ cup mixed nuts   **180 ml**
1 cup light brown sugar   **240 ml**
1 teaspoon cinnamon   **5 ml**

- Preheat oven to 350° (176° C). Core apples without cutting through to bottom. Using potato peeler, peel 1-inch (2.5 cm) strip around top of apple. Combine nuts, sugar and cinnamon and stuff cavities and place apples in greased 2-quart (2 L) baking dish. Drizzle apple with 2 tablespoons (30 ml) water and bake about 25 minutes. Serve warm or at room temperature.

Wild West Corn

3 (15 ounce) cans whole kernel corn, drained	3 (425 g)
1 (10 ounce) can tomatoes and green chilies, drained	280 g
1 (8 ounce) package shredded Monterey Jack cheese	227 g
1 cup cheese cracker crumbs	240 ml

- In large bowl, combine corn, tomatoes and green chilies and cheese and mix well. Pour into buttered 2½-quart (2.5 L) baking dish.

- Sprinkle cracker crumbs over casserole. Bake uncovered at 350° (176° C) for 25 minutes.

Corn Au Gratin

3 (15 ounce) cans mexicorn, drained	3 (425 g)
1 (4 ounce) can sliced mushrooms, drained	114 g
1 (10 ounce) can cream of mushroom soup	280 g
1 cup shredded cheddar cheese	240 ml

- Mix all ingredients in saucepan and heat slowly until cheese melts. Serve hot.

Mushrooms and Corn

½ cup fresh mushrooms, sliced	120 ml
3 chopped green onions with tops	
2 tablespoons butter	30 ml
1 (16 ounce) package frozen whole kernel corn	.5 kg

- Place all ingredients in 2-quart (2 L) saucepan and cook on medium heat for 5 to 10 minutes. Add salt and pepper to taste.

Italian Corn

1 (16 ounce) package frozen whole kernel corn	.5 kg
2 slices bacon, cooked, diced	
1 onion, chopped	
1 (15 ounce) can Italian stewed tomatoes	425 g

- Place all ingredients in 2-quart (2 L) pan. Cook until most liquid in tomatoes cooks out. Add a little salt and pepper and serve hot.

Corn Pudding

1 (8 ounce) package corn muffin mix	227 g
1 (15 ounce) can cream-style corn	425 g
½ cup sour cream	120 ml
3 eggs, slightly beaten	

- Combine all ingredients and pour into buttered 2-quart (2 L) baking dish.

- Bake uncovered at 350° (176° C) for about 30 minutes.

Stuffed Corn

1 (15 ounce) can cream-style corn	425 g
1 (15 ounce) can whole kernel corn, drained	425 g
½ cup (1 stick) butter, melted	120 ml
1 (6 ounce) package chicken stuffing mix	168 g

- Combine all ingredients plus seasoning packet and ½ cup (120 ml) water and mix well. Spoon into buttered 9 x 13-inch (23 x 33 cm) baking pan. Bake at 350° (176° C) for 30 minutes.

Atomic Salsa-Corn

1 (8 ounce) jar hot salsa	227 g
1 (16 ounce) package frozen whole kernel corn, thawed	.5 kg
¼ teaspoon garlic powder	1 ml
½ cup grated Monterey Jack cheese	120 ml

• Combine hot salsa, corn, garlic powder and ¼ cup (60 ml) water in saucepan. Cook on low-medium heat, stirring occasionally, for 6 minutes. Pour into serving bowl and sprinkle with cheese.

Shoe-Peg Corn

1 (8 ounce) package cream cheese, softened	227 g
½ cup (1 stick) butter, softened	120 ml
3 (15 ounce) cans shoe-peg corn	3 (425 g)
1 (4 ounce) can chopped green chilies	114 g

• With mixer beat cream cheese and butter. Add corn and green chilies; mix well. Spoon into 7 x 11-inch (18 x 28 cm) greased baking dish. Bake covered at 350° (176° C) for 25 minutes.

Hot Corn Bake

3 (15 ounce) cans whole kernel corn, drained	3 (425 g)
1 (10 ounce) can cream of corn soup	280 g
1 cup salsa	240 ml
1 (8 ounce) package shredded Mexican-cheese blend, divided	227 g

• Combine corn, soup, salsa and half cheese and mix well. Pour into buttered 3-quart (3 L) baking dish and sprinkle remaining cheese on top. Bake at 350° (176° C) for 20 to 30 minutes.

Corn Maize

¼ cup (½ stick) butter, melted	60 ml
1 (3 ounce) package cream cheese, softened	84 g
2 (15 ounce) cans whole kernel corn, drained	2 (425 g)
⅓ cup salsa	80 ml

- Beat together butter and cream cheese. Add corn and salsa.

- Pour into 2-quart (2 L) buttered baking dish.

- Bake covered at 350° (176° C) for 25 minutes. Serve hot.

Quick Corn-on-the-Cob

1 fresh ear corn-on-the-cob
Salt
Butter

- Microwave 1 ear of corn in its husk for 2 minutes on HIGH (the silky threads come off more easily after corn is cooked) turning once halfway through cooking.

- Or remove husk and silks and wrap ear in wax paper and cook 2 minutes on HIGH, turning once halfway through.

- For multiple ears, double or triple time for two or three ears.

Herb Butter for Corn-on-the-Cob

½ cup (1 stick) butter, softened	120 ml
1 teaspoon dried oregano	5 ml
1 teaspoon basil	5 ml
1 tablespoon dried parsley	15 ml
1 teaspoon lemon juice	5 ml

- In bowl, combine butter, oregano, basil, parsley, lemon juice and ½ teaspoon (2 ml) salt, mix well. Transfer to piece of wax paper and roll into a log and refrigerate until firm. When ready to serve, slice herbed butter and serve with the corn.

Calico Corn

1 (16 ounce) package frozen whole kernel corn	.5 kg
1 bell pepper, chopped	
⅓ cup chopped celery	80 ml
1 (10 ounce) can cream of cheddar cheese soup	280 g

- Cook corn in microwave according to package directions and drain well.

- Add bell pepper and celery. Stir in soup and mix well.

- Pour into buttered 2-quart (2 L) baking dish and bake covered at 350° (176° C) for 30 minutes.

Creamy Succotash

2 onions, chopped	
2 tablespoons (¼ stick) butter	30 ml
1 (10 ounce) package frozen baby lima beans, thawed	280 g
1 (10 ounce) package frozen whole kernel corn, thawed	280 g
⅔ cup heavy cream	160 ml

- Place onions in skillet with butter and saute until onions are clear, but not brown. Add lima beans and cook 5 minutes, stirring occasionally. Add corn with ample amount of salt and pepper; cook about 2 minutes.

- Stir in heavy cream and cook but do not boil, stirring, until cream is simmering, about 3 minutes or until vegetables are tender.

Spicy Hominy

1 (15 ounce) can yellow hominy, drained	425 g
1 (8 ounce) carton sour cream	227 g
1 (4 ounce) can chopped green chilies	114 g
1¼ cups grated cheddar cheese	300 ml

- Combine all ingredients and add a little salt. Pour into 1-quart (1 L) baking dish and bake at 350° (176° C) for about 20 minutes.

Fresh Asparagus with Vinaigrette

6 cups diagonally cut asparagus, steamed, chilled	1.5 L
1 tablespoon sesame seeds, toasted	15 ml
2 tablespoons minced shallots	30 ml

Dressing:

1 tablespoon olive oil	15 ml
1 tablespoon rice vinegar	15 ml
1 teaspoon fresh peeled, grated ginger	5 ml
½ teaspoon soy sauce	2 ml
½ teaspoon dried rosemary	2 ml
1 tablespoon honey	15 ml

- Place steamed asparagus, sesame seeds and shallots in serving bowl. Combine all dressing ingredients and pour over asparagus mixture and toss.

Asparagus Caesar

3 (15 ounce) cans asparagus spears, drained	3 (425 g)
¼ cup (½ stick) butter, melted	60 ml
3 tablespoons lemon juice	45 ml
½ cup grated parmesan cheese	120 ml

- Place asparagus in 2-quart (2 L) baking dish. Drizzle on butter and lemon juice. Sprinkle cheese and bake at 400° (204° C) for 15 to 20 minutes.

Sesame Asparagus

6 fresh asparagus spears, trimmed	
1 tablespoon butter	15 ml
1 teaspoon lemon juice	5 ml
1 teaspoon sesame seeds	5 ml

- Place asparagus in skillet. Sprinkle with salt if desired. Add ¼ cup (60 ml) water and bring to boil. Reduce heat. Cover and simmer about 4 minutes. Melt butter and add lemon juice and sesame seeds. Drain asparagus and drizzle with butter mixture.

Quick Microwave Asparagus

1 bunch fresh asparagus	
2 tablespoons olive oil	30 ml

- Wash asparagus and dry with paper towels and place in microwave-safe bowl. Drizzle with olive oil and cover with paper towel. Microwave 2 minutes; asparagus should be tender-crisp; if not continue microwaving until tenderness is reached. (Time will vary depending on your microwave.)

- Slide asparagus to a serving plate and season with salt and pepper.

Parmesan Asparagus

1 bunch fresh asparagus
1 tablespoon olive oil   15 ml
2 tablespoons lemon juice   30 ml
⅓ cup freshly grated parmesan cheese   80 ml

- Trim asparagus of woody ends and discard. Place asparagus and
  oil in large skillet over medium-high heat and saute just until
  tender-crisp and still bright green in color. Remove from heat
  and add lemon juice and an ample amount of salt and pepper.
  Sprinkle with parmesan cheese and serve.

Oven Baked Asparagus

1 bunch fresh asparagus, trimmed
2 tablespoons extra-virgin olive oil   30 ml
2 tablespoons balsamic vinegar   30 ml
⅓ cup fresh grated parmesan cheese   80 ml

- Preheat oven to 400° (204° C). Arrange asparagus in single layer
  in shallow baking dish and drizzle olive oil over asparagus. Bake
  uncovered about 10 minutes. To serve, sprinkle with a little salt
  and pepper, vinegar and parmesan cheese.

Creamed Asparagus

2 bunches fresh asparagus
1 teaspoon dried basil   5 ml
2 (10 ounce) cans cream of asparagus soup   2 (280 g)
¾ cup prepared Italian breadcrumbs   180 ml

- Preheat oven to 325° (162° C). Cut off tough ends of stalks and
  place in greased baking dish. Sprinkle with basil and a little salt.
  Bake uncovered for 10 minutes. Place cream of asparagus soup
  in skillet with ⅓ cup (80 ml) water (or milk); heat just enough to
  mix with water. Spread over baked asparagus and sprinkle with
  Italian breadcrumbs. Bake for 30 minutes.

Baked Asparagus with Lemon Dressing

2 bunches fresh asparagus	
2 tablespoons olive oil	30 ml

Dressing:

¼ cup lemon juice	60 ml
2 tablespoons finely minced shallots	30 ml
⅓ cup olive oil	80 ml
2 eggs, hard-boiled, finely minced	

• Preheat oven to 375° (190° C). Place asparagus on rimmed baking sheet and drizzle with olive oil; then sprinkle with 1 teaspoon (5 ml) seasoned salt. Toss to spread oil evenly and bake for 15 minutes.

• To make dressing, mix together lemon juice, shallots, little salt and slowly whisk in oil to blend well. Arrange asparagus on serving platter and drizzle with lemon juice-olive oil mixture and garnish with minced eggs.

Asparagus Bake

2 (15 ounce) cans cut asparagus spears with liquid	2 (425 g)
3 eggs, hard-boiled, chopped	
½ cup chopped pecans	120 ml
1 (10 ounce) can cream of asparagus soup	280 g

• Arrange asparagus spears in buttered 2-quart (2 L) baking dish. Top with eggs and pecans. Heat asparagus soup and add liquid from asparagus spears. Spoon over eggs and pecans. Bake covered at 350° (176° C) for 25 minutes.

Almond Asparagus

⅓ cup butter   80 ml
1 - 1½ pounds fresh asparagus   .5 kg
⅔ cup slivered almonds   160 ml
1 tablespoon lemon juice   15 ml

• Melt butter in skillet and add asparagus and almonds and saute
  3 to 4 minutes. Cover and steam about 2 minutes or until tender-
  crisp. Sprinkle lemon and a little salt and pepper over asparagus.
  Serve hot.

Yummy Cauliflower

1 head cauliflower, cut into florets
1 teaspoon prepared minced garlic   5 ml
⅓ cup mayonnaise   80 ml
Dash hot sauce

• Steam cauliflower and garlic in 1½ quarts (1.5 L) water
  until tender; drain well. Transfer to food processor and add
  mayonnaise, ½ teaspoon (2 ml) salt and dash of hot sauce.
  Process until tender and creamy. Garnish with pepper.

Savory Cauliflower

1 head cauliflower
1 (1 ounce) envelope hollandaise sauce mix   28 g
Fresh parsley to garnish
Lemon slices to garnish, optional

• Cut cauliflower into small florets. Cook in salted water until
  barely tender. Do not overcook. Mix sauce according to package
  directions. Drain cauliflower, top with sauce and sprinkle with
  parsley. Garnish with lemon slices if you like.

Best Cauliflower

1 (16 ounce) package frozen cauliflower	.5 kg
1 (8 ounce) carton sour cream	227 g
1½ cups grated American or cheddar cheese	360 ml
4 teaspoons sesame seeds, toasted	20 ml

- Cook cauliflower according to package directions. Drain and place half cauliflower in 2-quart (2 L) baking dish. Sprinkle a little salt and pepper on cauliflower. Spread half sour cream and half cheese, top with 2 teaspoons (10 ml) sesame seeds and repeat layer. Bake at 350° (176° C) for about 15 to 20 minutes.

Souper Cauliflower

1 (16 ounce) package frozen cauliflower, cooked, drained	.5 kg
1 (10 ounce) can cream of celery soup	280 g
¼ cup milk	60 ml
1 cup shredded cheddar cheese	240 ml

- Place cauliflower in 2-quart (2 L) greased baking dish. In saucepan, combine soup, milk and cheese; heat and mix well. Pour over cauliflower. Bake at 350° (176° C) for 15 minutes.

Creamy Cauliflower

1 head cauliflower, broken into large florets	
1 red bell pepper, chopped	
1 small zucchini, chopped	
1 (10 ounce) can cream of celery soup	280 g
⅓ cup milk	80 ml

- Place cauliflower florets, red bell pepper and zucchini in saucepan with about ¾ cup (180 ml) water and a little salt. Cover and cook on high heat about 10 minutes or until cauliflower is tender. Drain. In smaller saucepan combine soup and milk and heat, stirring until well mixed. Spoon cauliflower, bell pepper and zucchini into serving bowl and pour soup mixture over vegetables.

Best Green Beans

2 pounds fresh green beans, trimmed	1 kg
½ pound bacon	227 g
1 bunch fresh green onions, sliced white parts only	
1 (4 ounce) can chopped pimentos, drained	114 g

- In large saucepan over high heat, cook beans in ⅓ cup (80 ml) water for 10 minutes or until tender-crisp. Drain

- Cook bacon in skillet until crisp and drain, but reserve about 2 tablespoons (30 ml) drippings. Crumble bacon and place in small bowl. Wipe skillet of drippings and add 2 tablespoons (30 ml) of reserved drippings. Saute onion over medium-high heat for 1 minute.

- Spoon green beans into skillet with onions. Add pimentos and crumbled bacon; heat mixture until thoroughly hot.

Green Beans and Almonds

2 (16 ounce) packages frozen french-cut green beans	2 (.5 kg)
2 tablespoons (¼ stick) butter	30 ml
2 (8 ounce) cans water chestnuts, chopped	2 (227 g)
½ cup slivered almonds, toasted	120 ml

- Cook beans according to package directions.

- Drain, add butter and heat just until butter melts. Fold in water chestnuts. Place in serving dish and sprinkle almonds over top.

Crunchy Green Beans

3 (15 ounce) cans whole green beans	3 (425 g)
2 (10 ounce) cans cream of mushroom soup	2 (280 g)
2 (11 ounce) cans water chestnuts, chopped	2 (312 g)
2 (3 ounce) cans french-fried onion rings	2 (84 g)

• Combine green beans, mushroom soup, water chestnuts, ½ teaspoon (2 ml) salt and a little pepper. Pour mixture into 2-quart (2 L) baking dish. Bake covered at 350° (176° C) for 30 minutes. Remove casserole from oven and sprinkle onion rings over top and bake 10 more minutes longer.

Green Beans

1 pound fresh green beans	.5 kg
2 tablespoons soy sauce	30 ml
¼ teaspoon ground nutmeg	1 ml
½ cup toasted sesame seeds	120 ml

• Cook green beans until tender-crisp, about 10 minutes in medium saucepan.

• Combine soy sauce, nutmeg and 2 tablespoons (30 ml) butter. Cook over medium heat for a few minutes. Add to green beans and toss lightly. Add sesame seeds and toss again.

Seasoned Green Beans

4 slices bacon, chopped	
1 medium onion, chopped	
2 (15 ounce) cans green beans, drained	2 (425 g)
1 teaspoon sugar	5 ml

• Saute bacon and onion in skillet; drain. Add green beans and sugar and heat thoroughly.

Green Beans With Blue Cheese

1½ pounds fresh green beans, trimmed	.7 kg
1½ cups chopped, cooked ham (can be leftover)	360 ml
¾ cup crumbled blue cheese	180 ml
½ cup chopped walnuts, toasted	120 ml

- Cut beans to 2-inch (5 cm) pieces and place in steamer basket. Over boiling water, steam beans for 5 minutes. Drain.

- In skillet saute ham in a little oil and add blue cheese and green beans, heat just until cheese has melted. Spoon into serving bowl and sprinkle walnuts over top.

Green Beans and Mushrooms

½ cup (1 stick) butter, divided	120 ml
1 small onion, chopped	
1 (8 ounce) carton fresh shiitake mushrooms, sliced	227 g
2 pounds fresh green beans, trimmed	1 kg
¾ cup chicken broth	180 ml

- In saucepan, melt half butter and saute onion and mushrooms and transfer to small bowl.

- In same saucepan, melt remaining butter and toss with green beans. Pour chicken broth over beans, bring to a boil; reduce heat, cover and simmer until liquid evaporates and green beans are tender-crisp. Stir in mushroom mixture and season with salt.

Cheddar Fresh Green Beans

1 (6 ounce) can cheddar french-fried onions	168 g
3 pounds fresh green beans, ends trimmed	1.3 kg
¼ cup (½ stick) butter	60 ml
2 teaspoons salt free seasoning blend	10 ml

- Preheat oven to 325° (162° C). Place cheddar onions in pan and heat for about 15 minutes.

- In large saucepan, cook green beans in lightly salted water about 10 minutes or until tender-crisp. Drain well.

- Place butter in small saucepan and over low heat, cook and stir about 5 minutes, being careful not to let butter burn. Remove from heat and add seasoning blend. Pour over beans and toss gently. When ready to serve, toss half cheddar onions with green beans and place in serving bowl. Sprinkle remaining onions over green beans.

Italian Green Beans

1 (16 ounce) package frozen Italian green beans	.5 kg
3 green onions with tops, chopped	
2 tablespoons butter	30 ml
1 teaspoon mixed Italian seasoning	5 ml

- Mix all ingredients in 2-quart (2 L) saucepan and cook according to package directions.

Corny Green Beans

1 (16 ounce) package frozen green beans, thawed, drained	.5 kg
1 (16 ounce) package frozen whole kernel corn, thawed, drained	.5 kg
1 (10 ounce) can cream of chicken soup	280 g
1 (8 ounce) carton sour cream	227 g
1 (8 ounce) package shredded 4-cheese blend	227 g
2 cups crushed round butter-flavored crackers	480 ml
2 tablespoons butter, melted	480 ml

- Preheat oven to 350° (176° C). In large bowl, combine green beans, corn, soup, sour cream, cheese and a little salt, mixing well. Spoon into a greased 9 x 13-inch (23 x 33 cm) baking dish. Combine cracker crumbs and melted butter and sprinkle over top of casserole. Bake uncovered for 30 minutes.

Tangy Carrot Coins

2 (15 ounce) cans sliced carrots	2 (425 g)
2 tablespoons (¼ stick) butter	30 ml
2 tablespoons brown sugar	30 ml
1 tablespoon dijon-style mustard	15 ml

- Place all ingredients in saucepan. Cook and stir over medium heat for about 2 minutes. Serve hot.

Brown-Sugar Carrots

2 (15 ounce) cans carrots	2 (425 g)
¼ cup (½ stick) butter	60 ml
3 tablespoons brown sugar	45 ml
½ teaspoon brown ginger	2 ml

- Drain carrots but reserve 2 tablespoons (30 ml) liquid. Combine liquid with butter, brown sugar and ginger. Heat thoroughly. Add carrots, stirring gently, and cook 3 minutes. Serve hot.

Creamy Carrots with Toasted Almonds

2 (15 ounce) cans sliced carrots	2 (425 g)
1 (10 ounce) can cream of celery soup	280 g
½ cup milk	120 ml
⅓ cup chopped almonds, toasted	80 ml

- In saucepan, combine carrots, soup and milk. Over medium heat stir to mix and heat thoroughly. Stir almonds before serving. Serve hot.

Glazed Carrots

1 (16 ounce) package frozen baby carrots	.5 kg
¼ cup apple cider	60 ml
¼ cup apple jelly	60 ml
1½ teaspoons dijon-style mustard	7 ml

- In saucepan place carrots and apple cider and bring to boil. Reduce heat. Cover and simmer about 8 minutes or until carrots are tender. Remove cover and cook on medium heat until liquid evaporates. Stir in jelly and mustard. Cook until jelly melts and carrots glaze.

Caramelized Carrots

1 (16 ounce) package baby carrots	.5 kg
2 teaspoons soy sauce	10 ml
2 tablespoons brown sugar	30 ml
1 tablespoon olive oil	15 ml

- Preheat oven to 425° (220° C). Place carrots in single layer in buttered 7 x 11-inch (18 x 28 cm) baking pan. Combine soy sauce, brown sugar, olive oil and a little salt. Spoon over carrots. Bake for 15 minutes, stirring once.

Simply Sweet Carrots

1 (16 ounce) package baby carrots	.5 kg
1 (14 ounce) can chicken broth	396 g
½ cup apricot preserves	120 ml
1 tablespoon soy sauce	15 ml
1 tablespoon fresh grated ginger	15 ml

- Place carrots and broth in saucepan and bring to a boil; reduce heat to medium and cook for about 14 minutes or until carrots are tender-crisp and liquid is reduced to about ¼ cup (60 ml).

- Stir in apricot preserves, soy sauce and fresh grated ginger; cook another 10 minutes, stirring constantly until mixture thickens and carrots are glazed.

Carrots and Peas

1 (15 ounce) can sliced carrots, drained	425 g
1 (15 ounce) can green peas, drained	425 g
¼ cup (½ stick) butter	60 ml
⅓ cup chopped cashew nuts	80 ml

- In saucepan, combine carrots, peas, butter and cashew nuts.

- Heat until butter melts and mix well. Serve hot.

Kid-Pleasing Carrots

1 (16 ounce) package baby carrots	.5 kg
¾ cup orange juice	180 ml
2 tablespoons butter	30 ml
2 tablespoon brown sugar	30 ml
½ teaspoon ground cumin	2 ml

- Combine all ingredients in saucepan with ¼ cup (60 ml) water. Cook on medium-high about 10 minutes or until carrots are tender and liquid is cooked out.

Dilled Baby Carrots

1 (12 ounce) package fresh baby carrots	340 g
3 chicken bouillon cubes or 2 teaspoons bouillon	
granules	10 ml
6 tablespoons (¾ stick) butter	90 ml
2 teaspoons dill weed	10 ml

- Boil carrots in water with dissolved bouillon cubes until tender (about 8 minutes). Drain.

- Place in skillet with melted butter. Cook on low heat for only a few minutes and make sure butter coats all carrots.

- Sprinkle dill weed over carrots and shake to make sure dill is on all carrots. Place in serving dish and serve immediately.

Cheddar-Broccoli Bake

1 (10 ounce) can cheddar cheese soup	280 g
½ cup milk	120 ml
1 (16 ounce) bag frozen broccoli florets, cooked	.5 kg
1 (3 ounce) can french-fried onion rings	84 g

- In 2-quart (2 L) baking dish, mix soup, milk and broccoli.

- Bake at 350° (176° C) for 20 minutes.

- Stir and sprinkle onions over broccoli mixture. Bake for 10 more minutes or until onions are golden.

Buttered Vegetables

½ cup (1 stick) butter   120 ml
2 yellow squash, sliced
1 (16 ounce) package broccoli florets   .5 kg
1 (10 ounce) box frozen corn   280 g

- Melt butter in large skillet and combine all vegetables. Saute
  vegetables for about 10 to 15 minutes or until tender-crisp.

Crunchy Broccoli

2 (10 ounce) packages frozen broccoli florets   2 (280 g)
1 (8 ounce) can sliced water chestnuts, drained,
   chopped   227 g
½ cup (1 stick) butter, melted   120 ml
1 (1 ounce) packet dry onion soup mix   28 g

- Place broccoli in microwave-safe dish, cover and microwave
  5 minutes. Turn dish and cook another 4 minutes. Add water
  chestnuts. Combine melted butter and soup mix and blend well.
  Toss with cooked broccoli.

Broccoli-Stuffed Tomatoes

4 medium tomatoes
1 (10 ounce) package frozen chopped broccoli   280 g
1 (6 ounce) roll garlic cheese, softened   168 g
½ teaspoon garlic salt   2 ml

- Cut tops off tomatoes and scoop out pulp. Cook broccoli
  according to package directions and drain well. Combine
  broccoli, cheese and garlic salt. Heat just until cheese melts.
  Stuff broccoli mixture into tomatoes and place on baking sheet.

- Bake at 375° (190° C) for about 10 minutes.

Broccoli with Jazzy Cheese Sauce

1 (24 ounce) package frozen broccoli florets, thawed	680 g
1 (10 ounce) can cream of celery soup	280 g
¾ cup milk	180 ml
¼ teaspoon garlic powder	1 ml
¼ teaspoon cayenne pepper	1 ml
1½ cups cubed processed cheese	360 ml

- Place broccoli in microwave-safe bowl and microwave on HIGH about 4 minutes or until tender. Keep warm.

- In saucepan, combine celery soup, milk, garlic powder and cayenne pepper. Heat, stirring until well blended. On low heat, stir in cheese until melted. Spoon over broccoli.

Broccoli Fritters

1 (16 ounce) package frozen chopped broccoli	.5 kg
2 eggs, lightly beaten	
1 small onion, chopped	
½ cup chopped pecans	120 ml
½ cup self-rising flour	120 ml

- Cook broccoli according to package directions and drain well. Combine broccoli, eggs, onion, pecans and flour, mixing well.

- Place about ¼ inch (.6 cm) of oil in skillet and heat. Drop broccoli mixture by tablespoonfuls into hot oil and cook, in batches 2 minutes on each side or until light brown. Remove to wire rack on baking pan and keep warm in 200° (93° C) oven until each batch is cooked.

Vegetable Medley

1 (16 ounce) package frozen broccoli, cauliflower and carrots	.5 kg
1 (16 ounce) package frozen corn	.5 kg
2 (10 ounce) cans fiesta nacho cheese soup	2 (280 g)
½ cup milk	120 ml

- Combine broccoli mixture and corn in 2-quart (2 L) greased baking dish.

- Combine fiesta nacho cheese soup and milk in saucepan and heat just enough to mix well. Pour over vegetables.

- Cover and bake at 350° (176° C) for about 20 minutes.

Creamy Vegetable Casserole

1 (16 ounce) package frozen broccoli, carrots and cauliflower	.5 kg
1 (10 ounce) can cream of mushroom soup	280 g
1 (8 ounce) carton garden-vegetable cream cheese	227 g
1 cup seasoned croutons	240 ml

- Cook vegetables according to package directions, drain and place in large bowl. In saucepan, place soup and cream cheese and heat just enough to mix easily. Pour into vegetable mixture and mix well. Pour into 2-quart (2 L) baking dish.

- Sprinkle with croutons. Bake uncovered at 375° (190° C) for 25 minutes or until bubbly.

Veggies To Love

1 (16 ounce) package frozen broccoli, cauliflower	
and carrots	.5 kg
1 (10 ounce) can cream of celery soup	280 g
⅓ cup milk	80 ml
1 (3 ounce) can french-fried onion rings	84 g

- Cook vegetables according to package directions. Add soup and milk, mix well. Pour into buttered 2-quart (2 L) baking dish and sprinkle french-fried onions over top. Bake at 350° (176° C) for 30 minutes or until bubbly.

Roasted Vegetables

1½ pounds assorted fresh vegetables (squash, carrots,	
red bell peppers, zucchini, cauliflower or broccoli)	.7 kg
1 (11 ounce) can water chestnuts, drained	312 g
2 tablespoons (¼ stick) butter, melted	30 ml
1 (1 ounce) packet savory herb with garlic soup mix	28 g

- Cut all vegetables in 2-inch (5 cm) pieces and place in greased 2-quart (2 L) baking dish with water chestnuts. Combine melted butter and soup mix, drizzle over vegetables and stir well. Cover and bake vegetables at 400° (204° C) for 20 to 25 minutes or until tender and stir once.

Creamy Cabbage Bake

1 head cabbage, shredded	
1 (10 ounce) can cream of celery soup	280 g
⅔ cup milk	160 ml
1 (8 ounce) package shredded cheddar cheese	227 g

- Place cabbage in 2-quart (2 L) buttered baking dish. Pour celery soup diluted with milk over top of cabbage. Bake covered at 325° (162° C) for 30 minutes. Remove from oven, sprinkle with cheese and bake uncovered until cheese melts.

Quick Fix Cabbage Supper

1 pound Polish sausage, cut in ⅓-inch slices   .5 kg/.8 cm
1 bell pepper, seeded, diced
1 red onion, diced
1 medium size cabbage, cut up
1 (15 ounce) can stewed tomatoes with liquid   425 g

- In large skillet, brown sausage slices and remove with slotted spoon; set aside. In same skillet with hot drippings, saute bell pepper and red onion for 3 minutes. Stir in cabbage, cover and cook, stirring occasionally, for 10 minutes.

- Stir in stewed tomatoes and sliced sausage; bring to a boil; reduce heat and cook for about 10 minutes or until thoroughly hot.

Scalloped Cabbage

2 small cabbages, cut up
1 (10 ounce) can cream of celery soup   280 g
1 cup shredded cheddar cheese   240 ml
⅓ cup crumbled saltine crackers   80 ml

- Preheat oven to 350° (176° C). Cut whole cabbages into quarters to easily remove thick white core. Place cut up cabbage in saucepan with 2 cups (480 ml) water and 1 teaspoon (2 ml) salt. Cook 8 minutes and drain. Transfer cabbage to 2-quart (2 L) buttered baking dish.

- In saucepan on medium heat, combine celery soup, ½ cup (120 ml) water and cheddar cheese; whisk, stirring constantly, until mixture is heated and cheese begins to melt. Pour mixture over cabbage and sprinkle with crumbled crackers. Bake uncovered 20 minutes.

Speedy Cabbage

1 head cabbage, shredded	
2 tablespoons (¼ stick) butter	30 ml
3 tablespoons sour cream	45 ml
½ teaspoon sugar	2 ml

- Saute cabbage in butter and about 2 tablespoons (30 ml) water until tender (about 3 to 4 minutes), stirring constantly.

- Stir in sour cream and about ½ teaspoon (2 ml) each of salt and pepper and a little sugar. Serve hot.

Spinach To Like

2 (10 ounce) packages frozen, chopped spinach	2 (280 g)
1 (8 ounce) carton sour cream	227 g
½ (1 ounce) packet dry onion soup mix	28 g
⅔ cup seasoned breadcrumbs	160 ml

- Cook spinach according to package directions and drain well. Add sour cream and onion soup mix to spinach.

- Pour into 2-quart (2 L) baking dish. Sprinkle breadcrumbs on top. Bake at 350° (176° C) for 30 minutes.

Favorite Spinach

2 (10 ounce) packages frozen chopped spinach, thawed, well drained	2 (280 g)
1 (1 ounce) packet dry onion soup mix	28 g
1 (8 ounce) carton sour cream	227 g
⅔ cup shredded Monterey Jack cheese	160 ml

- Combine spinach, onion soup mix and sour cream. Pour into buttered 2-quart (2 L) baking dish. Bake at 350° (176° C) for 20 minutes. Take out of oven, sprinkle cheese over top and place casserole back in oven for 5 minutes.

Super Spinach Bake

¼ cup (½ stick) butter	60 ml
⅔ cup cracker crumbs	160 ml
2 (10 ounce) packages frozen chopped spinach, thawed, drained	2 (280 g)
1 (8 ounce) package shredded cheddar cheese, divided	227 g
1 (8 ounce) carton sour cream	227 g
1 tablespoon dry onion soup mix	15 ml

- Preheat oven to 325° (162° C). Melt butter in skillet over medium heat and add cracker crumbs. Cook, stirring often, for 5 minutes or until crumbs are light brown; set aside.

- In medium bowl, combine spinach, 1 cup (240 ml) cheese, sour cream and soup mix. Spoon into sprayed 7 x 11-inch (18 x 28 cm) baking dish. Top with browned crumbs.

- Bake uncovered for 25 minutes. Remove from oven, sprinkle remaining cheese over top and return to oven for 5 minutes.

Herbed Spinach

2 (16 ounce) packages frozen chopped spinach	2 (.5 kg)
1 (8 ounce) package cream cheese, softened	227 g
¼ cup (½ stick) butter, melted	60 ml
1 (6 ounce) package herbed-seasoned stuffing	168 g

- Cook spinach according to package directions. Drain and add cream cheese and half butter. Season with a little salt and pepper. Pour into buttered baking dish. Spread herb stuffing on top and drizzle with remaining butter. Bake at 350° (176° C) for 25 minutes.

Easy Spinach Bake

2 (8 ounce) packages cream cheese, softened	2 (227 g)
1 (10 ounce) can cream of chicken soup	280 g
2 (16 ounce) packages frozen chopped spinach, thawed, well drained	2 (.5 kg)
1 cup round crushed, buttery crackers	240 ml

• In mixing bowl, beat cream cheese until smooth. Add soup and mix well. Stir in spinach. Spoon into well greased 3-quart (3 L) baking dish. Sprinkle cracker crumbs over top of casserole. Bake uncovered at 325° (162° C) for 35 minutes.

Wilted Spinach with Walnuts

2 (8 ounce) packages baby spinach	2 (227 g)
1 teaspoon minced garlic	5 ml
2 tablespoons olive oil	30 ml
¼ cup whole walnuts, toasted	60 ml

• In large skillet, saute spinach and garlic in hot oil on medium-high heat for 6 minutes or until spinach is wilted. Sprinkle a little seasoned salt over spinach and mix. Toss with whole toasted walnuts. (To toast walnuts, place in a 300°/148° C oven for about 6 minutes.)

Creamy Spinach

1 (16 ounce) package frozen chopped spinach	.5 kg
1 (8 ounce) carton whipping cream	227 g
3 tablespoons butter	45 ml
½ cup grated parmesan cheese	120 ml

• Cook spinach according to package directions. Place whipping cream in heavy saucepan and cook on medium heat until cream is reduced by half. Stir in spinach, stirring well to coat spinach. Add butter and cheese while heat is still on medium and stir until mixture is thoroughly hot. Stir in a little salt and pepper.

Spinach and Ravioli Supreme

1 (6 ounce) package baby spinach	168 g
½ cup extra-virgin olive oil	120 ml
⅔ cup pine nuts	160 ml
2 (10 ounce) packages refrigerated cheese ravioli	2 (280 g)

- In food processor, combine spinach, oil, pine nuts and an ample amount of salt and pepper. Pulse until mixture is well blended. Place mixture in pint jar.

- In boiling water, cook cheese ravioli according to package directions and drain. Stir in ¾ cup (180 ml) spinach mixture and toss gently. Serve hot. Refrigerate remaining spinach mixture for another use; it can be kept for 1 week.

Creamed Spinach Bake

1 (16 ounce) package frozen chopped spinach	.5 kg
2 (3 ounce) packages cream cheese, softened	2 (84 g)
3 tablespoons butter	45 ml
1 cup Italian-style seasoned breadcrumbs	240 ml

- In saucepan, cook spinach with ¾ cup (180 ml) water for 6 minutes, drain thoroughly and pat dry with paper towels. Add cream cheese and butter and heat until they melt and mix well with spinach.

- Pour into greased 2-quart (2 L) baking dish. Sprinkle a little salt over spinach and cover with breadcrumbs.

- Bake uncovered at 350° (176° C) for 15 to 20 minutes.

Eggplant in Marinara Sauce

1 medium size eggplant	
Olive oil	
1 (16 ounce) carton marinara sauce	.5 kg
1 (8 ounce) package shredded mozzarella cheese	227 g

- Cut eggplant into ½-inch (1.2 cm) slices and brush with olive oil. Place slices on greased baking pan and broil 6 to 8 minutes.

- While eggplant is broiling, spoon marinara sauce in 9 x 13-inch (23 x 33 cm) baking dish. Top with half eggplant slices and layer eggplant and cheese twice. Repeat layers and bake at 325° (162°) about 10 minutes or until hot and bubbly.

Cheesy Baked Eggplant

1 eggplant	
½ cup mayonnaise	120 ml
1 cup seasoned breadcrumbs	240 ml
¼ cup grated parmesan cheese	60 ml

- Peel eggplant and slice ½-inch (1.2 cm) thick. Spread both sides with mayonnaise and dip in mixture of crumbs and cheese. Coat both sides well. Place in single layer in shallow baking dish. Bake at 400° (204° C) for 20 minutes.

Baked Eggplant

1 medium eggplant	
¼ cup (½ stick) butter, melted	60 ml
1 (5 ounce) can evaporated milk	143 g
1½ cups cracker crumbs	360 ml

- Peel, slice and boil eggplant until tender enough to mash. Season with a little salt and pepper. Add all other ingredients.

- Pour into 2-quart (2 L) buttered baking dish. Bake at 350° (176° C) for 25 minutes.

Brussels Sprouts and Onions

1 (10 ounce) container brussels sprouts	280 g
1 (10 ounce) bag pearl onions	280 g
3 slices bacon	
1 teaspoon chopped fresh thyme	5 ml

- In large saucepan, bring to a boil 1½ quarts (1.5 L) water and a little salt. Add brussels sprouts and onions and cook 2 minutes, drain. (Some of the onion outer layer may need to be removed).

- Cook bacon until crisp in skillet, drain on paper towels, returning bacon drippings to skillet. Add sprouts, onions, fresh thyme and salt to taste and stir to coat vegetables with drippings. Heat just until ingredients are warm and spoon into serving dish. Top with crumbled bacon.

Creamy Brussels Sprouts

2 pints fresh brussels sprouts	1 kg
1 onion, chopped	
¼ cup (½ stick) butter	60 ml
1 pint carton sour cream	.5 kg

- Take each brussels sprouts and cut a crisscross gash on bottom of each so that the tougher ends cook as quickly as the tops. In saucepan, steam or boil sprouts until tender.

- Saute onion in skillet with butter; add sour cream and heat, stirring constantly. Gently mix in sprouts. Serve immediately.

Baked Squash

5 cups squash, cooked, drained	1.3 L
¾ cup grated Monterey Jack cheese	180 ml
1 (10 ounce) can cream of chicken soup	280 g
1 (16 ounce) box herb dressing mix	.5 kg

- Place cooked squash in mixing bowl and season with salt to taste. Add cheese and soup; blend well. Mix dressing according to package directions. Place half dressing in 9 x 13-inch (23 x 33 cm) greased baking dish. Spoon squash mixture on top and sprinkle remaining dressing on top. Bake uncovered at 375° (190° C) for 30 minutes.

Creamy Squash

6 - 8 medium yellow squash, cut in small pieces	
1 (8 ounce) package cream cheese, cubed, softened	227 g
2 tablespoons (¼ stick) butter	30 ml
½ teaspoon sugar	2 ml

- Place squash in large saucepan. Cover with water and boil for 10 to 15 minutes or until tender. Drain liquid, and add cream cheese, butter, ¾ teaspoon (4 ml) each of salt, pepper and sugar. Cook over low heat and stir until cream cheese melts. Serve hot.

Posh Squash

8 medium yellow squash, sliced	
½ green bell pepper, seeded, chopped	
1 small onion, chopped	
1 (8 ounce) package cubed Mexican processed cheese	227 g

- Combine squash, bell pepper and onion in large saucepan and just barely cover with water. Cook 10 to 15 minutes until tender. Drain and add cheese. Stir until cheese melts and pour into buttered 2-quart (2 L) baking dish. Bake at 350° (176° C) for 15 minutes.

Seasoned Squash and Onion

8 yellow squash, sliced
2 onions, chopped
¼ cup (½ stick) butter   60 ml
1 cup grated American cheese   240 ml

- Cook squash and onion in small amount of water until tender and drain. Add butter and cheese and toss. Serve hot.

Stir-Fry Squash-Onions

¼ cup extra-virgin olive oil   60 ml
4 medium zucchini, sliced
3 medium yellow squash, sliced
1 red and 1 green bell pepper, julienned
2 yellow onions, sliced, cut into rings

- Heat skillet with oil on medium heat and stir-fry zucchini, squash, bell peppers and onions about 30 minutes, tossing several times to allow vegetables to brown lightly. Season with 2 teaspoons (2 ml) salt and pepper and serve immediately.

Sunny Yellow Squash

6 - 8 medium yellow squash, cut up
1 (8 ounce) package cream cheese, softened, cubed   227 g
2 tablespoons (¼ stick) butter   30 ml
1 teaspoon sugar   5 ml

- In saucepan, add squash with a little water and boil until tender. Drain. Add cream cheese, butter, sugar and a little salt and pepper. Cook over low heat and stir until cream cheese melts.

Creamed Yellow Squash

6 medium size yellow squash	
2 tablespoons butter	30 ml
1 (8 ounce) package cream cheese	227 g
½ cup seasoned breadcrumbs, optional	120 ml

- Cut squash into small chunks and place in saucepan. Just barely cover with water and bring to a boil. Reduce heat to medium, stirring several times and cook about 10 to 15 minutes or until some chunks become very soft. Drain. Spoon into serving dish and keep warm. While saucepan is still on medium heat, stir in butter, cream cheese and salt and pepper to taste; stir and heat until butter and cream cheese is creamy. Pour over squash and sprinkle seasoned breadcrumbs over top.

Seasoned Zucchini and Leeks

¼ cup (½ stick) butter	60 ml
2 large leeks, finely chopped	
6 small-medium zucchini, chopped	
1 teaspoon garlic powder	5 ml

- Place butter in skillet and saute leeks about 2 minutes. Stir in zucchini, garlic powder and 1 teaspoon (5 ml) salt. Cover and cook on medium heat for 15 minutes, stirring occasionally.

Fried Zucchini

3 large zucchini, grated	
5 eggs	
⅓ (12 ounce) box round buttery crackers, crushed	⅓ (340 g)
½ cup grated parmesan cheese	120 ml

- Combine zucchini, eggs and cracker crumbs; mix well. Add cheese and a little salt and pepper. Drop by spoonfuls into skillet with a little oil. Fry about 15 minutes; brown each side.

Zucchini and Creamy Penne

4 medium zucchini, sliced
1 (16 ounce) package penne pasta   .5 kg
1 (8 ounce) carton whipping cream   227 g
6 ounces crumbled goat cheese   168 g

- In saucepan, cook zucchini in a little salted water, drain and add
  1 tablespoon (15 ml) olive oil. Cook penne according to package
  directions. Drain and add another tablespoon olive oil.

- While zucchini and pasta are still hot, combine and stir in
  whipping cream and goat cheese; toss. Serve hot.

Walnut Zucchini

6 - 8 zucchini, julienned
½ red bell pepper, julienned
¼ cup (½ stick) butter   60 ml
1 cup chopped walnuts   240 ml

- Saute zucchini and bell pepper in butter until tender. Shake pan
  and toss zucchini to cook evenly. Pour off any excess butter.

- Add chopped walnuts and a little salt and pepper. When walnuts
  blend and heat, serve immediately.

Creamy Zucchini

6 - 8 medium zucchini, sliced
1 teaspoon beau monde seasoning   5 ml
1 (8 ounce) carton sour cream   227 g
¼ cup grated parmesan cheese   60 ml

- Saute zucchini in 2 tablespoons (30 ml) butter. Cook on low for
  5 minutes. Stir in seasoning, sour cream and cheese. Heat but
  do not boil.

Speedy Zucchini and Fettuccine

1 (9 ounce) package refrigerated fettuccine	255 g
⅓ cup extra-virgin olive oil, divided	80 ml
1 tablespoon minced garlic	15 ml
4 small zucchini, grated	
1 tablespoon lemon juice	15 ml
½ cup pine nuts, toasted	120 ml
⅓ cup grated parmesan cheese	80 ml

- Cook fettuccine according to package directions, drain and place in serving bowl. Heat large skillet over high heat and add 2 tablespoons (30 ml) oil, garlic and zucchini. Saute for 1 minute.

- Add zucchini mixture to pasta. Add lemon juice, pine nuts and salt and pepper to taste. Stir in remaining olive oil and toss to combine. To serve, sprinkle parmesan cheese over top of dish.

Zucchini Patties

1½ cups grated zucchini	360 ml
1 egg, beaten	
2 tablespoons flour	30 ml
⅓ cup finely minced onion	80 ml

- Mix all ingredients and add ½ teaspoon (2 ml) salt. Heat skillet with 3 tablespoons (45 ml) oil. Drop zucchini mixture by tablespoons onto skillet at medium to high heat. Turn and brown both sides. Remove and drain on paper towels.

Zucchini and Fettuccine Toss

2 pounds small zucchini, cubed	1 kg
¼ cup (½ stick) butter	60 ml
2 (9 ounce) packages fresh fettuccine	2 (255 g)
⅓ cup grated parmesan cheese	80 ml

• In skillet, saute zucchini in butter about 5 minutes, stirring several times. Cook fettuccine according to package directions; drain well and combine with cooked zucchini. Sprinkle dish with parmesan cheese. Serve hot. If you like to make this a main dish, stir in 2 cups (480 ml) cubed leftover cooked ham.

Swiss Cheesy Peas

3 (15 ounce) cans green peas and onions, drained	3 (425 g)
1 (8 ounce) carton sour cream	227 g
1 (8 ounce) package grated Swiss cheese	227 g
2 cups crushed corn flakes	480 ml

• In large bowl, combine peas, onions, sour cream, Swiss cheese and salt to taste. Spoon into buttered 3-quart (3 L) baking dish. Sprinkle corn flakes over top. Bake uncovered at 350° (176° C) for 35 minutes.

Sesame Peas

1 (10 ounce) package frozen green peas	280 g
2 tablespoons sesame seeds	30 ml
1 teaspoon sugar	5 ml
¼ cup (½ stick) butter	60 ml

• Cook peas according to package directions and drain.

• In saucepan, heat remaining ingredients. Pour over peas. Serve hot.

Parmesan Peas

2 (10 ounce) packages frozen green peas	2 (280 g)
3 tablespoons butter, melted	45 ml
1 tablespoon lemon juice	15 ml
⅓ cup grated parmesan cheese	80 ml

- Microwave peas in 2 tablespoons (30 ml) water for 3 minutes. Rotate bowl and cook another 3 minutes. Stir in butter, lemon juice and parmesan.

Minted Peas

1 teaspoon dried mint leaves	5 ml
Pinch of sugar	
1 (10 ounce) package frozen tiny peas, thawed	280 g

- In saucepan, combine ½ cup (120 ml) water, mint, sugar, salt and pepper to taste and bring to boil. Add peas and cook for 2 minutes. Drain slightly and add lump of butter.

Creamed Peas and Potatoes

2 pounds small new potatoes, quartered	1 kg
1 (10 ounce) can cream of mushroom soup	280 g
⅓ cup milk	80 ml
1 (10 ounce) package frozen peas with pearl onions	280 g

- Cook new potatoes in boiling water for 25 minutes; drain. Add soup, milk, peas and ½ teaspoon (2 ml) pepper, stir occasionally.

Cheesy Peas Please

1 (10 ounce) can cream of mushroom soup	280 g
1 (6 ounce) roll garlic cheese	168 g
2 (15 ounce) cans green peas, drained	2 (425 g)
⅛ teaspoon red pepper	.5 ml

- In saucepan, heat soup and cheese until cheese melts. Add peas and red pepper and heat.

Italian White Beans

1 onion, coarsely chopped	
1 bell pepper, seeded, chopped	
2 teaspoons minced garlic	10 ml
2 tablespoons olive oil	30 ml
2 (15 ounce) cans great northern beans, drained	2 (425 g)
1 teaspoon sugar	5 ml
1 teaspoon white wine vinegar	5 ml
1 roll commercially prepared polenta	
½ cup grated parmesan cheese	120 ml

- In large saucepan, saute onion, bell pepper and garlic in olive oil. Stir in beans, sugar, vinegar and salt and pepper to taste. Cook and stir over medium heat until mixture is hot. Serve over sliced, heated polenta sprinkled with parmesan cheese.

Southwest Bean Bake

1 (15 ounce) can kidney beans, rinsed, drained	425 g
1 (15 ounce) can navy beans, rinsed, drained	425 g
1 (15 ounce) can Mexican stewed tomatoes	425 g
¾ cup salsa	180 ml
¼ cup packed light brown sugar	60 ml

- Heat oven to 400° (204° C). Combine all ingredients and pour into 3 quart (3 L) greased baking dish. Bake for 20 minutes.

Chili-Baked Beans

2 (15 ounce) cans pork and beans	2 (425 g)
1 (15 ounce) can chili with beans	425 g
¼ cup molasses	60 ml
1 teaspoon chili powder	5 ml

- Pour visible liquid from can of pork and beans. In 2-quart (2 L) baking dish, combine pork and beans, chili, molasses and chili powder. Heat until bubbly.

Classic Baked Bean Stand-By

3 (18 ounce) cans baked beans	3 (510 g)
½ cup chili sauce	120 ml
⅓ cup packed brown sugar	80 ml
4 slices bacon, cooked, crumbled	

- In buttered 3-quart (3 L) baking dish, combine baked beans, chili sauce and brown sugar. Bake at 325° (162° C) for 30 minutes. When ready to serve, sprinkle bacon on top.

Lima Beans

1 (16 ounce) package frozen baby lima beans	.5 kg
1 cup chopped celery	240 ml
3 tablespoons butter	45 ml
2 teaspoons lemon juice	10 ml

- Place all ingredients in 2-quart (2 L) saucepan and add ⅓ cup (80 ml) water. Cook until vegetables are tender-crisp.

Barbecued Baby Limas

1 (10 ounce) package frozen baby lima beans	280 g
⅓ cup chili sauce	80 ml
¼ teaspoon chili powder	1 ml
2 tablespoons brown sugar	30 ml

- Cook lima beans according to package directions, drain and add chili sauce, chili powder and brown sugar, mixing gently.

- Simmer ingredients together for about 10 minutes to blend flavors.

Fried Green Tomatoes

1 pound green tomatoes	.5 kg
1 cup flour	240 ml
1 - 2 tablespoons light brown sugar	15 ml
Canola oil	

- Cut ends off tomatoes, slice ⅓-inch (.8 cm) thick and lay on paper towels to drain. Mix flour, brown sugar, ½ teaspoon (2 ml) each of salt and pepper in shallow bowl.

- Dredge tomatoes in flour thoroughly. Heat oil and carefully place each slice in skillet. When 1 side of tomato is crispy and golden turn to brown other side. Drain on paper towels and serve immediately.

Baked Tomatoes with Basil

3 large tomatoes	
1½ cups seasoned breadcrumbs	360 ml
4 tablespoons butter	60 ml
Dried basil	

- Cut tomatoes in half or slice tomatoes in ½ to 1-inch (1.2 cm) thick slices and place on baking sheet. Sprinkle slices generously with breadcrumbs and top with butter and basil. Bake at 350° (176° C) for 10 to 15 minutes or until light brown on top.

Stewed-Tomato Casserole

2 (15 ounce) cans Mexican-style stewed tomatoes	2 (425 g)
2 onions, sliced	
1¼ cups cracker crumbs	300 ml
1 cup shredded cheddar cheese	240 ml

- In 2-quart (2 L) baking dish layer tomatoes, onions, cracker crumbs and cheese and repeat layers. Sprinkle with a little salt and pepper. Bake at 350° (176° C) for 35 minutes.

Stewed Okra and Tomatoes

2 tablespoons oil	30 ml
1 small onion, chopped	
4 - 5 cups okra pods, trimmed	1 L
1 (15 ounce) can stewed tomatoes with liquid	425 g

- In skillet on medium heat, place oil and chopped onion and saute for 5 minutes. Add okra, stewed tomatoes and bring to a boil. Reduce heat, cover and simmer for 15 minutes.

Fried Okra

Small, fresh garden okra
Milk or buttermilk
Cornmeal

- Thoroughly wash and drain okra. Cut off top and ends and slice. Toss okra with a little milk or buttermilk (just enough to make cornmeal stick). Sprinkle cornmeal and a little salt and pepper over okra and toss. Heat 2 or 3 tablespoons (30 ml) oil in skillet. Fry okra, turning several times, until okra is golden brown and crisp.

Black-Eyed Peas and Okra

3 (15 ounce) cans black-eyed peas, drained	3 (425 g)
¾ cup shredded ham	180 ml
1 onion, chopped	
1 pound small fresh whole okra pods	.5 kg

- In large saucepan, combine peas, ham and onion and bring to a boil.

- Place all okra on top of pea-onion mixture and do not stir.

- Bring to boil again, lower heat, cover and simmer about 5 to 10 minutes or until okra is tender. Serve hot.

Southern Hoppin' John

1 pound bulk sausage	.5 kg
1 (16 ounce) package frozen chopped onion and	
bell peppers	.5 kg
1 (14 ounce) can chicken broth	396 g
1¼ cups instant white rice	300 ml
2 (15 ounce) cans black-eyed peas	2 (425 g)

- In large pot, brown and cook sausage, onions and bell peppers over medium-high heat. Drain and add chicken broth, rice and salt and pepper to taste. Bring to a boil, reduce heat and simmer 15 minutes, stirring occasionally.

- Drain and rinse peas and add to pot. Simmer an additional 10 minutes or until liquid is absorbed.

Hoppin' John

4 slices bacon	
1 onion, chopped	
1 cup uncooked instant rice	240 ml
1 (15 ounce) can black-eyed peas with liquid	425 g

- Fry bacon and drain. Saute onion in bacon grease.

- In large saucepan, combine onion, bacon grease, a little salt, rice and 1½ cups (360 ml) water. Bring to boil. Cover, lower heat and simmer for 10 minutes. Add bacon and black-eyed peas and simmer 5 more minutes. Remove from heat and allow to stand for 5 more minutes until juice absorbs.

Caramelized Onions

2 tablespoons butter   30 ml
2 tablespoons bacon drippings   30 ml
3 yellow onions, sliced

- Melt butter with bacon drippings in large skillet over medium-high heat. Add onions with a little salt and ¼ teaspoon (1 ml) black pepper and saute about 20 minutes or until light golden brown.

Cheesy Baked Onions

4 yellow onions, peeled, sliced
½ cup (1 stick) butter   120 ml
25 round, buttery crackers, crushed
⅓ cup grated parmesan cheese   80 ml

- Saute onions in butter until transparent. Spread half onions in buttered 2-quart (2 L) buttered casserole dish. Top with half crackers and half cheese. Repeat layers.

- Bake uncovered at 325° (162° C) for 30 minutes.

Cheesy Onion Casserole

5 sweet onions, sliced
½ cup (1 stick) butter   120 ml
1 cup shredded cheddar cheese   240 ml
22 saltine crackers, crushed

- Saute onions in butter until soft. In buttered 2-quart (2 L) baking dish layer half onions, half cheese, half crackers and repeat layers. Bake at 325° (162° C) for 30 minutes.

Onion Tart

Frozen 8-inch piecrust (from 15 ounce package of 2)　20 cm/425 g
2 medium-size onions, sliced
¼ cup (½ stick) butter　　　　　　　　　　　60 ml
5 eggs, well beaten

- Preheat oven to 375° (190° C). Line pie pan with crust and chill while making filling.

- In skillet, saute onion in butter; cook only until onions are transparent but still firm. Sprinkle with an ample amount of salt and pepper and spoon onions into piecrust. Pour beaten eggs over onions. Cook 5 minutes and then reduce heat to 250° (121° C) and bake another 25 minutes or until custard is set and light brown on top.

Creamed Onions and Peas

1 (10 ounce) can cream of celery soup	280 g
½ cup milk	120 ml
3 (15 ounce) jars tiny white onions, drained	3 (425 g)
1 (10 ounce) package frozen peas	280 g
½ cup slivered almonds	120 ml
3 tablespoons grated parmesan cheese	45 ml

- Preheat oven to 350° (176° C). In large saucepan, combine soup and milk, heat and stir until bubbly. Gently stir in onions, peas and almonds, mixing well. Spoon into greased 2-quart (2 L) baking dish. Sprinkle with parmesan cheese.

- Cover and bake for 30 minutes.

Onion Rings

1 yellow onion, sliced	
2⅓ cups biscuit mix, divided	560 ml
1 cup beer	240 ml
2 eggs, slightly beaten	

- Separate onion rings and toss with the ⅓ cup (80 ml) biscuit mix. Stir remaining biscuit mix, beer, eggs and a little salt.

- Heat oil to 375° (190° C) in deep fryer or large saucepan. Dip onion rings, a few at a time into batter, letting excess drip into bowl. Fry about 2 minutes and turning with fork, fry until golden brown and drain on paper towels.

Celery with Water Chestnuts

1 bunch celery, chopped diagonally	
1 (8 ounce) can water chestnuts, drained, chopped	227 g
¼ cup almonds, toasted	60 ml
¼ cup (½ stick) butter, melted	60 ml

- Boil celery in salted water just until tender-crisp and drain. Saute water chestnuts and almonds in melted butter. Toss celery with water chestnut-almond mixture. Serve hot.

Herb-Seasoned Vegetables

1 (14 ounce) can seasoned chicken broth with Italian herbs	396 g
½ teaspoon garlic powder	2 ml
1 (16 ounce) package frozen vegetables	.5 kg
½ cup grated parmesan cheese	120 ml

- Heat broth, garlic and vegetables to boil. Cover and cook over low heat for 5 minutes or until tender-crisp and drain. Place in serving dish and sprinkle cheese over vegetables.

Cheesy Macaroni Stuffed Peppers

4 large green bell peppers
1 (22 ounce) carton refrigerated macaroni
   and cheese   624 g
1 cup shredded cheddar cheese   240 ml

- Preheat oven to 350° (176° C). Cut peppers in half lengthwise and remove seeds and veins. Steam, covered in simmering water for 8 minutes; drain well. Heat macaroni and cheese in microwave as instructed on package and generously fill each pepper half with macaroni and cheese and place in greased baking dish. Bake about 10 minutes or just until macaroni and cheese is bubbly. Remove from oven and sprinkle 1 tablespoon (15 ml) cheddar cheese over each pepper and return to oven for 5 minutes and sprinkle a little paprika over top of each pepper.

Hot Mustard Sauce for Vegetables

1 (10 ounce) can cream of celery soup   280 g
½ cup milk   120 ml
2 tablespoons prepared mustard   30 ml
Pinch of sugar

- In saucepan, combine soup, milk, mustard and pinch of salt and sugar. Heat until well blended. Serve over cooked vegetables.

Black Bean Salsa

1 (15 ounce) can black beans with jalapeno, rinsed,
   drained   425 g
1 (8 ounce) can whole kernel corn, drained   227 g
⅓ cup chopped red onion   80 ml
⅓ cup lime juice   80 ml
1 teaspoon minced garlic and fajita seasoning   5 ml

- Place half of beans in shallow bowl and mash slightly. Combine mashed beans, whole beans and all remaining ingredients and chill 30 minutes before serving.

Rush-Hour
Main Dishes

Chicken
Beef
Pork
Seafood

Adobe Chicken

2 cups cooked brown rice	480 ml
1 (10 ounce) can chopped tomatoes and green chilies, drained	280 g
3 cups chopped cooked chicken	710 ml
1 (8 ounce) package shredded Monterey Jack cheese, divided	227 g

- Combine rice, tomatoes and green chilies, chicken and half cheese.

- Spoon into buttered, 7 x 11-inch (18 x 28 cm) baking dish. Cook covered at 325° (162° C) for 30 minutes.

- Uncover, sprinkle remaining cheese over casserole and return to oven for 5 minutes.

Alfredo Chicken

5 - 6 boneless, skinless chicken breast halves	
1 (16 ounce) package frozen broccoli florets, thawed	.5 kg
1 red bell pepper, seeded, chopped	
1 (16 ounce) jar alfredo sauce	5 kg

- Preheat oven to 325° (162° C). Brown and cook chicken breasts in large skillet with a little oil until juices run clear. Transfer to greased 9 x 13-inch (23 x 33 cm) baking dish.

- Microwave broccoli according to package directions and drain. (If broccoli stems are extra long, trim and discard.) Spoon broccoli and bell pepper over chicken.

- In small saucepan, heat alfredo sauce with ¼ cup (60 ml) water. Pour over chicken and vegetables. Cover and cook 15 to 20 minutes.

Almond Crusted Chicken

1 egg	
¼ cup seasoned breadcrumbs	60 ml
1 cup sliced almond	240 ml
4 boneless, skinless chicken breast halves	
1 (5 ounce) package grated parmesan cheese	143 g

Sauce:

1 teaspoon minced garlic	5 ml
⅓ cup finely chopped onion	80 ml
2 tablespoons oil	30 ml
1 cup white wine	240 ml
¼ cup teriyaki sauce	60 ml

• Preheat oven to 350° (176° C). Place egg and 1 teaspoon
  (5 ml) water in shallow bowl and beat. In another shallow bowl,
  combine breadcrumbs and almonds. Dip each chicken breast
  in egg, then in almond mixture and place in greased 9 x 13-inch
  (23 x 33 cm) baking pan. Bake uncovered for 20 minutes.
  Remove chicken from oven and sprinkle parmesan cheese over
  each breast and cook another 15 minutes or until almonds and
  cheese are golden brown.

• While chicken is cooking, saute garlic and onion in oil in small
  saucepan. Add wine and teriyaki; bring to a boil, reduce heat
  and simmer about 10 minutes or until mixture is reduced by half.
  When serving, divide sauce among four plates and place chicken
  breast on top.

Wild Rice and Chicken

1 (6 ounce) package long grain-wild rice mix	168 g
4 boneless, skinless chicken breast halves	
½ cup (1 stick) butter, divided	120 ml
1 large red bell pepper, chopped	

• Prepare rice according to package directions. In large skillet, cook
  chicken in 2 tablespoons (30 ml) butter and make sure each chicken
  breast browns on both sides. Remove chicken and keep warm.
  Add remaining butter to pan drippings and saute red pepper until
  tender. Add to rice. Serve with cooked chicken breasts.

Wine and Chicken

6 - 8 boneless, skinless chicken breast halves	
1 (10 ounce) can cream of mushroom soup	280 g
1 (10 ounce) can cream of onion soup	280 g
1 cup white wine	240 ml

• In skillet, brown chicken in little bit of oil. Place in 9 x 13-inch
  (23 x 33 cm) baking dish. Combine soups and wine and pour over
  chicken. Bake covered at 375° (190° C) for 25 minutes. Uncover
  and bake another 20 minutes.

Chicken and Orzo Supper

1 (5.6 once) box chicken-flavored orzo	155 g
1 (7 ounce) package cooked chicken strips	198 g
1 (10 ounce) package frozen corn	280 g
1 (10 ounce) package frozen cut green beans	280 g
¼ cup extra-virgin olive oil	60 ml
1 teaspoon minced garlic	240 ml

• Cook orzo according to package directions. Add remaining
  ingredients, ¼ cup (60 ml) water and a little salt and pepper,
  mixing well. Cook on low heat, stirring several times, until
  mixture is hot (about 10 to 15 minutes).

Alfredo Chicken Spaghetti

1 (8 ounce) package thin spaghetti, broken in thirds	227 g
2 teaspoons minced garlic	10 ml
1 (16 ounce) jar alfredo sauce	.5 kg
About ¼ cup milk	60 ml
1 (10 ounce) box broccoli florets, thawed	280 g
2 cups cooked, diced chicken	480 ml

- Cook spaghetti according to package directions and drain. Place back in saucepan and stir in garlic, alfredo sauce and milk, mixing well. Add drained broccoli florets and cook on medium heat (about 5 minutes), stirring several times or until broccoli is tender, adding more milk if mixture gets too dry.

- Stir in diced chicken and spoon into serving bowl.

Asparagus-Cheese Chicken

1 tablespoon butter	15 ml
4 boneless, skinless chicken breast halves	
1 (10 ounce) can broccoli-cheese soup	280 g
1 (10 ounce) package frozen asparagus cuts	280 g
⅓ cup milk	80 ml

- Heat butter in skillet and cook chicken 10 minutes or until brown on both sides. Remove chicken and set aside.

- In same skillet, combine soup, asparagus and milk. Heat to boil, return chicken to skillet and reduce heat to low.

- Cover and cook another 25 minutes until chicken is no longer pink and asparagus is tender.

Bacon-Wrapped Chicken

6 boneless, skinless chicken breast halves
1 (8 ounce) carton cream cheese with onion
   and chives   227 g
Butter
6 bacon strips

- Flatten chicken to ½-inch (1.2 cm) thickness. Spread
  3 tablespoons (45 ml) cream cheese over each. Dot with butter
  and a little salt; roll. Wrap each with bacon strip. Place seam-
  side down in greased 9 x 13-inch (23 x 33 cm) baking dish.

- Bake uncovered at 375° (190° C) for 35 to 40 minutes or until
  juices run clear. To brown, broil 6 inches (15 cm) from heat for
  about 3 minutes or until bacon is crisp.

Cheesy Crusted Chicken

¾ cup mayonnaise (not light)   180 ml
½ cup grated parmesan cheese   120 ml
5 - 6 boneless, skinless chicken breast halves
1 cup Italian seasoned dry breadcrumbs   240 ml

- Preheat oven to 400° (204° C). Combine mayonnaise and
  cheese. Place chicken breasts on sheet of wax paper and spread
  mayonnaise-cheese mixture over chicken. Sprinkle heavily with
  dry breadcrumbs and turn breasts over and sprinkle heavily with
  breadcrumbs.

- Place chicken on large greased baking pan making sure pieces
  do not touch. Bake 20 minutes (25 minutes if chicken pieces are
  fairly large). Chicken pieces can be sliced and placed on serving
  platter.

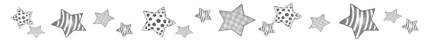

Glazed Chicken

4 skinless, boneless chicken breast halves
½ cup refrigerated dijon-style honey-mustard   120 ml
1 green and 1 red bell pepper, thinly sliced
1 (20 ounce) can pineapple chunks with juice   567 g

- Cut chicken breasts into strips, add a little salt and pepper and brown in large skillet with a little oil. Add juice from pineapple, cover and simmer for 15 minutes.

- Add honey-mustard, pepper slices and pineapple chunks to chicken. Bring to a boil, reduce heat, cover and simmer for another 15 minutes. Serve over hot, cooked couscous.

Chicken and Shrimp Curry

2 (10 ounce) cans cream of chicken soup   2 (280 g)
⅓ cup milk   80 ml
1½ teaspoons curry powder   7 ml
1 (12 ounce) can boned chicken   340 g
1 (6 ounce) can shrimp, drained, veined   168 g
Hot, cooked rice

- In saucepan, heat soup, milk and curry powder; stir in chicken pieces and shrimp. Serve over rice.

Chicken for Lunch

4 thick cooked deli chicken breast slices
1 (3 ounce) package cream cheese, softened   84 g
3 tablespoons salsa   45 ml
2 tablespoons mayonnaise   30 ml

- Place chicken slices on a bed of shredded lettuce on individual salad plates. Use mixer, blend cream cheese, salsa and mayonnaise. Place heaping tablespoon (15 ml) on top of chicken slices. Serve cold.

Baked Chicken and Mushrooms

2 (10 ounce) cans cream of mushrooms soup	2 (280 g)
1 soup can milk	
2 teaspoons curry powder	10 ml
1 (4 ounce) can sliced mushrooms	114 g
2½ cups cooked rice (use instant)	600 ml
1 (8 ounce) can green peas, drained	227 g
3 cups cooked, cubed chicken	710 ml
2 cups slightly crushed potato chips	480 ml

- Preheat oven to 350° (176° C). In large bowl, combine soup, milk, curry powder, mushrooms, rice, peas, chicken and salt and pepper to taste; mix well. Spoon into greased 9 x 13-inch (23 x 33 cm) baking pan. Cover and bake 20 minutes. Remove from oven and sprinkle with crushed potato chips and return to oven for another 15 minutes.

Cheesy Swiss Chicken

4 boneless, skinless chicken breast halves	
⅓ cup refrigerated honey-mustard dressing	80 ml
1 (8 slices) package fully cooked bacon	
4 slices Swiss cheese	

- In large skillet with a little oil, cook chicken breasts on medium-high heat for 5 minutes. Remove chicken to cutting board and liberally spread each breast with honey-mustard dressing.

- Top with 2 slices bacon for each breast and cover with 1 slice of Swiss cheese. Carefully lift each chicken breast back into skillet and place 1 tablespoon (15 ml) water in skillet. Cover and cook on low-medium heat for 10 minutes.

Zesty Orange Chicken

½ cup white wine	120 ml
½ cup orange juice concentrate	120 ml
½ cup orange marmalade	120 ml
½ teaspoon each ground ginger and cinnamon	2 ml
1 large fryer chicken, quartered	
2 (11 ounce) cans mandarin oranges, drained	2 (312 g)
½ cup green grapes, halved	120 ml
1½ cups instant brown rice, cooked	360 ml

- Preheat oven to 350° (176° C). Combine wine, orange juice concentrate, marmalade, ginger and cinnamon in greased 9 x 13-inch (23 x 33 cm) baking dish. Add chicken quarters, turning to coat chicken. Bake uncovered, basting occasionally, for 35 minutes. Add oranges and grapes to dish during last 5 minutes of cooking. Serve over brown rice.

Curried Chicken Casserole

1 (10 ounce) box chicken flavor rice and macaroni	280 g
2 (5 ounce) cans chunk white chicken with liquid	2 (143 g)
1 teaspoon curry powder	5 ml
⅓ cup raisins, optional	80 ml

- In skillet, prepare the rice and macaroni according to package directions. Once rice cooks, add curry powder and chicken plus liquid and raisins and mix well. Cover and remove from heat. Let stand for 10 minutes and serve.

Creamy Tarragon Chicken

1½ cups flour, divided	360 ml
6 boneless, skinless chicken breast halves	
2 tablespoons oil	30 ml
1 (10 ounce) can chicken broth	280 g
1 cup milk	240 ml
2 teaspoons dried tarragon	10 ml
1 (4 ounce) can sliced mushrooms, drained	114 g
2 (8 ounce) packages (microwavable) roasted chicken	
rice	2 (227 g)

- Mix flour and a little salt and pepper on wax paper and coat chicken, saving extra flour. Heat oil in large skillet over medium-high heat and cook chicken breasts, turning once, about 10 minutes or until light brown. Transfer to plate.

- In the same skillet, stir in 2 tablespoon (30 ml) flour-salt mixture. Whisk in chicken broth, milk and tarragon, heat, stirring constantly, until bubbly. Add mushrooms and return chicken to skillet. Cover and simmer for 10 to 15 minutes or until sauce has thickened.

- Microwave rice according to package directions and place on serving platter. Spoon chicken and sauce over rice.

Chicken Curry

2 (10 ounce) cans cream of mushroom soup	2 (280 g)
2 teaspoons curry powder	10 ml
⅓ cup chopped almonds	80 ml
4 boneless, skinless chicken breast halves,	
cooked, cubed	
Hot, cooked white rice	

- In large saucepan combine soup, 1 soup can water, curry powder, almonds and cubed chicken. Cook on medium heat, stirring often for 15 to 20 minutes. Serve over rice.

Cashew Chicken and Veggies

1 pound boneless, skinless chicken breasts	.5 kg
2 tablespoons cornstarch	30 ml
1 tablespoon soy sauce	15 ml
1 teaspoon grated fresh ginger	5 ml
1(16 ounce) package frozen broccoli florets, thawed	.5 kg
1 (10 ounce) package frozen green peas, thawed	280 g
1 (1.2 ounce) packet savory herb with garlic soup mix	28 g
⅔ cup whole cashews	160 ml
1 (6 ounce) package chicken and herb-flavored rice, cooked	168 g

- Cut chicken crosswise into ¼-inch (.6 cm) wide strips. In medium bowl, combine cornstarch, soy sauce and ginger, mixing well. Add chicken strips, stirring to coat well. Set aside. In large skillet with a little oil, stir-fry broccoli and peas for 3 minutes, remove vegetables to warm plate.

- In same skillet with a little oil, stir-fry chicken until all pieces change color. Stir in ½ cup (120 ml) water and soup mix. Cook on medium heat about 5 minutes until chicken is well coated with soup mix. Return cooked vegetables and add cashews to skillet and cook until thoroughly hot. Serve chicken and vegetables over hot flavored rice.

Chicken-Broccoli Skillet

3 cups cubed, cooked chicken	710 ml
1 (16 ounce) package frozen broccoli florets	.5 kg
1 (8 ounce) package cubed processed cheese	227 g
⅔ cup mayonnaise	160 ml
Hot, cooked rice	

- In skillet, combine chicken, broccoli, cheese and ¼ cup (60 ml) water. Cover and cook over medium heat until broccoli is tender-crisp and cheese melts. Stir in mayonnaise and heat through, but do not boil. Serve over rice.

Chicken Ala Orange

1 (11 ounce) can mandarin oranges, drained	312 g
1 (6 ounce) can frozen orange juice concentrate	168 g
1 tablespoon lemon juice and cornstarch	15 ml
4 boneless, skinless chicken breast halves	
1 tablespoon Mrs. Dash® garlic and herb seasoning	15 ml
2 tablespoons butter	30 ml

- In saucepan, combine oranges, orange juice concentrate, lemon juice, ⅔ cup (160 ml) water and cornstarch. Cook on medium heat, stirring constantly until mixture thickens. Set aside.

- Sprinkle chicken breasts with Mrs. Dash® seasoning and place in skillet with butter. Cook about 7 minutes on each side until brown. Lower heat and spoon orange juice mixture over chicken, cover and simmer about 20 minutes, adding a little water if sauce gets too thick.

Chicken Quesadillas

3 boneless, skinless chicken breast halves, cubed	
1 (10 ounce) can cheddar cheese soup	280 g
⅔ cup chunky salsa	160 ml
10 flour tortillas	

- Cook chicken in skillet, stirring often until juices evaporate. Add soup and salsa; heat thoroughly. Spread about ⅓ cup (80 ml) soup mixture on half tortilla within ½-inch (1.2 cm) of edge. Moisten edge with water, fold over and seal. Place tortillas on 2 baking sheets. Bake at 400° (204° C) for 5 to 6 minutes.

Chicken and Brown Rice Supper

3 cups instant brown rice	710 ml
¼ cup (½ stick) butter	60 ml
3 cups cooked, cubed chicken breasts	710 ml
½ cup golden raisins	120 ml
½ cup chopped red bell pepper	120 ml

Dressing:

2 tablespoons lemon juice	30 ml
1 tablespoon dijon-style mustard	15 ml
3 tablespoons honey	45 ml
¼ cup toasted, slivered almonds	60 ml

- Preheat oven to 350° (176° C). Cook brown rice according to package directions, adding butter and salt and pepper to taste. While rice is still hot, stir in cubed chicken, raisins and chopped bell pepper. Transfer to greased 7 x 11-inch (18 x 28 cm) baking dish. In jar with lid, combine all dressing ingredients and shake until well blended. Drizzle over rice-chicken mixture and sprinkle with almonds. Bake uncovered for 15 minutes.

Chile Pepper Chicken

5 boneless, skinless chicken breast halves	
1 (1 ounce) package hot and spicy recipe Shake'N Bake® coating mixture	28 g
1 (4 ounce) can chopped green chilies	114 g
Chunky salsa	

- Dredge chicken in coating mixture and place in greased 9 x 13-inch (23 x 33 cm) baking dish. Bake at 375° (190° C) for 25 minutes. Remove from oven, spread green chilies over chicken breasts and bake for 5 minutes. Serve with salsa over each chicken breast.

Chicken and Green Chile Casserole

1 green bell pepper, seeded, chopped	
3 ribs celery, chopped	
¾ cup chopped green onions	180 ml
½ cup (1 stick) butter	120 ml
1 (7 ounce) can chopped green chilies	198 g
1½ cups uncooked instant rice	360 ml
1 (8 ounce) carton sour cream	227 g
3 cooked chicken breasts, sliced	
1 (14 ounce) can chicken broth	396 g

- Preheat oven to 325° (162° C). Combine bell pepper, celery and green onions in skillet with butter and saute 5 minutes. Transfer to mixing bowl. Stir in green chilies, rice, sour cream, chicken, chicken broth, ¼ cup (60 ml) water and salt and pepper to taste. Pour into greased 9 x 13-inch (23 x 33 cm) baking dish. Cover and bake 20 minutes; uncover and cook another 10 minutes.

Parmesan Chicken

1 (1 ounce) package dry Italian salad dressing mix	28 g
½ cup grated parmesan cheese	120 ml
¼ cup flour	60 ml
¾ teaspoon garlic powder	4 ml
5 boneless, skinless chicken breast halves	

- Preheat oven to 375° (190° C). In shallow bowl, combine salad dressing mix, cheese, flour and garlic. Moisten chicken with a little water and coat with cheese mixture. Place in sprayed 9 x 13-inch (23 x 33 cm) baking pan. Bake for 25 minutes or until chicken is light brown and cooked thoroughly.

Chicken Cacciatore

1 (2½ pound) frying chicken	1.2 kg
2 onions, sliced	
Hot cooked noodles or spaghetti	
1 (15 ounce) can stewed tomatoes	425 g
1 (8 ounce) can tomato sauce	227 g
1 teaspoon dried oregano	5 ml
1 teaspoon celery seed	5 ml

• Quarter chicken and sprinkle with plenty of salt and black pepper. Place in large skillet on medium-high heat, with a little oil. Add sliced onions and cook until chicken is tender, about 15 minutes.

• Add stewed tomatoes, tomato sauce, oregano and celery seed. Bring mixture to a boil; reduce heat and simmer uncovered for about 20 minutes.

• Serve chicken over hot cooked noodles or spaghetti.

Chicken-Mushroom Bake

1 (4 ounce) can sliced mushrooms	114 g
1 (10 ounce) can cream of chicken soup	280 g
1 (8 ounce) carton sour cream	227 g
½ cup cooking sherry	120 ml
1 (1 ounce) packet dry onion soup mix	28 g
2 cups cooked, cubed chicken	480 ml
Hot, cooked rice	

• Preheat oven to 350° (176° C). In large bowl, combine mushrooms, soup, sour cream, sherry, onion soup mix and chicken. Spoon into greased 3-quart (3 L) baking dish and bake 30 minutes. Serve over hot, cooked rice.

Chicken Parmesan and Spaghetti

1 (14 ounce) package frozen, cooked, breaded chicken cutlets, thawed	396 g
1 (28 ounce) jar spaghetti sauce	794 g
2 (5 ounce) packages grated parmesan cheese, divided	2 (143 g)
1 (8 ounce) package thin spaghetti, cooked	227 g

- Preheat oven to 400° (204° C). Place cutlets in buttered 9 x 13-inch (23 x 33 cm) baking dish and top each with about ¼ cup (60 ml) spaghetti sauce and 1 heaping tablespoon (15 ml) parmesan. Bake 15 minutes.

- Place cooked spaghetti on serving platter and top with cutlets. Sprinkle remaining cheese over cutlets. Heat remaining spaghetti sauce and serve with chicken and spaghetti.

Chicken Couscous

1 (5.6 ounce) package toasted pine nut couscous, cooked	155 g
1 rotisserie chicken, skinned, boned, cubed	
1 (15 ounce) can baby green peas, drained	425 g
⅓ cup golden raisins	80 ml
1 (2.8 ounce) can french-fried onion rings	84 g

- Combine couscous, chicken, peas and raisins in microwaveable dish. Heat on medium about 2 minutes, stirring once, until mixture is warmed. Spoon into greased 7 x 11-inch (18 x 28 cm) baking dish. Place under broiler and broil about 3 minutes or just until onions are slightly brown.

Chicken Squares

2 (12 ounce) cans chicken breast chunks with liquid	2 (340 g)
1 (8 ounce) carton cream cheese, softened	227 g
¼ cup finely chopped onion	60 ml
2 tablespoons sesame seeds	30 ml
1 (8 count) package refrigerated crescent rolls	

- Preheat oven to 350° (176° C). Drain chicken and pour liquid in mixing bowl. Combine chicken liquid with cream cheese and beat until creamy. Add chicken, onion, sesame seeds and salt and pepper to taste.

- Open package of crescent rolls, but do not divide into triangles. Keep 2 triangles together to form 4 squares. Pinch seam in middle of each square together and pat into larger square.

- Spoon about ½ cup (120 ml) chicken mixture into center of each square. Fold corners up into center and lay like flower petals so roll seals. Repeat for all squares. Place each roll on sprayed baking sheet and bake about 15 minutes or until golden brown.

Glazed Chicken Over Rice

4 boneless, skinless chicken breast halves, cubed	
1 (20 ounce) can pineapple chunks with juice	567 g
½ cup honey-mustard grill-and-glaze sauce	120 ml
1 red bell pepper, seeded, chopped	
2 cups instant white rice, cooked	480 ml

- Place a little oil in skillet and brown chicken. Reduce heat to medium and cook 15 minutes. Add pineapple, honey-mustard sauce and bell pepper and bring to a boil.

- Reduce heat to low and simmer 15 minutes or until sauce thickens slightly. Serve over rice.

Chicken-Broccoli Casserole

2 (3 ounce) packages ramen chicken-flavor noodles	2 (84 g)
1 (10 ounce) can cream of chicken soup	280 g
⅔ cup milk	160 ml
1 cup shredded mozzarella cheese	240 ml
2 cups cooked, cubed chicken breasts	480 ml
1 (10 ounce) package frozen broccoli florets, thawed	280 g
¼ cup roasted sunflower kernels	60 ml

- In large saucepan, prepare noodles according to package directions, adding seasoning packets. Drain off most of liquid.

- Stir in soup, milk and cheese and mix well. Add chicken and broccoli and heat thoroughly, while stirring occasionally. Transfer to serving dish and sprinkle sunflower kernels over top of casserole. Serve immediately.

Chicken and Noodles

1 (3 ounce) package chicken-flavored ramen noodles	84 g
1 (16 ounce) package frozen broccoli, cauliflower and carrots	.5 kg
⅔ cup sweet-and sour-sauce	160 ml
3 boneless, skinless chicken breast halves, cooked, cut into thin strips	

- Reserve seasoning packet from noodles. In saucepan, cook noodles and vegetables in 2 cups (480 ml) boiling water for 3 minutes, stirring occasionally and drain.

- Combine noodle-vegetable mixture with seasoning packet, sweet-and-sour sauce and a little salt and pepper. (You may want to add 1 tablespoon/15 ml soy sauce.) Add chicken and heat thoroughly.

Honey-Glazed Chicken

4 skinless, boneless chicken breast halves	
1 (20 ounce) can pineapple chunks with juice	567 g
½ cup refrigerated dijon-style honey-mustard	120 ml
1 green and 1 red bell pepper, thinly sliced	
Hot, cooked couscous	

- Cut chicken breasts into strips, add a little salt and pepper and brown in large skillet with a little oil. Add juice from pineapple, cover and simmer for 15 minutes.

- Add honey-mustard, pepper slices and pineapple chunks to chicken. Bring to a boil, reduce heat, cover and simmer for 15 minutes. Serve over hot, cooked couscous.

Chicken and Sausage Casserole

1 pound pork sausage	.5 kg
1 pound carton fresh mushrooms, sliced	.5 kg
2 sweet red bell peppers, seeded, chopped	
3 cups cooked, cubed chicken	710 ml
1 (6 ounce) box long-grain and wild rice mix, cooked	168 g
1 (10 ounce) can cream of chicken soup	280 g
1 (10 ounce) can chicken broth	280 g
2 cups buttery cracker crumbs	480 ml

- Preheat oven to 350° (176° C). In large skillet, brown and cook sausage, drain. Add mushrooms and bell peppers and saute 5 minutes. Stir in chicken and mix well.

- In large saucepan, combine chicken soup, chicken broth and cooked rice. Stir in sausage-chicken mixture and gently mix to blend well. Spoon into greased 9 x 13-inch (23 x 33 cm) baking dish. Sprinkle buttery crumbs over top and bake 30 minutes.

Chicken and Sauerkraut

6 large, boneless, skinless chicken breast halves
1 (16 ounce) can sliced potatoes, drained .5 kg
1 (16 ounce) can sauerkraut, drained .5 kg
¼ cup pine nuts or ½ teaspoon caraway seeds 60 ml/2 ml

- In prepared large skillet, season chicken with pepper to taste and cook over medium heat until chicken browns on both sides, about 15 minutes.

- Add potatoes to skillet. Spoon sauerkraut over potatoes, cover and cook over low heat about 35 minutes until chicken is done. Toast pine nuts in dry skillet on medium heat, stirring constantly, until golden brown. Sprinkle chicken and sauerkraut with toasted pine nuts or caraway seeds and serve.

Honey-Roasted Chicken

3 tablespoons soy sauce 45 ml
3 tablespoons honey 45 ml
2½ cups crushed wheat cereal 600 ml
½ cup very finely minced walnuts 120 ml
5 - 6 boneless, skinless chicken breast halves

- Preheat oven to 400° (104° C). In shallow bowl, combine soy sauce and honey and set aside. In another shallow bowl, combine crushed cereal and walnuts.

- Dip both sides of each chicken breast in soy sauce-honey mixture and dredge in cereal-walnut mixture. Place each piece on sprayed foil-lined baking sheet. Bake for 25 minutes (about 35 minutes if breasts are very large).

Chicken Taco Pie

1½ pounds boneless, skinless chicken breast halves	.7 kg
1 (1.5 ounce) packet taco seasoning mix	45 g
1 green and 1 red bell pepper, finely chopped	
1½ cups shredded Mexican 3-cheese blend	360 ml
1 (8 ounce) package corn muffin mix	227 g
1 egg	
⅓ cup milk	80 ml

- Preheat oven to 400° (204° C). Cut chicken into 1-inch (2.5 cm) chunks and cook on medium-high heat in large skillet with a little oil. Cook about 10 minutes, drain.

- Stir in taco seasoning, bell peppers and ¾ cup (180 ml) water. Reduce heat and simmer, stirring several times for another 10 minutes. Spoon into buttered 9-inch (23 cm) deep-dish pie pan and sprinkle with cheese.

- Prepare corn muffin mix with egg and milk, mixing well. Spoon over top of pie and bake for 20 minutes or until top is golden brown. Let set about 5 minutes before serving.

Honey-Mustard Chicken

⅓ cup dijon-style mustard	80 ml
½ cup honey	120 ml
2 tablespoons dried dill	30 ml
1 (2½ pound) chicken, quartered	1.2 kg

- Combine mustard, honey and dill. Arrange chicken quarters in 9 x 13-inch (23 x 33 cm) baking dish. Pour mustard mixture over chicken. Turn chicken over and make sure mustard mixture covers chicken.

- Bake covered at 375° (190° C) for 30 minutes. Uncover and bake another 10 minutes.

Chicken Stir-Fry

1 pound chicken tenders, cut in half lengthwise	.5 kg
2 tablespoons cornstarch	30 ml
1 (16 ounce) package frozen broccoli, cauliflower and carrot medley, thawed	.5 kg
1 (10 ounce) package sugar snap peas	280 g
1 (15 ounce) can pineapple chunks, reserve liquid	425 g
⅔ cup prepared stir-fry sauce	160 ml

• Place chicken tenders, cornstarch and salt and pepper to taste, in large ziplock bag; seal and shake to coat chicken. In large skillet with a little oil on medium-high heat, stir-fry chicken about 10 minutes or until thoroughly cooked. Transfer to plate.

• In same skillet with a little oil, add vegetables and stir-fry about 3 minutes. Add pineapple and cook until vegetables are tender-crisp. Add stir-fry sauce and pineapple liquid and simmer about 10 minutes. Add chicken to vegetable mixture and toss to mix.

Honey-Mustard Grilled Chicken

½ teaspoon lemon pepper	2 ml
¾ cup mayonnaise	180 ml
2 tablespoons country dijon-style mustard	30 ml
¼ cup honey	60 ml
4 - 5 boneless, skinless chicken breast halves	

• In bowl, combine lemon pepper, mayonnaise, mustard and honey, mixing well. Brush about half mayonnaise mixture over each piece of chicken and sprinkle with lemon pepper and grill over hot coals until done. Serve with remaining mayonnaise-mustard mixture.

Grilled Chicken with Broccoli Slaw

1 (3 pound) chicken, quartered	1.3 kg
3 tablespoons olive oil	45 ml
⅔ cup bottled barbecue sauce	160 ml
¼ cup mayonnaise	60 ml
3 tablespoons cider vinegar	45 ml
2 tablespoons sugar	30 ml
1 (12 ounce) package broccoli slaw	340 g
1 cup shredded carrots	240 ml

• Brush chicken quarters with oil and sprinkle with salt and pepper. Grill 30 to 35 minutes, turning once or twice or until juices run clear when thigh part is pierced and a meat thermometer inserted registers 170° (76° C). Brush with barbecue sauce and grill just until sauce is brown, but not charred.

• Combine mayonnaise, vinegar and sugar, mixing well. Spoon over broccoli slaw and carrots and toss. Chill.

Spicy Chicken and Rice

3 cups cooked, sliced chicken	710 ml
2 cups cooked brown rice	480 ml
1 (10 ounce) can fiesta nacho cheese soup	280 g
1 (10 ounce) can chopped tomatoes and green chilies	280 g

• Combine chicken, rice, cheese soup, tomatoes and green chilies and mix well. Spoon mixture into buttered 3-quart (3 L) baking dish.

• Cook covered at 350° (176° C) for 35 minutes.

Grilled Chicken with Raspberry-Barbecue Sauce

1 (12 ounce) jar seedless raspberry preserves	340 g
½ cup bottled barbecue sauce	120 ml
2 tablespoons raspberry vinegar	30 ml
2 tablespoons dijon-style mustard	30 ml
1 (2½ pound) chicken, quartered	1.2 kg

- In bowl, combine preserves, barbecue sauce, vinegar and mustard and have ready when chicken quarters are nearly done.

- Season chicken quarters liberally with seasoned salt and pepper. Grill chicken, covered with grill lid, over medium-high heat for about 8 minutes on each side. Baste sauce over quarters last 2 minutes of cooking. Serve with remaining sauce.

Sunday Chicken

5 - 6 boneless, skinless chicken breast halves	
½ cup sour cream	120 ml
¼ cup soy sauce	60 ml
1 (10 ounce) can French onion soup	280 g

- Place chicken in greased 9 x 13-inch (23 x 33 cm) baking dish.

- In saucepan, combine sour cream, soy sauce and soup and heat just enough to mix well. Pour over chicken breasts.

- Bake covered at 375° (190° C) for 35 minutes.

Glazed Drumsticks

1 (20 ounce) package frozen chicken drum sticks	567 g
½ cup hoisin sauce	120 ml
2 tablespoons light soy sauce	30 ml
1 teaspoon minced garlic	5 ml

- Preheat broiler. Place drumsticks in a single layer, in greased 9 x 13-inch (23 x 33 cm) baking dish and broil for 10 minutes. Turn drumsticks and broil another 10 minutes. Reduce heat to 325° (162° C).

- In bowl, combine hoisin sauce, soy sauce and garlic, mixing well. Brush chicken drumsticks lightly with sauce and bake for 25 minutes. During baking time, remove from oven and brush with remaining sauce and continue cooking until glaze bubbles and browns.

Tempting Chicken

3 boneless, skinless chicken breast halves	
3 boneless, skinless chicken thighs	
1 (16 ounce) jar tomato-alfredo sauce	.5 kg
1 (10 ounce) can tomato-bisque soup	280 g

- Preheat oven to 350° (176° C). In large skillet, brown chicken pieces in little oil and place in sprayed 9 x 13-inch (23 x 33 cm) baking pan.

- Combine tomato-alfredo sauce, tomato-bisque soup and ½ cup (120 ml) water and pour over chicken. Cover and simmer about 20 minutes; uncover chicken and cook another 15 minutes.

Tasty Skillet Chicken

5 large boneless, skinless chicken breast halves, cut in strips
1 green and 1 red bell pepper, julienned
2 small yellow squash, seeded, julienned
1 (16 ounce) bottle thick-and-chunky salsa   .5 kg

• With a little oil in large skillet, saute chicken for about 5 minutes.
  Add peppers and squash and cook another 5 minutes or until
  peppers are tender-crisp. Stir in salsa and bring to a boil; lower
  heat and simmer for 10 minutes. Serve over rice.

Sunshine Chicken

1 chicken, quartered
Flour
1 cup barbecue sauce   240 ml
½ cup orange juice   120 ml

• Place chicken in bowl of flour and coat well. In skillet with a
  little oil, brown chicken and place in sprayed, shallow 9 x 13-inch
  (23 x 33 cm) baking pan. Combine barbecue sauce and orange
  juice. Pour over chicken. Bake covered at 350° (176° C) for
  30 minutes. Remove from oven, spoon sauce over chicken and
  bake uncovered another 15 minutes.

Sweet-Spicy Chicken Thighs

3 tablespoons each chili powder and honey   45 ml
3 tablespoons honey   45 ml
2 tablespoons lemon juice   30 ml
10 - 12 chicken thighs

• Preheat oven to 425° (220° C). Line 10 x 15-inch (25 x 38 cm)
  shallow baking pan with heavy foil and set metal rack on top.
  Combine chili powder, honey, lemon juice and lots of salt and
  pepper. Brush mixture over chicken thighs, place on rack and
  turn thighs to coat. Bake, turning once, for about 35 minutes.

So-Good Chicken

4 - 5 boneless, skinless chicken breasts
1 (10 ounce) can golden mushroom soup   280 g
1 cup white cooking wine   240 ml
1 (8 ounce) carton sour cream   227 g

- Wash, dry chicken breasts with paper towels and sprinkle a little
  salt and pepper over each. Place chicken in sprayed 9 x 13-inch
  (23 x 33 cm) baking dish. Preheat over to 375° (190° C). In
  bowl, combine mushroom soup, wine and sour cream and mix
  well. Spoon over chicken breasts. Cook covered for 30 minutes.
  Uncover, and cook another 10 minutes.

Sweet-and-Sour Chicken

2 - 3 pounds chicken pieces   1 kg
1 (1 ounce) packet dry onion soup mix   28 g
1 (6 ounce) can frozen orange juice concentrate,
   thawed   168 g

- In skillet, brown chicken pieces on both sides in a little oil. Place in
  9 x 13-inch (23 x 33 cm) baking dish. In small bowl, combine onion
  soup mix, orange juice and ⅔ cup (160 ml) water and stir well. Pour
  over chicken. Bake uncovered at 375° (190° C) for 30 minutes.

Requested Favorite Chicken

6 boneless, skinless chicken breast halves
1 (16 ounce) jar thick-and-chunky hot salsa   .5 kg
1 cup packed light brown sugar   240 ml
1 tablespoon dijon-style mustard   15 ml
Cooked brown rice

- Preheat oven to 350° (176° C). In large skillet with a little
  oil, brown chicken breasts and place in greased 9 x 13-inch
  (23 x 33 cm) baking dish. Combine salsa, brown sugar, mustard
  and ½ teaspoon (2 ml) salt and pour over chicken. Cover and
  bake 35 minutes. Serve over brown rice.

Italian Crumb Chicken

5 - 6 boneless, skinless chicken breast halves
¾ cup mayonnaise   180 ml
⅓ cup grated parmesan cheese   80 ml
½ cup prepared Italian seasoned breadcrumbs   120 ml

- Preheat oven to 400° (204° C). Place all chicken breasts on foil-
  lined baking pan. Combine mayonnaise, 2 teaspoons (10 ml)
  pepper and parmesan cheese in bowl; mix well. Spread mixture
  over chicken breasts and sprinkle breadcrumbs on both sides.
  Place in oven uncovered and bake 20 to 25 minutes.

Quick Chicken Supper

1 (16 ounce) package frozen broccoli florets, thawed   .5 kg
1 (10 ounce) can cream of chicken soup   280 g
⅔ cup mayonnaise   160 ml
1 cup shredded cheddar cheese   240 ml
3 cups cooked, cubed chicken   710 ml
2 cups crushed cheese crackers   480 ml

- Preheat oven to 375° (190° C). In large bowl, combine broccoli,
  soup, mayonnaise, cheese and chicken, mixing well. Pour into
  greased 3-quart (3 L) baking dish; cover and bake 20 minutes.
  Uncover, sprinkle crackers over casserole and bake 10 minutes.

Saucy Chicken

5 - 6 boneless, skinless chicken breast halves
2 cups thick, chunky salsa   480 ml
⅓ cup packed light brown sugar   80 ml
1½ tablespoons dijon-style mustard   22 ml
Hot, cooked rice

- Place chicken breasts in greased 9 x 13-inch (23 x 33 cm) baking
  dish. Combine salsa, sugar and mustard and pour over chicken.
  Cover and bake at 350° (176° C) for 45 minutes. Serve over rice.

Italian Chicken and Rice

3 boneless, chicken breast halves, cut into strips	
1 (14 ounce) can chicken broth seasoned with	
Italian herbs	396 g
¾ cup uncooked instant rice	180 ml
¼ cup grated parmesan cheese	60 ml

• Cook chicken in non-stick skillet until brown and stir often. Remove chicken. To skillet add broth and rice. Heat to boiling point. Cover and simmer over low heat for 15 minutes. (Check to see if it needs more water.) Stir in cheese. Return chicken to pan. Cover and cook for 5 minutes or until done.

Skillet Chicken and Peas

4 - 5 boneless, skinless chicken breast halves	
2 (10 ounce) can cream of chicken soup	2 (280 g)
2 cups uncooked instant rice	480 ml
1 (10 ounce) package frozen green peas	280 g

• Heat a little oil in very large skillet. Add chicken and cook until it browns. Transfer chicken to plate and keep warm. To skillet, add soup, 1¾ cups (420 ml) water and ½ teaspoon (2 ml) pepper and paprika. Heat to a boil, stir in rice and peas, reduce heat. Place chicken on top and cook on low heat for 15 minutes.

Skillet Chicken and Stuffing

1 (6 ounce) box stuffing mix for chicken	168 g
1 (16 ounce) package frozen whole kernel corn	.5 kg
¼ cup (½ stick) butter	60 ml
4 boneless, skinless chicken breast halves, cooked	

• In large skillet, combine contents of seasoning packet in stuffing mix, corn, 1⅔ cups (400 ml) water and butter. Bring to a boil Reduce heat, cover and simmer for 5 minutes. Stir in stuffing mix just until moist. Cut chicken into thin slices. Mix with stuffing-corn mixture. Cook on low heat until thoroughly hot.

Chicken-Green Bean Bake

2 cups instant rice	480 ml
1 (16 ounce) package shredded processed cheese	.5 kg
1 (16 ounce) package frozen cut green beans, thawed	.5 kg
3 cups cooked, cubed chicken	710 ml
2 cups coarsely crushed potato chips	480 ml

- Preheat oven to 325° (162° C). Cook rice in large saucepan according to package directions and stir in cheese and extra ¼ cup (60 ml) water. Stir and mix until cheese melts.

- Cook green beans according to package directions; drain. Stir in rice-cheese mixture and add cubed chicken; mix well. Spoon into sprayed 9 x 13-inch (23 x 33 cm) baking dish. Top with potato chips and bake 20 minutes until chips are light brown.

Creamy Chicken and Veggies

6 small boneless, skinless chicken breast halves	
1 (16 ounce) bottle creamy Italian dressing	.5 kg
1 (16 ounce) package frozen broccoli, cauliflower and carrots, thawed	.5 kg

- Sprinkle chicken with pepper and salt to taste. Place a little oil in large, heavy non-stick skillet over medium-high heat. Add chicken breasts and cook 4 minutes on each side. Pour about ³/₄ dressing over chicken; cover and simmer for about 8 minutes. Add vegetables, cover and cook another 10 minutes or until vegetables are tender.

Chop Suey Veggies and Chicken

3 cups cooked, cubed chicken	710 ml
2 (10 ounce) cans cream of chicken soup	2 (280 g)
2 (15 ounce) cans chop suey vegetables, drained	2 (425 g)
1 (8 ounce) can sliced water chestnuts, drained	227 g
1 (16 ounce) package frozen seasoning blend onions and bell peppers	.5 kg
½ teaspoon hot sauce and curry powder	2 ml
2 cups chow mein noodles	480 ml

- Preheat oven to 350° (176° C). In large bowl, combine all ingredients, saving noodles for topping. Spoon into greased 9 x 13-inch (23 x 33 cm) baking dish. Sprinkle chow mein noodles over top and bake uncovered for 30 minutes.

Confetti Squash and Chicken

1 pound yellow squash, sliced	.5 kg
1 pound zucchini, sliced	.5 kg
2 cups cooked, cubed chicken	480 ml
1 (10 ounce) can cream of chicken soup	280 g
1 (8 ounce) carton sour cream	227 g
1 (4 ounce) can chopped pimento, drained	114 g
½ cup (1 stick) butter, melted	120 ml
1 (6 ounce) box herb stuffing mix	168 g

- Preheat oven to 350° (176° C). In large saucepan, cook squash and zucchini in salted water about 10 minutes. Drain and stir in chicken, soup, sour cream and pimentos, mixing well.

- Combine melted butter and stuffing mix and add to vegetable-chicken mixture and mix well. Spoon into greased 9 x 13-inch (23 x 33 cm) baking dish. Cover and bake 30 minutes.

Creamy Chicken and Broccoli

5 large chicken breast halves, thawed
2 (10 ounce) cans creamy chicken verde soup   2 (280 g)
½ cup milk   120 ml
1 (16 ounce) package frozen broccoli florets, thawed   .5 kg
Cooked instant brown rice

- In very large skillet (with lid) sprinkle chicken with salt and
  pepper and brown breasts in a little oil.   On medium-high heat,
  stir into skillet both cans of soup and milk. Stir to mix and as
  you are stirring, spoon soup mixture over top of chicken breasts.
  When mixture is well mixed and hot, reduce heat to low, cover
  and simmer for 20 minutes.

- Place broccoli florets around chicken and into creamy sauce.
  Return heat to high until broccoli is heated; again reduce heat
  and simmer about 10 minutes or until broccoli is tender-crisp.

- Serve chicken and sauce over brown rice.

Creamy Chicken and Pasta

1 (10 ounce) package penne pasta   280 g
1 tablespoon olive oil   15 ml
2 (12 ounce) cans white chicken meat, drained   2 (340 g)
2 tablespoons prepared pesto   30 ml
¾ cup whipping cream   180 ml

- In large saucepan, cook penne pasta according to package
  directions. Drain and place back in saucepan. Gently stir in oil,
  chicken, prepared pesto, whipping cream and salt and pepper to
  taste. Place saucepan over low heat and simmer, stirring often,
  (but do not let mixture boil) until cream is absorbed into pasta.
  Spoon into serving bowl and serve immediately.

Easy Chicken and Dumplings

3 cups cooked, chopped chicken	710 ml
2 (10 ounce) cans cream of chicken soup	2 (280 g)
3 teaspoons chicken bouillon granules	15 ml
1 (8 ounce) can refrigerated buttermilk biscuits	227 g

- Combine chopped chicken, both cans of soup, chicken bouillon granules and 4½ cups (1.1 L) water in large kettle or Dutch oven. Boil mixture and stir to mix well.

- Separate biscuits and cut in half, cut again making 4 pieces out of each biscuit. Drop biscuit pieces, 1 at a time, into boiling chicken mixture, stir gently. When all biscuits are dropped, reduce heat to low and simmer, stirring occasionally, for about 15 minutes.

Crunchy Chip Chicken

1½ cups crushed sour cream potato chips	360 ml
1 tablespoon dried parsley	15 ml
1 egg, beaten	
1 tablespoon Worcestershire	15 ml
4 large boneless, skinless chicken breast halves	
¼ cup oil	60 ml

- In shallow bowl, combine potato chips and parsley. In another shallow bowl, combine beaten egg, Worcestershire sauce and 1 tablespoon (15 ml) water. Dip chicken pieces in egg mixture, then dredge chicken in potato chip mixture. Heat oil in heavy skillet and fry chicken pieces in skillet for about 10 minutes; turn each piece over and cook another 10 minutes until golden brown or until juice of chicken is no longer pink.

Moist-Crunchy Baked Chicken

¼ pound (1 stick) butter, melted	114 g
2 tablespoons mayonnaise	30 ml
2 tablespoons white wine Worcestershire sauce	30 ml
1 (6 ounce) can french-fried onions, crushed	168 g
6 boneless, skinless chicken breasts halves	

- Preheat oven to 375° (190° C). In shallow bowl, combine melted butter, mayonnaise and Worcestershire sauce. Place crushed onions in another shallow bowl.

- Dry chicken breasts with paper towels and dip first into butter mixture and dredge each chicken breast in crushed onions. Place in large baking pan, arranging so pieces do not touch.

- Bake 25 minutes or until chicken juices run clear.

Lemony Chicken and Noodles

½ (16 ounce) package wide egg noodles	½ (.5 kg)
1 (10 ounce) package frozen sugar snap peas, thawed	280 g
1 (10 ounce) can chicken broth	280 g
1 teaspoon fresh grated lemon peel	5 ml
2 cups cubed skinless rotisserie chicken meat	480 ml
½ cup whipping cream	120 ml

- In large saucepan with boiling water, cook noodles according to package directions, but add snap peas to noodles 1 minute before noodles are done. Drain and return to saucepan. Add chicken broth, lemon peel, chicken pieces and ½ teaspoon (2 ml) each of salt and black pepper; heat, stirring constantly until thoroughly hot. Over low heat, gently stir in heavy cream. Serve hot.

Roasted Chicken

1 (14 ounce) can chicken broth	396 g
1 (8 ounce) can whole kernel corn, drained	227 g
2 cups cooked, cubed chicken breast	480 ml
1 (5 ounce) box couscous	143 g
1 cup prepared roasted red bell peppers	240 ml
¼ cup toasted pine nuts	60 ml

- In saucepan over medium-high heat, combine chicken broth, corn, chicken, couscous and bell peppers. Cover and simmer 10 minutes. Sprinkle pine nuts over top.

Parmesan Crusted Chicken

1 egg white, beaten	
1½ cups dry breadcrumbs	360 ml
1 teaspoon dried parsley	5 ml
½ cup grated parmesan cheese	120 ml
4 small boneless, skinless chicken breast halves	
¼ cup minced shallots	60 ml
½ cup dry white wine	120 ml
½ cup heavy cream and chicken broth	120 ml
¼ cup (½ stick) butter, cut in chunks	60 ml
¾ teaspoon dried sage	4 ml

- Preheat oven to 425° (220° C). Combine beaten egg white and 1 tablespoon (15 ml) water. In shallow bowl, combine breadcrumbs, parsley, cheese and salt and pepper to taste. Dip each piece of chicken in egg white; dredge in crumb mixture. Place in heavy skillet with a little oil and saute chicken until golden. Transfer to greased baking dish and bake, uncovered for 15 minutes. Saute shallots in a little oil in saucepan. Add wine, cream and chicken broth; simmer until reduced by half. Stir in butter and sage. Serve over parmesan chicken.

Sassy Red Pepper Chicken

4 boneless, skinless chicken breast halves
1½ cups seasoned breadcrumbs   360 ml
1 teaspoon garlic powder   5 ml
1 large egg, beaten
½ cup oil, divided   120 ml

Red Pepper Sauce:
¾ cup drained, diced roasted red peppers   180 ml
½ cup vinegar   120 ml
½ cup ketchup   120 ml
⅔ cup sugar   160 ml
1 teaspoon paprika   5 ml

- Place chicken breasts between 2 sheets plastic wrap and, using a meat mallet, flatten chicken to ¼-inch (.6 cm); set aside. In shallow bowl, combine breadcrumbs and garlic powder and place beaten egg with 2 tablespoons (30 ml) water in second shallow bowl. Dip chicken in egg mixture and then dredge chicken in breadcrumbs.

- Pour ¼ cup (60 ml) of oil in large skillet and cook 2 chicken breasts for 5 minutes on each side. Remove from skillet to keep warm. Repeat procedure with remaining oil and chicken.

- Place all pepper sauce ingredients in saucepan, bring to a boil, reduce heat and cook 25 minutes, stirring often. Spoon sauce over chicken to serve.

Rolled Chicken Florentine

6 boneless, skinless chicken breast halves
6 thin slices deli ham
6 thin slices Swiss cheese
1 (10 ounce) package frozen chopped spinach,
   thawed, drained   280 g
2 (10 ounce) cans cream of chicken soup   2 (280 g)
4 fresh green onions, finely chopped
1 (10 ounce) box chicken flavored Rice-a-Roni®   280 g

- With flat side of meat mallet, pound chicken to ¼-inch (.6 cm) thickness. Place ham slice, cheese slice and one-fourth well drained spinach on each chicken piece and roll chicken from short end, jelly-roll style. Secure with wooden toothpicks. Place chicken in buttered 9 x 13-inch (23 x 33 cm) glass baking dish. Cover with plastic wrap and microwave on HIGH for 4 minutes.

- Preheat oven to 325° (162° C). In bowl, stir together chicken soup, onions, ⅔ cup (160 ml) water and black pepper to taste, stirring to blend well. Pour over chicken rolls, cover and bake for 25 minutes or until chicken is fork-tender.

- Cook rice according to package directions and place on serving platter and spoon chicken and sauce over rice.

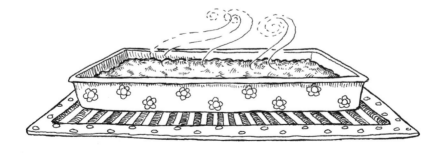

Skillet Chicken and More

4 boneless, skinless chicken breast halves
2 (10 ounce) cans cream of chicken soup   2 (280 g)
2 cups uncooked, instant white rice   480 ml
1 (16 ounce) package broccoli florets   .5 kg

- Brown chicken breasts on both sides in very large skillet with
  a little oil and simmer 10 minutes. Remove chicken and keep
  warm. Add soup and 2 cups (480 ml) water. Heat to boiling.

- Stir in instant rice and broccoli florets. Use a little salt, pepper
  and paprika (if you have it) on chicken and place on top of rice.
  Cover dish and cook on low 15 minutes or until liquid evaporates.

Stir-Fry Cashew Chicken

1 pound chicken tenders, cut into strips   .5 kg
1 (16 ounce) package frozen broccoli,
   cauliflower and carrots   .5 kg
1 (8 ounce) jar stir-fry sauce   227 g
⅓ cup cashew halves   80 ml
1 (12 ounce) package chow mein noodles   340 g

- In 12-inch (32 cm) wok, place a little oil and stir-fry chicken
  strips over high heat about 4 minutes. Add vegetables and stir-fry
  another 4 minutes or until vegetables are tender.

- Stir in stir-fry sauce and cashews. Cook just until mixture is hot.
  Serve over chow mein noodles.

Luncheon Chicken Pie

1 (12 ounce) package shredded cheddar cheese, divided	340 g
1 (10 ounce) package frozen peas and carrots, thawed	280 g
1 red bell pepper, seeded, chopped	
2 cups cooked, finely diced chicken breasts	480 ml
3 large eggs, beaten	
¾ cup baking mix	180 ml
1½ cups half-and-half cream	360 ml

- In large bowl, combine 2 cups (480 ml) cheese, peas and carrots, bell pepper and chicken. Spread into buttered 10-inch (25 cm) deep-dish pie plate. In mixing bowl, combine eggs and baking mix, whisk until smooth. Stir in cream and salt to taste. Spoon mixture over cheese-vegetable mixture, but do not stir.

- Cover and bake 30 minutes or until center of pie is firm. Sprinkle remaining cheese over top and bake for 5 more minutes.

Stir-Fry Chicken and Veggies

1¼ cups instant rice	300 ml
¼ cup (½ stick) butter	60 ml
1½ pounds chicken tenderloin strips	.7 kg
1 (16 ounce) package frozen broccoli, cauliflower and carrots	.5 kg
2 sweet red bell peppers, julienned	
½ cup stir-fry sauce	120 ml
Hot, cooked rice	

- Cook rice according to package directions and keep warm. In large non-stick skillet, melt butter and stir-fry chicken strips about 5 minutes, or until light brown.

- Stir in vegetables and cook 8 minutes longer. Pour in stir-fry sauce, mixing well; cover and cook 2 minutes or until thoroughly hot. Serve over rice.

Pimento Cheese-Stuffed Chicken

4 large skinless, boneless chicken breast halves
½ cup milk   120 ml
1 large egg, beaten
2 cups seasoned breadcrumbs   480 ml
1 (16 ounce) carton pimento cheese   .5 kg

- Preheat oven to 350° (176° C). Dry chicken breasts with paper towels and sprinkle well with salt and pepper.

- Combine milk and beaten egg in shallow bowl, mixing well and place breadcrumbs in second shallow bowl. Dip chicken in milk mixture and dredge in breadcrumbs.

- In large skillet over medium-high heat, pour in a little oil to -inch (.4 cm) depth and cook chicken about 10 to 12 minutes on each side. Transfer to baking sheet. Hold chicken with tongs and cut slit in 1 side of each chicken breast to form a pocket. Spoon about ¼ cup (60 ml) pimento cheese into each pocket and bake another 5 minutes or until cheese melts.

Swiss-Cheesy Chicken

4 boneless, skinless chicken breast halves
½ cup refrigerated honey-mustard dressing   120 ml
1 package (8 slices) fully cooked bacon
4 slices Swiss cheese

- In large skillet with a little oil, cook chicken breasts on medium-high heat for 5 minutes. Remove chicken to cutting board and liberally spread each breast with honey-mustard dressing.

- Top with 2 slices of bacon for each breast and cover with a slice of Swiss cheese. Carefully lift each chicken breast back into skillet and place 1 tablespoon (15 ml) water in skillet. Cover and cook on low-medium heat for 10 minutes.

Ranch Chicken To Go

1 (8 ounce) package of your favorite pasta	227 g
½ cup (1 stick) butter, melted	120 ml
1 (10 ounce) can cream of chicken soup	280 g
1 (1 ounce) packet ranch-style salad dressing mix	28 g
2 (15 ounce) cans peas and carrots, drained	2 (425 g)
3 cups cooked, cubed chicken	710 ml
1 (2.8 ounce) can french-fried onion rings	84 g

- Preheat oven to 350° (176° C). Cook pasta according to package directions. In a saucepan, combine butter, soup, dry dressing mix, peas and carrots. Heat on medium, stirring occasionally, until all ingredients are well mixed and thoroughly hot. Toss with cooked pasta and chicken and spoon into greased 3-quart (3 L) baking dish. Cover and bake 15 minutes. Sprinkle on onion rings and bake 15 more minutes.

Sweet'n Spicy Chicken

1 pound boneless, skinless chicken breast halves	.5 kg
1 (1 ounce) packet taco seasoning	28 g
1 (16 ounce) jar chunky salsa	.5 kg
1½ cups peach preserves	360 ml
Hot, cooked rice	

- Cut chicken into ½-inch (1.2 cm) cubes and place in large, plastic bag. Add taco seasoning and toss to coat. In skillet, brown chicken in a little oil. Combine salsa and preserves, stir into skillet and bring mixture to a boil. Reduce heat, cover and simmer until juices run clear, for 15 minutes. Serve over rice.

Skillet Roasted Chicken

1 (2½ - 3 pound) chicken, quartered	1.2 kg
2 teaspoons sage	10 ml
2 teaspoons prepared minced garlic	10 ml
2 (10 ounce) cans cream of chicken soup	2 (280 g)
Hot, buttered rice	

• Dry chicken quarters with paper towels. Sprinkle with sage and salt and pepper to taste. Place in large skillet with a little oil. Cook on both sides over medium-high heat for about 15 minutes. Combine garlic, chicken soup and ½ cup (120 ml) water in saucepan. Heat just enough to blend ingredients.

• Pour over chicken, cover and cook on low heat for 10 minutes or until chicken heats thoroughly. Serve over rice.

Special Chicken Couscous

1¼ cups chicken broth	300 ml
1 (5.6 ounce) package pine nut couscous mix	155 g
1 rotisserie chicken, skinned, boned, cut up	
1 (4 ounce) can chopped pimento	114 g
½ cup crumbled feta cheese	120 ml
1 (10 ounce) package frozen green peas, drained,	
optional	280 g
1 tablespoon dried basil	15 ml
1 tablespoon lemon juice	15 ml

• Heat broth and seasoning packet from couscous in microwave on HIGH for 4 minutes or until broth begins to boil. Place couscous in large bowl and stir in broth, cover and let stand 5 minutes. Fluff couscous with fork and add chicken, pimento, cheese, peas, basil and lemon juice. Toss and serve warm.

Spicy Orange Chicken

1 pound boneless skinless chicken tenders	.5 kg
2 tablespoons oil	30 ml
2 tablespoons soy sauce	30 ml
1 (16 ounce) package frozen stir-fry vegetables, thawed	.5 kg
1 (6 ounce) package chow mein noodles	168 g
⅔ cup orange marmalade	160 ml
1 tablespoon olive oil	15 ml
2 teaspoons lime juice	10 ml
½ teaspoon dried ginger and cayenne pepper	2 ml

• In large skillet over medium-high heat, lightly brown chicken tenders in oil. Add soy sauce and stir-fry vegetables and cook about 8 minutes or until vegetables are tender-crisp. In saucepan, combine marmalade, oil, lime juice, ginger and cayenne pepper and mix well. Heat and pour over stir-fry and toss. Serve over chow mein noodles.

Cheesy Chicken and Potatoes

1 (20 ounce) package frozen has browns with peppers and onions, thawed	567 g
1 tablespoon minced garlic	15 ml
2-2½ cups bite-size chunks rotisserie chicken	480 ml
1 bunch green onions, sliced	
1 cup shredded cheddar cheese	240 ml

• Add a little oil to large skillet over medium-high heat, cook potatoes for 7 minutes and turn frequently.

• Add garlic, chicken, green onions and ⅓ cup (80 ml) water and cook 5 to 6 minutes. Remove from heat and stir in cheese. Serve immediately right from skillet.

Stir-Fry Chicken Spaghetti

1 pound boneless, skinless chicken breast halves	.5 kg
1½ cups sliced mushrooms	360 ml
1½ cups bell pepper strips	360 ml
1 cup sweet-and-sour stir-fry sauce	240 ml
1 (16 ounce) package spaghetti, cooked, drained	.5 kg
¼ cup (½ stick) butter	60 ml

- Salt and pepper chicken and cut into thin slices. In large skillet with a little oil, brown chicken slices and cook for 5 minutes on low-medium heat. Transfer to plate and reserve.

- In same skillet adding a little more oil, stir-fry mushrooms and bell pepper strips for 5 minutes. Add chicken strips and sweet-and-sour sauce, stirring until ingredients are thoroughly hot.

- While spaghetti is still hot and drained, add butter, stirring until butter is melted. Place in large bowl and toss with chicken mixture.

Sunny Chicken Supper

4 boneless, skinless chicken breast halves	
1½ teaspoons curry powder	7 ml
1½ cups orange juice	360 ml
2 tablespoons brown sugar	30 ml
1 cup uncooked rice	240 ml
1 teaspoon mustard	5 ml

- Rub chicken breasts with curry powder and a little salt and pepper. In large skillet, combine remaining ingredients and mix well. Top with chicken breasts and bring to a boil. Reduce heat, cover and simmer for 30 minutes.

- Remove from heat and let stand, covered until all liquid has absorbed, about 10 minutes.

Supreme Chicken

1 (16 ounce) package seasoning blend of onions and bell peppers	.5 kg
3 cup cooked, diced chicken	710 ml
1 (6 ounce) package long-grain and wild rice, cooked	168 g
1 (10 ounce) can cream of chicken soup	280 g
1 (4 ounce) can chopped pimentos	114 g
1 (15 ounce) can French-style green beans, drained	425 g
½ cup slivered almonds	120 ml
1 cup mayonnaise	240 ml
3 cups lightly crushed potato chips	710 ml

- Preheat oven to 350° (176° C). In skillet with a little oil, saute onions and bell peppers. In large bowl, combine onions and bell peppers, chicken, rice, chicken soup, pimentos, green beans, almonds, mayonnaise and salt and pepper to taste. Mix until well blended.

- Butter a deep 9 x 13-inch (23 x 33 cm) baking dish and spoon mixture into dish. Sprinkle crushed potato chips over casserole and bake for 35 minutes or until chips are light brown.

Spaghetti Toss

1 (10 ounce) package thin spaghetti	280 g
1 (10 ounce) package frozen sugar snap peas	280 g
2 tablespoons butter	30 ml
3 cups rotisserie cooked chicken strips	710 ml
1 (11 ounce) can mandarin oranges, drained	312 g
⅔ cup stir-fry sauce	160 ml

- Cook spaghetti according to package directions; peas and cook an additional minute. Drain and stir in butter until butter melts. Spoon into bowl. Add chicken strips, oranges and stir-fry sauce; toss to coat.

Summertime-Limeade Chicken

6 large boneless, skinless chicken breast halves	
1 (6 ounce) can frozen limeade concentrate, thawed	168 g
3 tablespoons brown sugar	45 ml
½ cup chili sauce	120 ml
Hot, buttered rice	

- Sprinkle chicken breasts with a little salt and pepper and place in lightly greased skillet. Cook on high heat and brown on both sides for about 10 minutes. Remove from skillet, set aside and keep warm.

- Add limeade concentrate, brown sugar and chili sauce to skillet. Boil, stirring constantly, for 10 minutes.

- Return chicken to skillet and spoon sauce over chicken. Reduce heat, cover and simmer for 15 minutes. Serve over rice.

Southwest Pizza

1 (12 inch) pre-baked pizza crust	32 cm
¾ cup prepared guacamole	180 ml
1 (10 ounce) package cooked southwest-style chicken breast, sliced	280 g
½ cup roasted red peppers, drained, sliced	120 ml
1 (4 ounce) can sliced ripe olives	114 g
1 (8 ounce) package shredded Mexican 4-cheese blend	227 g

- Preheat oven to 350° (176° C). Place pizza crust on greased cookie sheet and spread guacamole over crust. Top with chicken, red peppers and olives, spreading evenly. Top with cheese. Bake 15 minutes or just until cheese bubbles and is slightly brown. Cut pizza into wedges to serve.

Ginger-Orange Glazed Cornish Hens

1 cup fresh orange juice	240 ml
2 tablespoons peeled, minced fresh ginger	30 ml
1 tablespoon soy sauce	15 ml
3 tablespoons honey	45 ml
2 (about 1½ pounds) cornish hens, halved	2 (.7 kg)
½ teaspoon ground ginger	2 ml

• Preheat oven to 450° (230° C). In saucepan, combine orange juice, minced ginger, soy sauce and honey and cook on high heat, stirring constantly, for 3 minutes or until thick and glossy.

• Place hens in greased baking pan and sprinkle with ground ginger, ½ teaspoon (2 ml) each of salt and pepper. Spoon glaze mixture over hens and bake 25 minutes, brushing glaze over hens several times during cooking.

Jambalaya

1 (8 ounce) package jambalaya mix	227 g
1 (6 ounce) package frozen chicken breast strips, thawed	168 g
1 (11 ounce) can mexicorn	312 g
1 (2 ounce) can chopped black olives	57 g

• Combine jambalaya mix and 2¼ cups (540 ml) water in soup or large saucepan. Heat to boiling, reduce heat and cook slowly 5 minutes. Add chopped chicken, corn and black olives. Heat to boiling, reduce heat and simmer about 20 minutes.

Tortellini and Chicken Supper

1 (9 ounce) package refrigerated cheese tortellini	255 g
1 (10 ounce) package frozen green peas, thawed	280 g
1 (8 ounce) carton cream cheese with chives	
and onion	227 g
½ teaspoon Creole seasoning	2 ml
½ cup sour cream	120 ml
1 (9 ounce) package frozen cooked chicken breasts	255 g

- Cook cheese tortellini in saucepan according to package directions. Place peas in colander and pour hot pasta water over green peas. Return tortellini and peas to saucepan.

- Combine cream cheese, Creole seasoning and sour cream in smaller saucepan and heat on low, stirring well until cream cheese melts. Spoon mixture over tortellini and peas and toss, keeping heat on low. Heat cooked chicken in microwave according to package directions. Spoon tortellini and peas in serving bowl and place chicken on top.

Family Night Spaghetti

6 frozen breaded, cooked chicken breast	
1 (8 ounce) package spaghetti, cooked	227 g
1 (18 ounce) jar spaghetti sauce	510 g
1 (26 ounce) package shredded mozzarella cheese,	
divided	737 g

- Bake chicken breast according to package directions; keep warm. Cook spaghetti as instructed on package; drain and arrange on platter. Place spaghetti sauce in saucepan with 1 cup (240 ml) of mozzarella cheese and heat slightly, not boiling. Spoon about half sauce over spaghetti and arrange chicken breast over top. Spoon remaining spaghetti sauce over chicken and sprinkle remaining cheese over top.

Turkey and Rice Supper

¾ pound cooked, sliced deli turkey	340 g
2 cups cooked instant brown rice	480 ml
1 (10 ounce) can cream of chicken soup	280 g
1 (10 ounce) can chopped tomatoes and green chilies	280 g
1½ cups crushed tortilla chips	360 ml

- Preheat oven to 350° (176° C). Place turkey slices in bottom of sprayed 7 x 11-inch (18 x 28 cm) baking dish. In bowl, combine rice, chicken soup and tomatoes and green chilies and mix well. Spoon over turkey slices. Sprinkle crushed tortilla chips over top of casserole and bake, uncovered, for 30 minutes.

Baked Turkey and Dressing

1 (6 ounce) package turkey stuffing	168 g
3 cups diced, cooked turkey	710 ml
2 tablespoons dried parsley flakes	30 ml
1 (10 ounce) can cream of chicken soup	280 g
1 (8 ounce) carton sour cream	227 g
¼ cup (½ stick) butter, melted	60 ml
1 teaspoon ground cumin	5 ml
1½ cups shredded mozzarella cheese	360 ml

- Preheat oven to 350° (176° C). In large mixing bowl, combine all ingredients except mozzarella cheese. Mix well and spoon into greased 9 x 13-inch (23 x 33 cm) baking dish. Cover and bake 30 minutes. Uncover and sprinkle with cheese and bake just until cheese begins to melt.

Turkey Casserole

1 (7 ounce) package herb-seasoned stuffing	198 g
1 cup whole cranberry sauce	240 ml
1 (12 ounce) can turkey	340 g
1 (10 ounce) can turkey gravy	280 g

- Prepare stuffing according to package directions. Combine prepared stuffing and cranberry sauce in medium bowl and set aside.

- In buttered, 2-quart (2 L) baking dish place turkey. Pour gravy over turkey and spoon stuffing mixture over casserole. Bake uncovered at 375° (190° C) for 20 minutes or until hot.

Chilly Night's Turkey Bake

1 (6 ounce) package stuffing mix for chicken, divided	168 g
1½ pounds cooked turkey, cut into 1-inch strips	360 ml/2.5 cm
1 (10 ounce) can cream of chicken soup	280 g
½ cup sour cream	120 ml
1 (16 ounce) package frozen mixed vegetables, thawed, drained	.5 kg

- Preheat oven to 350° (176° C). Sprinkle ½ cup (120 ml) dry stuffing mix evenly over bottom of sprayed 9 x 13-inch (23 x 33 cm) baking dish and set aside. In bowl, combine remaining stuffing and 1 cup (240 ml) water and stir just until moist and set aside.

- Place turkey strips (deli turkey can be used) over dry stuffing mix in baking dish. In bowl, mix soup, sour cream and vegetables, spoon over turkey strips and top with prepared stuffing. Bake, uncovered, for 25 minutes.

Turkey and the Works

1 (6 ounce) stuffing mix for turkey	168 g
½ (16 ounce) can whole cranberry sauce	½ (.5 kg)
1 pound turkey tenderloin, cut in thin slices	.5 kg
1 (12 ounce) jar turkey gravy	340 g

- Preheat oven to 325° (162° C). Prepare stuffing mix according to package directions; (besides water, you will need ½ stick butter). Measure 1 cup (240 ml) of cranberry sauce and stir into prepared stuffing mix.

- In skillet with a little oil, brown turkey slices and let them simmer, covered for about 10 minutes or until liquid has evaporated.

- Place turkey slices in 7 x 11-inch (18 x 28 cm) buttered baking dish. Cover with turkey gravy and then spoon prepared stuffing mix over turkey and gravy. Cover and bake for 25 minutes.

Turkey and Noodles

1 (8 ounce) package noodles	227 g
2½ cups diced, cooked turkey	600 ml
1 (1 ounce) package prepared chicken gravy	28 g
2 cups round, buttery cracker crumbs	480 ml

- Boil noodles according to package directions and drain.

- Arrange alternate layers of noodles, turkey and gravy in greased 2-quart (2 L) baking dish. Cover with crumbs.

- Bake uncovered at 350° (176° C) for 35 minutes.

Turkey Tenders

1 pound turkey tenders	.5 kg
1 (6 ounce) package roasted-garlic long grain, wild rice	168 g

Glaze:

⅔ cup honey	160 ml
2 teaspoons grated, peeled fresh ginger	10 ml
1 tablespoon white wine Worcestershire sauce	15 ml
1 tablespoon soy sauce and lemon juice	15 ml

- Place a little oil in heavy skillet and cook turkey tenders about 5 minutes on each side or until brown.

- Combine all glaze ingredients, mix well and pour into skillet. Bring mixture to a boil, reduce heat and simmer for 15 minutes; spoon glaze over turkey every 5 minutes. Prepare rice according to package directions and serve turkey over rice.

Turkey-Asparagus Alfredo

1 bunch fresh asparagus	
1 sweet red bell pepper, julienned	
1 (16 ounce) jar alfredo sauce	.5 kg
½ pound deli smoked turkey, cut into strips	227 g

- In large skillet bring ½ cup (120 ml) water to a boil. Cut off woody ends of asparagus and cut into thirds. Add asparagus and bell peppers to skillet and cook on medium-high heat for 4 minutes or until tender-crisp, drain. With skillet on medium-high heat, stir in alfredo sauce and turkey strips. Bring to a boil, reduce heat and simmer until mixture is thoroughly hot.

Turkey-Broccoli Bake

1 (16 ounce) package frozen broccoli spears, thawed	.5 kg
2 cups cooked, diced turkey	480 ml
1 (10 ounce) can cream of chicken soup	280 g
½ cup mayonnaise	120 ml
2 tablespoons lemon juice	30 ml
⅓ cup grated parmesan cheese	80 ml

- Preheat oven to 350° (176° C). Arrange broccoli spears in bottom of sprayed 9 x 13-inch (23 x 33 cm) baking dish and sprinkle with diced turkey.

- In saucepan, combine chicken soup, mayonnaise, lemon juice, cheese and ¼ cup (60 ml) water. Heat just enough to mix well. Spoon over broccoli and turkey. Cover and bake for 20 minutes, uncover and continue baking for another 10 minutes.

Turkey-Rice Olé

1 pound ground turkey	.5 kg
1 (5.5 ounce) package Mexican rice mix	155 g
1 (15 ounce) can black beans, rinsed, drained	425 g
1 cup thick and chunky salsa	240 ml
1 (10 ounce) package small original corn chips	280 g
1 cup shredded pepper Jack cheese	240 ml

- Brown turkey in large skillet and break up large pieces with fork. Add rice mix and 2 cups (480 ml) water, bring to a boil, reduce heat and simmer about 8 minutes or until rice is tender.

- Stir in beans and salsa; cook just until mixture is thoroughly hot. Place corn chips in individual salad or serving bowl and spoon turkey mixture over corn. Sprinkle cheese over each serving.

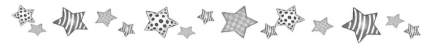

Pizza Pies

½ pound bulk turkey sausage	227 g
⅔ cup prepared pizza sauce	160 ml
1 (10 ounce) package refrigerated pizza dough	280 g
½ cup shredded mozzarella cheese	120 ml

• Preheat oven to 400° (204° C). Brown sausage in skillet and stir to break up pieces of meat. Drain fat, add pizza sauce and heat until bubbly.

• Unroll pizza dough, place on flat surface and pat into an 8 x 12-inch (20 x 32 cm) rectangle. Cut into 6 squares.

• Divide sausage mixture evenly among squares and sprinkle with cheese. Lift one corner of each square and fold over filling to make triangle. Press edges together with tines of fork to seal. Bake 12 minutes or until light brown. Serve immediately.

Dipping Sauce for Chicken Nuggets

1 (18 ounce) package frozen, cooked chicken nuggets	510 g
1 cup bottled barbecue sauce	240 ml
½ teaspoon mustard	2 ml
¾ cup apricot preserves	180 ml

• Place number of chicken nuggets you will need in a 325° (162° C) oven and heat for 20 minutes. Place barbecue sauce, mustard and preserves in microwave-safe bowl and microwave on HIGH for 30 seconds, stirring occasionally or until hot.

Chicken Dipping

1½ cups cornbread stuffing mix, plus half	
seasoning packet	360 ml
4 tablespoons oil	60 ml
4 boneless, skinless chicken breast halves	

- Place stuffing mix in plastic bag and crush with rolling pin.

- Add oil to center of 9 x 13-inch (23 x 33 cm) baking pan and spread around entire pan.

- Cut chicken breasts into 3 or 4 pieces, dip in stuffing mix and place in baking pan. Arrange chicken, making sure pieces are not touching. Bake at 350° (176° C) uncovered for 25 minutes. Remove from oven, turn pieces and bake another 15 minutes.

Dipping Sauce:

4 tablespoons honey	60 ml
3 tablespoons spicy brown mustard	45 ml

- To serve, dip chicken in dipping sauce and enjoy.

Smothered Beef Patties

1½ pounds lean ground beef	.7 kg
½ cup chili sauce	120 ml
½ cup buttery cracker crumbs	120 ml
1 (14 ounce) can beef broth	396 g

- Combine beef, chili sauce and cracker crumbs and form into 5 or 6 patties. In skillet, brown patties and pour beef bouillon over patties.

- Bring to a boil. Reduce heat and cover and simmer for 35 minutes.

Bueno Taco Casserole

2 pounds lean ground beef	1 kg
1½ cups taco sauce	360 ml
2 (15 ounce) cans Spanish rice	2 (425 g)
1 (8 ounce) package shredded Mexican 4-cheese blend, divided	227 g

- In skillet, brown ground beef and drain. Add taco sauce, Spanish rice and half cheese. Spoon into buttered 3-quart (3 L) baking dish. Cover and bake at 350° (176° C) for 35 minutes. Uncover and sprinkle remaining cheese on top and return to oven for 5 minutes.

Yummy Creamy Pasta Shells

1¼ pounds lean ground beef	567 g
1 onion, chopped	
1 (10 ounce) can cream of celery soup	280 g
1 package shells and cheese sauce	

- In skillet, brown beef and onion and stir until beef crumbles.

- Add a little pepper and garlic salt if desired. Add soup and mix.

- Prepare shells and cheese according to package directions. Stir into beef mixture. Simmer for 20 minutes.

Cheesy Beefy Gnocchi

1 pound lean ground beef	.5 kg
1 (10 ounce) can cheddar cheese soup	280 g
1 (10 ounce) can tomato-bisque soup	280 g
2 cups uncooked gnocchi or shell pasta	480 ml

- In skillet, cook beef until brown and drain. Add soups, 1½ cups (360 ml) water and pasta. Bring mixture to a boil. Cover and cook over medium heat for 10 to 12 minutes, stirring often.

Tex-Mex Supper

1 pound lean ground beef	.5 kg
1 large onion, chopped	
1 (15 ounce) can pinto beans, drained	425 g
2 teaspoons cumin	10 ml
½ head lettuce, torn	
2 large tomatoes, chopped, drained	
2 avocado, peeled, diced	
1 (8 ounce) package shredded cheddar cheese	227 g
1 (10 ounce) package small chips	280 g
1 (8 ounce) bottle Catalina salad dressing	227 g

• Saute beef and onion in skillet. Drain grease and add beans, cumin, salt and pepper to taste and ½ cup (120 ml) water and simmer until water cooks out.

• In large serving bowl, combine lettuce, tomatoes and avocado and toss. When ready to serve, toss salad with warm beef mixture, cheese, chips and dressing. Serve immediately.

Quick Skillet Supper

1½ pounds lean ground beef	.7 kg
⅔ cup stir-fry sauce	160 ml
1 (16 ounce) package frozen stir-fry vegetables	.5 kg
2 (3 ounce) packages Oriental-flavor ramen noodles	2 (84 g)

• Brown and crumble ground beef in large skillet. Add 2½ cups (600 ml) water, stir-fry sauce to taste, vegetables and seasoning packets with ramen noodles. Cook and stir on low-medium heat about 5 minutes.

• Break noodles, add to beef-vegetable mixture and cook about 6 minutes. Stir to separate noodles as they soften.

Taco Pie Pan Bake

1 pound lean ground beef	.5 kg
1 (11 ounce) can mexicorn, drained	312 g
1 (8 ounce) can tomato sauce	227 g
1 (1.25 ounce) packet taco seasoning	38 g
1 (9-inch) frozen piecrust	23 cm
1 cup shredded cheddar cheese	240 ml

- Preheat oven to 350° (176° C). In large skillet, brown and cook ground beef until no longer pink. Stir in corn, tomato sauce and taco seasoning. Keep warm.

- Place piecrust in pie pan and bake 5 minutes. Remove from oven and spoon ground beef mixture onto piecrust, spreading evenly. Sprinkle cheese over top and bake another 20 minutes or until filling is bubbly. Let stand 5 minutes before slicing.

Potato-Beef Bake

1 pound ground beef	.5 kg
1 (10 ounce) can sloppy Joe sauce	280 g
1 (10 ounce) can fiesta nacho cheese soup	280 g
1 (32 ounce) package frozen hash brown potatoes,	
thawed	1 kg

- In skillet, cook beef over medium heat until no longer pink and drain. Add sloppy Joe sauce and fiesta nacho cheese soup.

- Place hash browns in greased 9 x 13-inch (23 x 33 cm) baking dish. Top with beef mixture. Cover and bake at 400° (204° C) for 25 minutes. Uncover and bake 10 minutes longer.

Southern Taco Pie

1 pound lean ground beef	.5 kg
1 large bell pepper, seeded, chopped	
2 jalapeno peppers, seeded, chopped	
1 (15 ounce) can Mexican stewed tomatoes	425 g
1 tablespoon chili powder	15 ml
1 (8 ounce) box corn muffin mix	227 g
1 egg	
⅓ cup milk	80 ml
1 (8 ounce) package shredded sharp cheddar cheese	227 g

- Brown ground beef, bell pepper and jalapeno peppers in large skillet with a little oil; drain. Stir in tomatoes, chili powder, ½ cup (120 ml) water and a little salt to taste. Cover and cook on medium heat for about 10 minutes or until most liquid cooks out, but not dry. Pour into greased 9 x 13-inch (23 x 33 cm) baking pan and sprinkle with cheese. Combine muffin mix, egg and milk and pour over meat mixture.

- Bake 20 minutes or until corn muffin mix is light brown.

Casserole Supper

1 pound lean ground beef	.5 kg
¼ cup uncooked white rice	60 ml
1 (10 ounce) can French onion soup	280 g
1 (3 ounce) can french-fried onion rings	84 g

- Brown ground beef, drain and place in buttered 7 x 11-inch (18 x 28 cm) baking dish. Add rice, onion soup and ½ cup (120 ml) water. Cover and bake at 325° (162° C) for 40 minutes. Uncover, sprinkle onion rings over top and return to oven for 10 minutes.

Beef Patties and Mushroom Gravy

1 pound lean ground beef	.5 kg
¼ cup chili sauce	60 ml
1 egg	
¾ cup crushed corn flakes	180 ml
2 (10 ounce) cans cream of mushroom soup	2 (280 g)

- In bowl, combine ground beef, chili sauce, egg, crushed corn flakes and salt and pepper to taste, mixing well. Shape into 4 patties, about ¾-inch (1.8 cm) thick.

- Place patties in skillet with a tiny bit of oil and on high heat, brown each patty on both sides. Reduce heat, cover and simmer for 10 to 15 minutes.

- Stir in both cans soup with ½ cup (120 ml) water, mixing well. Spoon gravy over patties and let simmer for about 10 minutes. This gravy is great served over mashed potatoes or hot biscuits.

Beef Patties in Creamy Onion Sauce

1½ pounds lean ground beef	.7 kg
⅓ cup salsa	80 ml
⅓ cup butter cracker crumbs	80 ml
1 (10 ounce) can cream of onion soup	280 g
Hot, cooked noodles	

- Combine beef, salsa and cracker crumbs and form into 5 to 6 patties. Brown in skillet and reduce heat. Add ¼ cup (60 ml) water and simmer for 15 minutes. In saucepan, combine onion soup and ½ cup (120 ml) water or milk, heat and mix. Pour over beef patties. Serve over hot, cooked noodles.

Mexican Casserole

1 (13 ounce) bag tortilla chips, divided	370 g
2 pounds lean ground beef	1 kg
1 (10 ounce) can Mexican stewed tomatoes	280 g
1 (8 ounce) package shredded Mexican 4-cheese blend	227 g

- Partially crush half bag chips and place in bottom of buttered 9 x 13-inch (23 x 33 cm) baking dish. Brown ground beef and drain.

- Add stewed tomatoes and cheese and mix well. Sprinkle finely crushed chips over casserole.

- Bake uncovered at 375° (190° C) for 30 minutes.

Speedy Steak Strombolis

1 (2 pound) package frozen pizza dough, thawed	1 kg
⅔ cup hot salsa	60 ml
½ pound sliced roast beef	227 g
1 (8 ounce) package cheddar cheese	227 g

- Preheat oven to 425° (220° C). On floured work surface, roll out half dough into 10 x 14-inch (25 x 36 cm) rectangle baking dish.

- Spread half of salsa over dough, leaving ½-inch (1.2 cm) border. Cover with half sliced roast beef and half cheese. Starting at long side, roll jellyroll style, pinching ends together. Place on greased baking sheet. Repeat with remaining ingredients for second roll. Bake 20 minutes or until light brown. Let cool about 20 minutes and slice to serve.

Steak with Horseradish Sauce

1 (2 pound) 1-inch thick sirloin steak	1 kg/2.5 cm
1 (8 ounce) carton sour cream	227 g
4 tablespoons horseradish	60 ml

- Preheat broiler. Pat steak dry and sprinkle liberally with salt and pepper. Broil steak on rack about 3 inches (8 cm) from heat for 5 minutes. Let stand 5 minutes before slicing. In bowl, combine sour cream, horseradish and a little salt and pepper, mixing well. Serve with sirloin steak.

Beef and Broccoli

1 pound beef sirloin steak	.5 kg
1 onion, chopped	
1 (10 ounce) can cream of broccoli soup	280 g
1 (10 ounce) package frozen chopped broccoli, thawed	280 g

- Slice beef across grain into very thin strips. In large skillet, brown steak strips and onion in a little oil and stir several times. Reduce heat and simmer for 10 minutes. Stir in soup and broccoli and heat. Serve over noodles.

Steak for Supper

1 pound round steak, cut in strips	.5 kg
1 (14 ounce) can beef broth	396 g
3 tablespoons cornstarch	45 ml
1 tablespoon soy sauce	15 ml
1 red and 1 green bell pepper, julienned	

- In large skillet brown steak strips; reduce heat, add ⅓ cup (80 ml) water, cover and simmer until liquid evaporates. Combine beef broth, cornstarch and soy sauce and pour over steak strips. Add bell peppers, stirring until mixture boils and thickens. Serve over hot, cooked rice.

Skillet Steak and Veggies

1 pound boneless sirloin steak, cut in strips	.5 kg
2 (15 ounce) cans Italian stewed tomatoes with liquid	2 (425 g)
1 (16 ounce) package frozen Italian green beans, thawed	.5 kg
1 (8 ounce) carton sour cream	227 g
Hot, cooked egg noodles	

• Place sirloin strips in large skillet with a little oil. Cook on high heat about 10 minutes. Add stewed tomatoes and green beans, bring to boiling, lower heat and cook 10 minutes.

• Just before serving, fold in sour cream. Serve over egg noodles.

Easy Salisbury Steak

1¼ pounds lean ground beef	567 g
½ cup flour	120 ml
1 egg	
1 (10 ounce) can beef gravy	280 g
Hot, cooked rice or noodles	

• In large bowl, combine beef, flour and egg. Add a little salt and pepper and mix well. Shape into 5 patties and place in shallow 7 x 11-inch (18 x 28 cm) baking dish.

• Bake uncovered at 350° (176° C) for 20 minutes and drain off any fat. Pour beef gravy over patties. Bake another 20 minutes. Serve with rice or noodles.

Thai Beef, Noodles And Veggies

2 (4.4 ounce) packages Thai sesame noodles	2 (128 g)
1 pound sirloin steak, cut in strips	.5 kg
1 (16 ounce) package frozen stir-fry vegetables, thawed	.5 kg
½ cup chopped peanuts	120 ml

• Cook noodles according to package directions, remove from heat and cover. Season sirloin strips with a little salt and pepper.

• Brown half sirloin strips in a little oil in skillet and cook about 2 minutes. Remove from skillet and drain. Add remaining sirloin strips, brown in skillet with a little oil and cook about 2 minutes.

• In same skillet place vegetables and ½ cup (120 ml) water, cover and cook 5 minutes or until tender-crisp. Remove from heat, add steak strips and toss to mix. To serve, sprinkle with chopped peanuts.

Skillet Sirloin

2 teaspoons oil	10 ml
2 teaspoons minced garlic	10 ml
½ teaspoon cayenne pepper	2 ml
2 tablespoons soy sauce	30 ml
2 tablespoons honey	30 ml
1 pound beef sirloin, thinly sliced	.5 kg

• Combine oil, garlic, cayenne pepper, soy sauce and honey and place in plastic freezer bag. Add sliced beef, seal and shake; refrigerate for 25 minutes. Place beef mixture in large greased skillet over medium-high heat and cook 5 to 6 minutes or until desired doneness, but do not over-cook. Serve over cooked rice.

Pepper Steak

1 (1¼ pound) sirloin steak, cut into strips	567 g
1 (16 ounce) package frozen bell pepper and onion strips, thawed	.5 kg
1 (16 ounce) package cubed Mexican processed cheese	.5 kg
Hot, cooked rice	

- Sprinkle steak with a little salt. Coat large skillet with non-stick vegetable spray. Cook steak strips about 10 minutes or until no longer pink. Remove steak from skillet and set aside.

- Stir in vegetables and ½ cup (120 ml) water. Simmer vegetables about 5 minutes until all liquid cooks out.

- Add cheese. Stir over low heat until cheese melts. Stir in steak and serve over rice.

Ginger Grilled Steak

1½ pound flank-steak	.7 kg
¼ cup low-sodium soy sauce	60 ml
¼ cup sugar	60 ml
¼ cup ketchup	60 ml
3 tablespoons cider vinegar	45 ml
1 tablespoon bottled ground fresh ginger	15 ml
¼ teaspoon cayenne pepper	1 ml

- Place flank-steak in a large baggie and pour the ¼ cup (60 ml) soy sauce over steak. Seal but move steak around getting soy sauce over all of steak.

- In bowl, combine sugar, ketchup, vinegar, ginger and cayenne pepper. Place steak on hot grill and cook about 5 minutes on each side, basting several times during cooking. Cut steak diagonally across grain; drizzle with remaining sauce mixture.

Grilled Steak with Garlic-Mustard Sauce

⅓ cup apple juice	80 ml
2 tablespoons dijon-style mustard	30 ml
1 tablespoon minced garlic	15 ml
4 (1-inch) thick boneless beef top strip steaks	4 (2.5 cm)

- Combine apple juice, mustard, garlic and 1 teaspoon (5 ml) pepper in bowl, and mix well. Remove and reserve ¼ cup (60 ml) sauce for basting. Brush steaks with remaining sauce.

- Grill steaks on grill over medium hot coals. Grill about 15 to 18 minutes or until desired doneness and turn occasionally.

- During last 8 to 10 minutes of grilling, baste steaks with the ¼ cup (60 ml) sauce set aside for basting.

Barbecued Pizza

1 (12-inch) purchased pizza crust	32 cm
1 (12 ounce) package Mexican style shredded cheese, divided	340 g
1 pound cooked and shredded barbecue	.5 kg
1 (4 ounce) sliced ripe olives, drained	114 g

- Preheat oven to 400° (204° C). Place pizza crust on baking sheet and sprinkle on half of cheese. Spread the shredded barbecue beef over top of cheese and sprinkle remaining cheese over top. Arrange olives over top of pizza.

- Bake 5 to 10 minutes or until hot and bubbly.

Texas Chili Pie

2 (20 ounce) cans chili without beans	2 (567 g)
1 (13 ounce) package small corn chips	370 g
1 onion, chopped	
1 (16 ounce) package shredded cheddar cheese	.5 kg

- Heat chili in saucepan. In 9 x 13-inch (23 x 33 cm) baking dish, layer corn chips, chili, onion and cheese one-third at a time. Repeat layers with cheese on top. Bake at 325° (162° C) for 20 minutes or until cheese bubbles.

Top-Notch Hot Dogs

10 (8-inch) flour tortillas	10 (20 cm)
10 beef hot dogs	
1 (15 ounce) can chili with beans, slightly heated	425 g
1 (16 ounce) can thick-and-chunky salsa	.5 kg
1 (8 ounce) package Mexican-style shredded cheese	227 g

- Preheat oven to 325° (162° C). Grease a 9 x 13-inch (23 x 33 cm) baking dish. Soften tortillas as directed on package.

- Place 1 hot dog and about 3 tablespoons (45 ml) chili on each tortilla and roll tortillas. Place seam-side down on baking dish. Pour salsa over tortillas. Cover with foil and bake 25 minutes. Remove from oven, uncover and sprinkle cheese over tortillas. Return to oven for 5 minutes.

Chihuahua Dogs

1 (10 ounce) can chili hot dog sauce	280 g
1 (10 count) package frankfurters	
10 pre-formed taco shells	
Shredded cheddar cheese	

- Place hot dog sauce in saucepan. Place frank in each taco shell. Top with heated chili sauce and cheese. Place in microwave and heat for 30 seconds or until frankfurters warm.

Winter Chili Supper

1 (40 ounce) can chili with beans	1.1 kg
1 (7 ounce) can chopped green chilies	198 g
1 bunch fresh green onions, sliced	
1 (8 ounce) package shredded Mexican 4-cheese blend	227 g
2½ cups crushed ranch-flavored tortilla chips, divided	600 ml

- Preheat oven to 350° (176° C). Combine chili, green chilies, onions, cheese and 2 cups (480 ml) crushed chips. Transfer to greased 3-quart (3 L) baking dish and bake 20 minutes.

- Remove from oven and sprinkle remaining chips over top of casserole and continue baking another 10 minutes.

Corny Chili and Beans

2 (15 ounce) cans chili with beans	2 (425 g)
1 (15 ounce) can Mexican-style stewed tomatoes	425 g
1 (11 ounce) can mexicorn, drained	312 g
2 diced ripe avocados	

- Combine chili, tomatoes and corn in microwave-safe bowl. Cover loosely and cook on high in microwave for about 4 minutes. Stir in diced avocados and serve hot.

Pan-Fried Liver and Onions

Calf liver	Canola Oil
Flour	2 large onions

- Slice calf liver in ¼-inch (.6 cm) thick. Season calf liver slices with salt and dredge with flour in shallow bowl. Brown both sides in small amount of oil in heavy skillet. Slice onions and separate into rings. Place rings on top of liver, cover and simmer for 20 minutes.

Quick-Friday-Night-Game Supper

2 (15 ounce) cans chili without beans	2 (425 g)
2 (15 ounce) cans pinto beans with liquid	2 (425 g)
2 (15 ounce) cans beef tamales without shucks	2 (425 g)
1 (8 ounce) package shredded Mexican 4-cheese	
blend, divided	227 g

- Preheat oven to 350° (176° C). In greased 9 x 13-inch (23 x 33 cm) baking pan, spoon both cans chili in pan and spread out with back of large spoon. Spread beans with liquid over chili. Spread tamales over beans. Sprinkle about ½ cup (120 ml) cheese over top, cover and bake 30 minutes. Sprinkle remaining cheese over top of casserole and bake for 5 minutes.

Zippy Tomato Sauce for Meat Loaf

1 (8 ounce) can tomato sauce	227 g
3 tablespoons brown sugar	45 ml
1 tablespoon vinegar	15 ml
1 tablespoon Worcestershire sauce	15 ml

- In saucepan, combine all ingredients and heat, stirring constantly until mixture is thoroughly hot. Mixture may be spooned over meatloaf last 10 minutes of cooking time or spooned over each serving.

White Barbecue for Brisket

1½ cups mayonnaise	.7 kg
¼ cup white wine vinegar	60 ml
1 tablespoon Creole mustard	15 ml
1 tablespoon each horseradish and minced garlic	15 ml
1 teaspoon sugar	5 ml

- In bowl, combine all barbecue ingredients and use as a marinade for the brisket or use it for basting the brisket. Bake or grill as you normally would when cooking a brisket.

Tortellini-Ham Supper

2 (9 ounce) packages fresh tortellini	2 (255 g)
1 (16 ounce) package frozen green peas, thawed	.5 kg
1 (16 ounce) jar alfredo sauce	.5 kg
2 - 3 cups cubed ham	480 ml

- Cook tortellini according to package directions. Add green peas about 5 minutes before tortellini are done and drain. In saucepan, combine alfredo sauce and ham; heat until thoroughly hot. Toss with tortellini and peas. Serve immediately.

Supper-in-a-Dish

2 (9 ounce) packages instant rice-in-a-bag	2 (255 g)
1½ cups cubed, cooked ham	360 ml
1½ cups shredded cheddar cheese	360 ml
1 (8 ounce) can green peas, drained	227 g

- Prepare rice according to package directions. In large bowl, combine rice, ham, cheese and peas. Pour into 3-quart (3 L) baking dish and bake at 350° (176° C) for 15 to 20 minutes.

Mustard Ham

1 (1-inch) center slice of cooked ham	2.5 cm
2 teaspoons of dry mustard	10 ml
⅓ cup honey	80 ml
⅓ cup cooking wine	80 ml

- Rub ham slice with 1 teaspoon (5 ml) mustard for each side. Place in shallow baking pan. Combine honey and wine; pour over ham. Bake uncovered at 350° (176° C) for 30 minutes.

Cherry Best Ham

1 (½-inch/1.2 cm) center-cut ham slice
⅔ cup cherry preserves   160 ml
½ teaspoon ground cinnamon   2 ml
⅓ cup chopped walnuts   80 ml

- Preheat oven to 325° (162° C). Place ham slice on 9 x 13-inch (23 x 33 cm) pyrex baking dish. Spread preserves over ham and sprinkle cinnamon over preserves. Top with chopped walnuts. Bake uncovered for 20 minutes.

The Perfect Potato

4 large baking potato, baked
4 tablespoons each butter and sour cream   60 ml
1 cup finely chopped ham (leftover or deli)   240 ml
1 (10 ounce) package frozen broccoli florets,
    coarsely chopped   280 g
1 cup shredded sharp cheddar cheese   240 ml

- Preheat oven to 400° (204° C). Slit potatoes down center, but not through to bottom. For each potato, use 1 tablespoon (15 ml) of butter and sour cream. With fork, work in ¼ cup (60 ml) ham, one-fourth broccoli and ¼ cup (60 ml) cheese. Before serving, place potatoes on baking sheet and heat for 10 minutes.

Peach-Pineapple Baked Ham

4 tablespoons dijon-style mustard, divided   60 ml
1 (3 - 4) pound boneless smoked ham   1.3 kg
1 cup each peach and pineapple preserves   240 ml

- Preheat oven to 325° (162° C). Spread 2 tablespoons (30 ml) mustard on ham. Place ham in prepared, shallow baking pan and bake for 20 minutes. Combine remaining 2 tablespoons (30 ml) mustard and both preserves and heat microwave oven for 20 seconds. Pour over ham and bake another 20 minutes.

Sweet Potato Ham

1 (16 ounce) ½-inch thick, center cut fully cooked ham slice	.5 kg (1.2 cm)
1 (15 ounce) can sweet potatoes, drained	425 g
½ cup packed brown sugar	120 ml
⅓ cup chopped pecans	80 ml

- Cut outer edge of ham fat at 1-inch (2.5 cm) intervals to prevent curling, but do not cut into ham. Place on 10-inch (25 cm) microwave-safe pie plate and broil with top 5 inches (13 cm) from heat for 5 minutes.

- Mash each piece of sweet potato in bowl with fork just once (not totally mashed) and add brown sugar, a little salt and chopped pecans, mix well. Spoon mixture over ham slice and cook at 350° (176° C) for 15 minutes.

Fruit-Covered Ham Slice

2 (15 ounce) cans fruit cocktail with juice	2 (425 g)
½ cup packed brown sugar	120 ml
2 tablespoons cornstarch	30 ml
1 (½-inch/1.2 cm) thick center-cut ham slice	

- Combine fruit cocktail, brown sugar and cornstarch and mix well. Cook about 15 minutes on medium heat, stirring frequently, until sauce thickens.

- Place ham slice in large non-stick skillet on medium heat. Cook about 5 minutes or just until ham thoroughly heats.

- Spoon fruit sauce over ham.

Stove-Top Ham Supper

1 (12 ounce) package spiral pasta	340 g
3 tablespoons butter, cut in slices	45 ml
2 - 3 cups cooked, cubed ham (leftover or deli)	480 ml
1 teaspoon minced garlic	5 ml
1 (10 ounce) package frozen green peas	280 g
½ cup sour cream	120 ml
1 (8 ounce) package shredded cheddar cheese, divided	227 g

• Preheat oven to 375° (190° C). Cook pasta in large saucepan, according to package directions, drain, while still hot, stir in butter. Add ham, garlic and 1 teaspoon (5 ml) seasoned salt.

• Cook peas in microwave according to package directions and stir, undrained into pasta-ham mixture. Stir in sour cream and half cheese, mix until well blended. Spoon into buttered 3-quart (3 l) baking dish. Bake 15 minutes or just until bubbly around edges. Sprinkle remaining cheese on top and let cheese melt.

Honey-Ham Slice

⅓ cup orange juice	80 ml
⅓ cup honey	80 ml
1 teaspoon prepared mustard	5 ml
1 (1-inch) thick slice fully cooked ham	2.5 cm

• Combine orange juice, honey and mustard in saucepan and cook slowly for 10 minutes, stir occasionally. Place ham in broiling pan about 3 inches (8 cm) from heat. Brush with orange glaze. Broil for 8 minutes on first side. Turn ham slice over. Brush with glaze again and broil for another 6 to 8 minutes.

Ham Quesadillas

2 cups shredded (leftover or deli) ham	480 ml
½ cup chunky salsa	120 ml
2 teaspoons chili powder	10 ml
¾ cup whole kernel corn	180 ml
1 (8 ounce) package shredded Mexican 4-cheese blend	227 g
8 large whole-wheat tortillas	

- In large bowl, combine shredded ham, salsa, chili powder and corn. Spread mixture over 4 tortillas to within ½-inch (1.2 cm) of edge and sprinkle cheese on top.

- Top with remaining tortillas and cook (1 at a time) on medium-high heat, in large non-stick skillet about 5 minutes, turning after 2 minutes or until light golden brown. Cut in wedges and serve with pinto beans and guacamole.

Cran-Apple Ham

1 cup apple juice, divided	240 ml
1 tablespoon cornstarch	15 ml
1 cup whole cranberry sauce	240 ml
1 center-cut (½-inch) thick ham slice	1.2 cm

- In medium saucepan over low heat, pour ¼ cup (60 ml) apple juice and cornstarch and stir until cornstarch is smooth. Add remaining apple juice. With medium heat, bring to boil and cook, stirring constantly, until mixture clears and thickens.

- Stir in cranberry sauce and heat for 2 to 3 minutes, stirring often.

- Place ham slice in shallow baking pan. Spread sauce over ham slice, bake at 350° (176° C) for 25 minutes and baste ham with sauce 2 to 3 times.

Broiled Ham with Sweet Potatoes

1 (½-inch thick) fully cooked, center-cut ham slice	1.2 cm
1 (15 ounce) can sweet potatoes, drained	425 g
⅔ cup packed brown sugar	160 ml
2 tablespoons melted butter	30 ml
1 teaspoon ground cinnamon	5 ml

- Slit edges of fat on ham slice at 1-inch (2.5 cm) intervals to prevent curling. Place ham on broiler pan and broil about 5 minutes.

- Spoon sweet potatoes into shallow dish and mash with fork and stir in brown sugar, butter and cinnamon. Spoon sweet potato mixture over ham and place under broiler. Broil about 5 minutes or until sweet potatoes are hot and beginning to brown.

Mac Cheese Casserole

4 eggs	
1½ cups milk	360 ml
12 ounces macaroni, cooked	340 g
1 (8 ounce) package shredded cheddar cheese	227 g
2 cups deli (or leftover) ham, cubed	480 ml
¾ cup seasoned breadcrumbs	180 ml

- Preheat oven to 350° (176° C). In large bowl, lightly beat eggs and milk with salt and pepper to taste. Stir in macaroni, cheese and ham. Spoon into buttered 7 x 11-inch (18 x 28 cm) baking dish and bake uncovered for 30 minutes.

Ham and Sweet Potatoes

3 tablespoons dijon-style mustard, divided	45 ml
1 (3 - 4 pound) boneless smoked ham	1.3 kg
½ cup packed brown sugar	120 ml
1 (29 ounce) can sweet potatoes, drained or	805 g
4 unpeeled, cooked sweet potatoes, quartered	

- Preheat oven at 350° (176° C). Spread 2 tablespoons (30 ml) mustard on ham. Place ham in prepared shallow baking pan and bake for 20 minutes. Combine remaining mustard with brown sugar and spread over ham. Add sweet potatoes, baste ham with sauce and bake for 15 minutes.

A Different Macaroni

1 cup uncooked shell macaroni	240 ml
½ cup heavy cream	120 ml
8 ounces shredded gorgonzola cheese	227 g
1 (10 ounce) package frozen green peas, thawed	280 g
2 cups cubed ham (deli or leftover)	480 ml

- Cook macaroni according to package directions and drain. Stir in cream and cheese, stirring until cheese melts. Fold in peas and ham and cook on low heat, stirring constantly, until mixture is hot.

Ham and Veggies

1 (16 ounce) package frozen mixed vegetables	.5 kg
2 (10 ounce) cans cream of celery soup	2 (280 g)
2 cups cubed, cooked ham	480 ml
½ teaspoon dried basil	2 ml
1 (22 ounce) package frozen buttermilk biscuits	624 g

- Cook vegetables according to package directions. Add soup, ham and basil. Bake biscuits according to package directions. Cut in half and spoon vegetable-ham mixture over biscuits.

Ham and Vegetable Supper

1½ cups dry corkscrew macaroni	360 ml
1 (16 ounce) package frozen broccoli, cauliflower and carrots	.5 kg
1 (10 ounce) can broccoli cheese soup	280 g
1 (3 ounce) package cream cheese with chives, softened	84 g
¾ cup milk	180 ml
1 (8 ounce) package cubed processed cheese	227 g
1 tablespoon dijon-style mustard	15 ml
2 cups cooked, cubed ham	480 ml

- In large saucepan, cook macaroni according to package directions. For last 5 minutes of cooking time, bring back to boiling, add vegetables and cook remaining 5 minutes. Drain in colander.

- In same saucepan, combine soup, cream cheese, milk, cheese and mustard over low heat, stirring until cream cheese melts. Gently stir in ham, macaroni-vegetable mixture and salt and pepper to taste, heat stirring often. Transfer to 3-quart (3 L) serving dish.

Hot Spiced Cherries for Baked Ham

1 (15 ounce) can pitted red sour cherries	425 g
1 (15 ounce) can crushed pineapple	425 g
2 tablespoons cornstarch	30 ml
½ cup sugar	2 ml
½ teaspoon allspice	2 ml

- Drain cherries and pineapple, reserving juices; set aside cherries and pineapple.

- In saucepan, combine cornstarch, sugar and allspice. Over medium heat, add reserved juices, stirring constantly and cook until mixture is thick and clear. Stir in cherries and pineapple and serve with baked ham.

Sweet-and-Sour Glaze for Ham or Wieners

1 (6 ounce) jar yellow mustard	168 g
1 (12 ounce) jar grape or plum jelly	340 g

- In saucepan, combine mustard and jelly and heat. Stir until mixture is smooth.

Baked Pork Chops

¾ cup ketchup   180 ml
¾ cup packed brown sugar   180 ml
¼ cup lemon juice   60 ml
4 butter-flied pork chops

- Combine ketchup, ½ cup (120 ml) water, brown sugar and lemon juice. Place pork chops in 7 x 11-inch (18 x 28 cm) buttered baking dish and pour sauce over pork chops.

- Bake covered at 350° (176° C) for 30 minutes. Uncover and continue cooking another 10 minutes.

Yee-Ha Pork Chops

1 (1 ounce) packet taco seasoning   28 g
4 (½-inch) boneless pork loin chops   4 (1.2 cm)
1 tablespoon oil   15 ml
Salsa

- Rub taco seasoning over pork chops. In skillet, brown pork chops in oil over medium heat.

- Add 2 tablespoons (30 ml) water, turn heat to low and simmer pork chops about 35 minutes. (Add water if needed.) Spoon salsa over pork chops to serve.

Stuffed Pork Chops

4 (1-inch) thick boneless center-cut pork chops	4 (2.5 cm)
2 slices rye bread, diced	
⅓ cup chopped each onion and celery	80 ml
⅓ cup dried apples, diced	80 ml
⅓ cup chicken broth	80 ml
½ teaspoon dried thyme	2 ml

- Preheat oven to 400° (204° C). Make 1-inch (2.5 cm) wide slit on side of each chop and insert knife blade to other side, but not through pork chop. Sweep knife back and forth and carefully cut pocket opening larger.

- In bowl, combine rye bread pieces, onion, celery, apples, broth and thyme and mix well. Stuff chops with stuffing mixture and press to use all stuffing mixture in pork chops.

- Place chops in heavy skillet with a little oil and saute each chop about 3 minutes on each side. Transfer to non-stick baking dish and bake uncovered for 15 minutes.

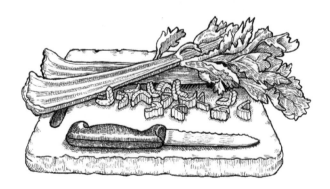

Sweet and Savory Pork Chops

4 - 6 (1-inch) thick boneless pork chops, trimmed	4 - 6 (2.5 cm)
½ cup grape, apple or plum jelly	120 ml
½ cup chili sauce or hot ketchup	120 ml

• Brown pork chops and season to taste with salt and pepper.
  Transfer browned pork chops to shallow baking dish, cover and
  place in oven and bake at 325° (162° C) for 15 minutes. Combine
  jelly and chili sauce or ketchup and spread over pork chops.
  Cook for 10 minutes, baste with sauce and cook another 15
  minutes more or until pork chops are tender.

Spicy Pork Chops

4 - 6 pork chops	
1 large onion	
1 bell pepper	
1 (10 ounce) can diced tomatoes and green chilies	280 g

• Brown pork chops in skillet with a little oil. Spray baking dish
  with non-stick spray. Place chops in dish. Cut onion and bell
  pepper into large chunks and place on chops. Pour tomato and
  green chilies over chops and sprinkle with 1 teaspoon (5 ml) salt
  over casserole. Bake covered at 350° (176° C) for 30 minutes.

Smoky Grilled Pork Chops

1 cup mayonnaise (not light)	240 ml
2 tablespoons lime juice	30 ml
1 teaspoon ground cilantro and chili powder	5 ml
2 teaspoons minced garlic	10 ml
8 (1-inch) thick bone-in, pork chops	8 (2.5 cm)

• Combine mayonnaise, lime juice, cilantro, chili powder and garlic
  and mix. Set ½ cup (120 ml) aside. Grill or broil pork chops
  6 minutes on each side and brush with ½ cup (120 ml) sauce.
  Serve remaining ½ cup (120 ml) sauce.

Skillet Pork Chops

⅔ cup baking mix	160 ml
½ cup crushed saltine crackers	120 ml
1 egg	
6 boneless (½-inch) thick pork chops	6 (1.2 cm)

- In shallow bowl, combine baking mix, crushed crackers and a generous amount of salt and pepper. In another shallow bowl, beat egg with 2 tablespoons (30 ml) water. Heat skillet with small amount of oil. Dip each pork chop in egg mixture and then in cracker mixture. Place in heated skillet and cook 8 to 10 minutes on each side.

Glazed-Grilled Pork Chops

1 cup mayonnaise	240 ml
2 tablespoons lime juice	30 ml
2 tablespoons chopped fresh cilantro	30 ml
1 teaspoon chili powder	5 ml
8 (½-inch) thick pork chops	8 (1.2 cm)

- Combine mayonnaise, lime juice, cilantro and chili powder and blend well. Reserve ½ cup (120 ml) and use remaining glaze to brush over pork chops while grilling.

Tangy Pork Chops

4 - 6 pork chops	
¼ cup Worcestershire sauce	60 ml
¼ cup ketchup	60 ml
½ cup honey	120 ml

- In skillet, brown pork chops. Place in shallow baking dish. Combine Worcestershire, ketchup and honey. Pour over pork chops. Cover and bake at 325° (162° C) for 20 minutes; uncover and bake another 15 minutes.

Saucy Pork Chops

4 (½-inch) thick pork chops	4 (1.2 cm)
1 tablespoon oil	15 ml
1 (10 ounce) can cream of onion soup	280 g
2 tablespoons soy sauce	30 ml

- In skillet, brown pork chops in oil and cook chops about 15 minutes and drain. Remove chops from skillet. Add soup and soy sauce. Heat to boil. Return chops to skillet. Reduce heat to low. Cover and simmer about 20 minutes.

"Giddy-Up" Pork Chops

6 boneless pork chops	
½ cup salsa	120 ml
½ cup honey or packed brown sugar	120 ml
1 teaspoon soy sauce	5 ml

- Brown pork chops in ovenproof pan. Combine salsa, honey or brown sugar and soy sauce and heat for 20 to 30 seconds in microwave. Pour salsa mixture over pork chops, cover and bake at 350° (176° C) for about 35 minutes or until pork chops are tender.

Potato-Pork Chops

6 boneless loin pork chops	
1 (14 ounce) can chicken broth	396 g
2 (1 ounce) packet dry onion gravy mix	2 (28 g)
6 red potatoes, thickly sliced	

- Season pork chops with a little pepper and brown in large skillet with a little oil. Combine chicken broth, gravy mix and ¾ cup (180 ml) water. Add potatoes to skillet with pork chops and cover with gravy mixture. Heat to a boil, reduce heat, cover and simmer 35 minutes or until pork chops and potatoes are tender.

Pork Chops with Black Bean Salsa

2 teaspoons chili powder	10 ml
2 tablespoons vegetable oil	30 ml
6 thin-cut, boneless pork chops	
1 (15 ounce) can black beans, rinsed, drained	425 g
1 (24 ounce) refrigerated citrus fruit, drained	680 g
1 ripe avocado, sliced	
⅔ cup Italian salad dressing	160 ml

- Combine chili powder and ½ teaspoon (2 ml) salt. Rub oil over pork chops, sprinkle chili powder mixture over chops and rub into meat. Place in skillet over medium heat and cook pork chops about 5 minutes on both sides.

- For salsa, combine beans, fruit and avocado and toss with salad dressing. Serve with pork chops.

Parmesan Covered Pork Chops

½ cup grated parmesan cheese	120 ml
⅔ cup Italian seasoned dried breadcrumbs	160 ml
1 egg	
4 - 5 thin-cut pork chops	

- Combine cheese and dried breadcrumbs in shallow bowl. Beat egg with 1 teaspoon (5 ml) water on shallow plate.

- Dip each pork chop in beaten egg then into breadcrumb mixture.

- Cook over medium-high heat in skillet with a little oil for about 5 minutes on each side or until golden brown.

Curried-Orange Pork Chops

¾ teaspoon curry powder, divided	4 ml
½ teaspoon paprika	2 ml
4 (½-inch) thick center-cut boneless pork chops	4 (1.2 cm)
Hot, cooked couscous	
½ cup orange marmalade	120 ml
1 heaping teaspoon horseradish	5 ml
1 teaspoon balsamic vinegar	5 ml
teaspoon cayenne pepper	.5 ml

• Combine ¼ teaspoon (1 ml) curry powder, paprika and ½ teaspoon (2 ml) salt and sprinkle over pork chops. Place chops in skillet on medium-high heat and cook 5 minutes on each side. Transfer chops to plate.

• In same skillet, combine remaining ½ teaspoon (2 ml) curry powder, marmalade, horseradish, vinegar and cayenne pepper. Cook this mixture for 1 minute and scrape pan to loosen browned bits in skillet.

• Spoon sauce over pork chops. Serve over couscous.

Pork-Potato Chop

6 boneless or loin pork chops	
1 (14 ounce) can chicken broth	396 g
2 (1 ounce) packets dry onion gravy mix	2 (28 g)
4 red potatoes, sliced	

• Brown pork chops in large skillet. Combine chicken broth and gravy mix. Place potatoes with pork chops and pour gravy mixture over pork chops and potatoes. Heat to boiling, cover and simmer about 35 minutes or until pork chops and potatoes are fork-tender.

Pork Chops with Ginger-Soy Sauce

Sauce:
¾ cup chili sauce	180 ml
2 teaspoons minced garlic	10 ml
1 tablespoon minced fresh ginger	15 ml
2 tablespoons Worcestershire sauce	30 ml

Pork Chops:
1 large egg, beaten	
¾ cup seasoned breadcrumbs	180 ml
2 tablespoons oil	30 ml
4 (¾-inch) thick boneless pork chops	4 (1.8 cm)

- In small bowl, combine all sauce ingredients and set aside for flavors to blend. Place egg with 1 tablespoon (15 ml) water, in shallow bowl. Place breadcrumbs in another shallow bowl. In skillet on medium heat, pour in oil.

- Dip each chop in beaten egg first, dredge in breadcrumbs and coat well. Cook in skillet about 5 minutes on each side. Serve with ginger-soy sauce.

Chops and Stuffing

1 (6 ounce) box savory herb stuffing mix	168 g
6 center-cut pork chops	
3 onions, halved	

- Make stuffing according to package directions and set aside.

- Fry pork chops in skillet with little oil. Brown chops on both sides and place in greased 9 x 13-inch (23 x 33 cm) baking dish.

- Divide stuffing and onions among pork chops and mound on top of each. Cover and bake at 350° (176° C) for about 30 minutes.

Pork Chops in Cream Gravy

4 (¼-inch) thick pork chops	4 (.6 cm)
Flour	
2¼ cups milk	540 ml
Hot, cooked noodles	

- Dip chops in flour with a little salt and pepper. Brown pork chops on both sides in a little oil. Remove chops from skillet.

- Add about 2 tablespoons (30 ml) flour to skillet, brown lightly and stir in a little salt and pepper. Slowly stir in milk to make gravy. Return chops to skillet with gravy. Cover and simmer on low burner for about 35 minutes. Serve over noodles.

Pork Chop Supper

1 (18 ounce) package smoked pork chops	510 g
1 (12 ounce) jar pork gravy	240 g
¼ cup milk	60 ml
1 (12 ounce) package very small new potatoes	340 g

- Brown pork chops in large skillet with a little oil. Pour gravy and milk or water into skillet and stir mixture around chops until mixed well. Add new potatoes around chops and gravy. Cover and simmer on medium heat for about 20 minutes.

Mexicali Pork Chops

1 (1 ounce) packet taco seasoning	28 g
4 (½-inch) thick boneless pork loin chops	4 (1.2 cm)
1 tablespoon oil	15 ml
Salsa	

- Rub taco seasoning over pork chops. In skillet, brown pork chops in oil over medium heat. Add 2 tablespoons (30 ml) water, turn heat to low, cover and simmer pork chops for 35 minutes. Add to more water if needed. Spoon salsa over pork chops.

Crunchy Pork Chops

1 cup crushed saltine crackers	240 ml
¼ cup biscuit mix	60 ml
1 egg, beaten	
5 - 6 boneless ½-inch thick pork chops	1.2 cm

- In shallow bowl, combine crushed crackers, biscuit mix and ¾ teaspoon (4 ml) seasoned salt. In second shallow bowl, combine beaten egg and 2 tablespoons (30 ml) water.

- Dip pork chops into egg mixture and dredge in cracker mixture. Heat a little oil in heavy skillet and cook pork chops about 15 minutes, turning once.

Apple Pork Chops

4 butter-flied pork chops	
2 apples, peeled, cored, halved	
2 teaspoons butter	10 ml
2 tablespoons brown sugar	30 ml

- Place pork chops in non-stick sprayed shallow baking dish. Season with salt and pepper. Cover and bake at 350° (176° C) for 30 minutes. Uncover and place apple halves on top of pork chops. Add a little butter and a little brown sugar on each apple.

- Bake for another 10 minutes.

Pineapple Salsa for Pork Chops

1 (20 ounce) can pineapple tidbits, drained	567 g
¼ cup balsamic vinegar	60 ml
⅓ cup maple syrup	80 ml
2 tablespoons Asian sesame oil	30 ml

- In saucepan, combine all ingredients. Bring mixture to a boil, lower heat and simmer for 5 minutes. Serve with grilled pork chops.

Pork Chop and Fried Rice

4 - 6 boneless pork chops
1 (11 ounce) box fried rice mix   312 g
⅓ cup frozen peas   80 ml
3 green onions with tops, sliced

- Dry pork chops and brown over medium heat in preheated, prepared large skillet. Add ¼ cup (60 ml) water and simmer until tender, adding water if needed.

- Remove pork chops from skillet and keep warm. In medium bowl, mix fried rice and ½ cup (120 ml) water. Add fried rice to skillet and heat for 10 minutes.

- Add peas and green onions to rice and cook an additional 5 minutes or until peas are tender-crisp.

Rosemary Pork Tenderloin

¼ cup finely chopped fresh rosemary   60 ml
2 teaspoons minced garlic   10 ml
2 (about 1 pound each) pork tenderloins   2 (.5 kg)

- Preheat oven to 450° (230° C). In small bowl, combine rosemary and minced garlic, mixing well. Make several deep slits in tenderloin and rub rosemary-garlic mixture into tenderloin. Sprinkle liberally with salt and pepper and place on greased baking pan. Bake uncovered for 20 minutes. Let stand for 10 minutes before slicing.

Spicy Glazed Pork Tenderloin

½ cup orange juice	120 ml
¼ cup lime juice	60 ml
½ cup packed brown sugar	120 ml
1 teaspoon each ground cumin and cayenne pepper	5 ml
2 (1 pound) pork tenderloins	2 (.5 kg)

- In a small bowl, combine orange juice, lime juice, brown sugar, cumin and cayenne pepper.

- Pat tenderloins dry with paper towels and season with salt and pepper. In large skillet over medium-high heat, place a little oil. Cook tenderloins, turning until browned on all sides, about 9 to 10 minutes total. Reduce heat to medium and add orange juice mixture and cook, rolling tenderloins to coat, until mixture is thick and syrupy, about 10 minutes

- Transfer to cutting board and cover tenderloins with foil and let rest 10 minutes before slicing crosswise into ½-inch (1.2 cm) slices. Arrange on serving plate and pour glaze over slices.

Pork Picante

1 pound pork tenderloin, cubed	.5 kg
2 tablespoons taco seasoning	30 ml
1 cup chunky salsa	240 ml
⅓ cup peach preserves	80 ml
Hot, cooked rice	

- Toss pork with taco seasoning and brown with a little oil in skillet. Stir in salsa and preserves. Bring to a boil.

- Lower heat and simmer 30 minutes. Pour over rice.

Rub for Pork Tenderloins

1 teaspoon chili powder	5 ml
1 teaspoon ground cumin	5 ml
1 teaspoon each Italian seasoning and garlic powder	5 ml
1 tablespoon oil	15 ml
1 package (about 2 pound) 2 pork tenderloins	1 kg

- Combine all seasoning mix plus 1 teaspoon (5 ml) salt and stir in oil. Rub on both tenderloins.

- Preheat oven to 425° (220° C). Place tenderloins on foil lined baking pan that has been sprayed with cooking spray. Roast for 25 minutes or until meat thermometer in tenderloins registers 160° (71° C). Slice after 5 minutes.

Pork and Veggie Stir-Fry

2 (12 ounce) whole pork tenderloins, thinly sliced	2 (340 g)
2 tablespoons peeled, grated fresh ginger	30 ml
1 (10 ounce) package frozen snow peas	280 g
2 small zucchini, cut lengthwise in half and sliced	
1 bunch green onions, cut in 3-inch pieces	8 cm
1 (10 ounce) can chicken broth	280 g
2 tablespoons teriyaki sauce	30 ml
1 tablespoon cornstarch	15 ml

- In large skillet with a little oil over medium-high heat, stir-fry pork slices and ginger just until pork loses its pink color. Transfer to serving bowl and keep warm. In same skillet with a little more oil, cook snow peas, zucchini and onions until tender-crisp. In small bowl, combine broth, teriyaki sauce and cornstarch, mixing well. Pour into skillet with vegetables and heat to boiling; boil, stir constantly, until sauce thickens. Return pork to skillet, stir to coat with sauce and heat thoroughly.

Grilled Pork Tenderloin with Rice

2 (about 1 pound each) pork tenderloins	2 (.5 kg)
1 tablespoon oil	15 ml
2 tablespoons jerk seasoning	30 ml
1 (6 ounce) package chicken-flavored rice	168 g
1 (15 ounce) can black beans, rinsed	425 g
½ cup roasted red bell pepper, sliced	120 ml
2 tablespoons chopped cilantro	30 ml

- Rub tenderloins with oil and sprinkle with jerk seasoning. Grill over medium-high heat about 25 minutes, browning on both sides until meat thermometer inserted in center registers 160° (71° C).

- Cook rice according to package directions and add beans, bell pepper, cilantro and salt and pepper to taste. Spoon on serving platter. Slice tenderloin and arrange on top of rice-bean mixture.

Ravioli and Tomatoes

1 (9 ounce) package sausage-filled ravioli	255 g
1 (15 ounce) can Italian-stewed tomatoes	425 g
2 (4 ounce) cans sliced mushrooms	2 (114 g)
1 (5 ounce) package grated parmesan cheese	143 g

- Cook ravioli according to package directions and drain well. Stir in stewed tomatoes and mushrooms; bring to a boil. Reduce heat to low and simmer for 5 minutes. Sprinkle cheese on each serving.

Italian Sausage and Ravioli

1 pound sweet Italian pork sausage, casing removed	.5 kg
1 (26 ounce) jar extra chunky mushroom and green pepper spaghetti sauce	737 g
1 (24 ounce) package frozen cheese-filled ravioli, cooked, drained	680 g

- In roasting pan over medium heat, cook sausage according to package directions or until brown and no longer pink and stir to separate meat. Stir in spaghetti sauce. Heat to boiling. Add ravioli and heat through, stirring occasionally. Pour into serving dish and sprinkle with parmesan cheese.

Sausage Casserole

1 pound pork sausage	.5 kg
2 (15 ounce) cans pork and beans	2 (425 g)
1 (15 ounce) can Mexican-style stewed tomatoes	425 g
1 (6 ounce) package corn muffin mix	168 g

- Brown sausage and drain fat. Add beans and tomatoes, blend and bring to a boil. Pour into 3-quart (3 L) greased baking dish. Prepare muffin mix according to package directions. Drop by spoonfuls over meat and bean mixture. Bake at 400° (204° C) for 30 minutes or until top browns.

Easy Pork Stew

1 (1 pound) pork tenderloin, cubed	.5 kg
2 (12 ounce) jars pork gravy	2 (340 g)
¼ cup chili sauce	60 ml
1 (16 ounce) package frozen stew vegetables, thawed	.5 kg

- Cook pork pieces in greased soup pot on medium to high heat for 10 minutes, stirring frequently. Stir in gravy, chili sauce and stew vegetables and bring to a boil. Reduce heat and simmer for 12 minutes or until vegetables are tender.

Colorful Sausage Supper

4 tablespoons olive oil, divided	60 ml
1 pound cooked Polish sausage, cut into ¼-inch slices	.5 kg/.6 cm
1 sweet red bell pepper, julienned	
3 small zucchini, sliced	
3 small yellow squash, sliced	
1 (16 ounce) package penne pasta	.5 kg
1 (26 ounce) jar spaghetti sauce, heated	737 g

- In large skillet with 2 tablespoons (30 ml) oil, saute sausage, bell pepper, zucchini and squash until vegetables are tender-crisp. Cook pasta according to package directions, drain and stir in remaining oil; add salt and pepper to taste. Spoon into large serving bowl and spread heated spaghetti sauce over pasta. Using slotted spoon, top with sausage-vegetable mixture.

Sausage-Bean Casserole Supper

1 pound pork sausage	.5 kg
2 (15 ounce) cans pork and beans with liquid	2 (425 g)
1 (15 ounce) can Mexican-style stewed tomatoes	2 (425 g)
1 (8 ounce) package corn muffin mix	227 g
1 egg	
⅓ cup milk	80 ml

- Preheat oven to 350° (176° C). Brown sausage in large skillet and drain. Add beans and stewed tomatoes; stir and bring to a boil. Pour into sprayed 3-quart (3 L) baking dish.

- Prepare muffin mix with egg and milk according to package directions. Drop by teaspoonfuls over meat-bean mixture and bake 25 minutes or until top is light brown.

Sausage Stuffed Bell Peppers

6 large green bell peppers	
1 pound pork sausage	.5 kg
1 (8 ounce) can tomato sauce	227 g
1 onion, finely chopped	
1 cup uncooked instant rice	240 ml

- Preheat oven to 325° (162° C). Slice peppers lengthwise in half through stem and scrape out centers.

- In bowl, combine sausage, tomato sauce, onion and rice, mixing well. Stuff pepper halves evenly with stuffing mixture and place in greased, shallow baking dish. Cover and bake 25 minutes; uncover and bake for 10 minutes.

Simple Sauce for Sassy Ribs

2 racks baby back ribs, cut into individual ribs

Sauce:

¼ cup hoisin sauce	60 ml
¼ cup wine vinegar	60 ml
2 tablespoons soy sauce	30 ml
⅓ cup apricot preserves	80 ml

- Preheat broiler to high and line large shallow baking pan with foil and place ribs, meaty side down, close together but not touching. In small bowl, combine all sauce ingredients, mixing well. Spoon one-third of sauce over ribs and broil 10 minutes (6 inches/15 cm from broiler). Spoon additional one-third sauce over ribs and broil an additional 6 minutes. Broil another 3 minutes or until ribs are crispy and done. Spoon on remaining sauce before serving.

Skillet Shrimp Scampi

2 teaspoons olive oil	10 ml
2 pounds uncooked shrimp, peeled, veined	1 kg
⅔ cup herb-garlic marinade with lemon juice	160 ml
¼ cup finely chopped green onions with tops	60 ml
Hot, cooked rice	

- Heat oil in large non-stick skillet. Add shrimp and marinade and cook, stirring often, until shrimp turns pink.

- Stir in green onions, Serve over rice.

Shrimp Supper

1½ pounds cooked, peeled shrimp	.7 kg
1 small head lettuce, shredded	
1 (14 ounce) jar artichokes, quartered, drained	396 g
2 avocados, peeled, sliced	
1 (8 ounce) bottle creamy ranch dressing	227 g

- Combine all ingredients and serve with dressing.

Shrimp Newburg

1 (10 ounce) can condensed cream of shrimp soup	280 g
1 teaspoon seafood seasoning	5 ml
1 (1 pound) package frozen cooked salad shrimp, thawed	.5 kg
Hot, cooked rice	

- In saucepan, combine soup, ¼ cup (60 ml) water and seafood seasoning and bring to boil. Reduce heat and stir in shrimp. Heat thoroughly. Serve over rice.

Thai Peanut Noodles

1 (5.5 ounce) box Thai stir-fry rice noodles with seasoning packet	155 g
1 pound peeled, veined shrimp	.5 kg
1 (10 ounce) package frozen broccoli florets, thawed	280 g
½ cup peanuts	120 ml

• Boil 3 cups (710 ml) water in saucepan and stir in noodles. Turn heat off and soak noodles about 5 minutes. Drain and rinse in cold water. Saute shrimp and broccoli in skillet with a little oil for about 8 minutes or just until shrimp turns pink.

• Add softened noodles, seasoning packet and peanuts.

Shrimp Florentine

2 (10 ounce) boxes frozen creamed spinach, thawed	2 (280 g)
1 (12 ounce) package penne pasta	340 g
2 tablespoons oil	30 ml
1 pound peeled, cleaned large shrimp	.5 kg
¼ cup grated parmesan cheese	60 ml

• Cook spinach according to package directions. Cook pasta according to package directions. In large skillet, over medium-high heat, place oil, a little black pepper and shrimp; cook 3 minutes or until shrimp is thoroughly cooked.

• Add cooked spinach, pasta and parmesan cheese, gently tossing. If pasta is too dry, gradually add 1 tablespoon (15 ml) of hot water. Spoon into serving bowl and serve hot.

Shrimp Cooked In Beer

2 (12 ounce) cans beer	2 (340 g)
3 tablespoons pickling spice	45 ml
Lemon slices	
2 pounds shrimp	1 kg

- In large saucepan or stew pot, pour beer in pot and turn on high heat.

- Add pickling spice, lemon slices and ½ teaspoon (2 ml) salt. When mixture is steaming, add shrimp and stir well. Make sure there is enough liquid to cover or almost cover shrimp.

- Cook just until shrimp turns pink, remove from pot and drain.

Shrimp and Rice Casserole

2 cups instant rice	480 ml
1½ pounds frozen cooked shrimp	.7 kg
1 (10 ounce) carton alfredo sauce	280 g
1 (4 ounce) can chopped pimento, drained	114 g
4 fresh green onions with tops, chopped	
1 (8 ounce) package shredded cheddar cheese,	
divided	227 g

- In saucepan, cook rice according to package directions and place in sprayed 9 x 13-inch (23 x 33 cm) baking dish. Thaw shrimp in colander under cold running water, drain well and remove tails. Set aside.

- In saucepan on medium heat, combine alfredo sauce, pimento and green onions. Stir in shrimp and spoon mixture over rice. Cover with about half cheese and bake about 15 minutes. Sprinkle remaining cheese on top and bake for 5 minutes.

Shrimp and Chicken Curry

2 (10 ounce) cans cream of chicken soup	2 (280 g)
⅓ cup milk	80 ml
1½ teaspoons curry powder	7 ml
1 (12 ounce) can chicken breast, drained	340 g
2 (6 ounce) cans shrimp, drained	2 (168 g)
Hot, cooked rice	

• In saucepan, heat soup, milk and curry powder. Stir in chicken
  pieces and shrimp. Heat, stirring constantly, until mixture is
  thoroughly hot. Serve over rice.

Pan-Seared Shrimp Ancho

3 - 4 ancho chilies	
6 - 8 cloves garlic, minced	
1½ cups extra virgin olive oil	360 ml
2 pounds fresh shrimp, shelled, veined	1 kg

• Clean ancho chilies well with dry cloth, heat for several minutes
  in lightly oiled skillet and soak in hot water for about 30 minutes.
  Dry chilies, remove stems and seeds and slice in long, thin strips.
  Place in large cast-iron or heavy skillet with garlic and about ¼ to
  ½ cup (60 ml) hot oil. Cook about 1 to 2 minutes. Add shrimp
  and cook until they turn pink. Season with salt and pepper.

Creamed Shrimp Over Rice

3 (10 ounce) cans cream of shrimp soup	3 (280 g)
1 pint sour cream	.5 kg
1½ teaspoons curry powder	7 ml
2 (5 ounce) cans veined shrimp	2 (143 g)
Hot, cooked rice	

• Combine all ingredients in top of double boiler. Heat, stirring
  constantly, but do not boil. Serve over rice.

Grilled Garlic Shrimp

¼ cup (½ stick) butter	60 ml
1 heaping teaspoon minced garlic	5 ml
1 teaspoon dried parsley	5 ml
¼ cup dry white wine	60 ml
1 pound medium fresh or frozen shrimp, peeled, veined	

- For sauce, in saucepan combine butter, garlic, parsley and wine, adding about ½ teaspoon (2 ml) black pepper. Cook mixture about 1 minute and set aside. Thread shrimp onto metal skewers and grill on uncovered grill directly over medium-hot coals for about 12 minutes or until pink. Brush shrimp frequently with sauce.

Florentine Shrimp and Pasta

2 (9 ounce) frozen boil-in-bag creamed spinach	2 (255 g)
1 (12 ounce) package penne pasta	340 g
¼ cup heavy cream	60 ml
1 teaspoon Cajun seasoning	5 ml
2 tablespoons olive oil	30 ml
1 pound peeled, medium shrimp	.5 kg

- Bring large pot of water to boil and add spinach pouches; cook according to package directions. In another large saucepan, cook pasta according to package directions; drain and add cream and Cajun seasoning, mixing until well blended.

- In skillet with olive oil, cook shrimp about 3 minutes or until thoroughly cooked (but not over-cooked). Cut spinach pouches and add to pasta; stir in shrimp and transfer to serving dish.

Shrimp Scampi

½ cup (1 stick) butter	120 ml
3 cloves garlic, pressed	
¼ cup lemon juice	60 ml
Hot sauce	
2 pounds raw shrimp, peeled	1 kg

- Melt butter, saute garlic and add lemon juice and a few dashes of hot sauce. Arrange shrimp in single layer in shallow pan, pour garlic-butter over shrimp and salt lightly.

- Broil 2 minutes, turn shrimp and broil 2 more minutes.

- Reserve garlic butter and serve separately.

Broiled Lemon-Garlic Shrimp

1 pound shrimp, peeled, veined	.5 kg
1 teaspoon garlic salt	5 ml
2 tablespoons lemon juice and butter	30 ml

- Place shrimp in shallow baking pan.

- Sprinkle with garlic salt and lemon juice and dot with butter.

- Broil on one side for 3 minutes. Turn and broil 3 minutes more.

Beer-Batter Shrimp

1 (12 ounce) can beer	340 g
1 cup flour	240 ml
2 teaspoons garlic powder	10 ml
1 pound shrimp, peeled, veined	.5 kg

- Make batter by mixing beer, flour and garlic powder and stir to creamy consistency. Dip shrimp into batter and deep-fry in hot oil.

Orange Roughy With Peppers

1 pound orange roughy	.5 kg
1 onion, sliced	
2 red bell peppers, cut into julienne strips	
1 teaspoon dried thyme leaves	5 ml

- Cut fish into 4 serving pieces. Heat a little oil in skillet. Layer onion and bell peppers in skillet. Sprinkle with half thyme and pepper. Place fish over peppers and sprinkle with remaining thyme and a little pepper. Turn burner on high until fish is hot enough to begin cooking. Lower heat, cover for 15 minutes or until fish flakes easily.

Seafood Delight

1 (6 ounce) can shrimp, drained	168 g
1 (6 ounce) can crabmeat, drained, flaked	168 g
1 (10 ounce) can corn or potato chowder	280 g
2 - 3 cups dry, seasoned breadcrumbs, divided	480 ml

- Preheat oven at 350° (176° C). Mix shrimp, crabmeat, chowder and ⅓ cup (80 ml) breadcrumbs. Place mixture in prepared 1½-quart (1.5 L) baking dish. Sprinkle with remaining breadcrumbs. Bake for 30 minutes or until casserole bubbles and breadcrumbs brown lightly.

Chipper Fish

2 pounds sole or orange roughy	1 kg
½ cup Caesar salad dressing	120 ml
1 cup crushed potato chips	240 ml
½ cup shredded cheddar cheese	120 ml

- Dip fish in dressing. Place in greased baking dish. Combine chips and cheese; sprinkle over fish. Bake at 375° (190° C) for 25 minutes.

Baked Orange Roughy

1 egg, beaten	
¼ cup milk	60 ml
1½ cups cracker crumbs	360 ml
⅓ cup grated parmesan cheese	80 ml
4 large orange roughy fillets	

- Preheat oven to 425° (220° C). In shallow bowl, beat together egg and milk. In another shallow, combine cracker crumbs and parmesan cheese.

- Dip fillets in egg mixture, then dredge both sides of fillets in crumb mixture, pressing to use all the crumb mixture. Place in greased 9 x 13-inch (23 x 33 cm) baking pan. Bake, uncovered for 15 to 20 minutes or until fish flakes easily with fork.

Extra-Special Fried Fish

1 (16 ounce) package frozen, cooked batter-dipped fried fish	.5 kg
¾ cup chili sauce	180 ml
1 bunch fresh green onions, chopped	
1 cup shredded cheddar cheese	240 ml

- Preheat oven to 325° (162° C). Arrange fish in greased 9 x 13-inch (23 x 33 cm) glass baking dish and heat about 20 minutes or just until fish heats thoroughly. Heat chili sauce in saucepan and spoon over each piece of fish. Top with chopped green onions and cheddar cheese.

Sunday Best Fried Fish

1 (16 ounce) package frozen, cooked, batter-dipped fried fish	.5 kg
1 cup prepared spaghetti sauce	240 ml
2 teaspoons Italian seasoning	10 ml
1 cup shredded mozzarella cheese	240 ml

- Heat fish according to package directions. While fish is heating, combine spaghetti sauce and Italian seasoning. When fish heats thoroughly, place each piece on serving plate and spoon spaghetti mixture over fish. Sprinkle cheese on top.

Snappy Catfish

4 teaspoons paprika	20 ml
1 teaspoon cayenne pepper	5 ml
2 teaspoons dried oregano	10 ml
3 tablespoons oil	45 ml
8 catfish fillets	

- In small bowl, combine paprika, cayenne pepper, oregano and 1 teaspoon (5 ml) salt. Line fillets on baking sheet, lined with non-stick foil and coat each fillet with oil. Rub spice-mixture evenly over both sides of fish. Broil 5 minutes on each side.

Fish and Chips

1 cup mayonnaise	240 ml
1 lime	
3 - 4 fish fillets, rinsed, dried	
1½ cups crushed corn chips	360 ml

- Preheat oven to 425° (220° C). Mix mayonnaise and 2 tablespoons (30 ml) lime juice. Spread on both sides of fish fillets. Place crushed corn chips on wax paper and dredge both sides of fish in chips. Shake off excess chips. Place fillets on foil-covered baking sheet and bake for 15 minutes or until fish flakes.

Pan Fried Flounder

¼ teaspoon cayenne	1 ml
⅔ cup flour	160 ml
¼ cup olive oil	60 ml
6 - 8 small flounder fillets	
¾ cup prepared tartar sauce	180 ml
⅓ cup ketchup	80 ml

- In shallow bowl, combine 1 tablespoon (15 ml) salt, cayenne pepper, ¼ teaspoon (1 ml) black pepper and flour. Heat oil over high heat in large skillet and dredge each fillet in flour-seasoning mixture and place in skillet (in batches) and fry about 3 minutes on each side, depending on thickness of fillets. Drain on paper towels. Combine tartar sauce, ketchup and ½ teaspoon (2 ml) salt and serve with fried flounder.

Lemon Dill Fish

½ cup mayonnaise	120 ml
2 tablespoons lemon juice	30 ml
½ teaspoon lemon peel	2 ml
1 teaspoon dill weed	5 ml
1 pound cod or flounder fillets	.5 kg

- Combine mayonnaise, lemon juice, peel and dill weed until they blend well. Place fish on greased grill or broiler rack. Brush with half sauce. Grill or broil 5 to 8 minutes, turn and brush with remaining sauce. Continue grilling or broiling 5 to 8 minutes or until fish flakes easily with fork.

Crispy Flounder

⅓ cup mayonnaise	80 ml
1 pound flounder fillets	.5 kg
1 cup seasoned breadcrumbs	240 ml
¼ cup grated parmesan cheese	60 ml

- Place mayonnaise in small dish. Coat fish with mayonnaise and dip in crumbs to coat well.

- Arrange in shallow baking dish. Bake uncovered at 375° (190° C) for 25 minutes. Before serving, sprinkle with parmesan.

Flounder Au Gratin

½ cup fine dry breadcrumbs	120 ml
¼ cup grated parmesan cheese	60 ml
1 pound flounder	.5 kg
⅓ cup mayonnaise	80 ml

- In shallow dish combine crumbs and cheese. Brush both sides of fish with mayonnaise. Coat with crumb mixture. Arrange in single layer in shallow pan. Bake at 375° (190° C) for 25 minutes or until fish flakes easily.

Baked Halibut

2 (1-inch) thick halibut steaks	2 (2.5 cm)
1 (8 ounce) carton sour cream	227 g
½ cup grated parmesan cheese	120 ml
¾ teaspoon dill weed	4 ml

- Place halibut in greased 9 x 13-inch (23 x 33 cm) baking dish.

- Combine sour cream, parmesan cheese, dill weed and salt and pepper if desired. Spoon over halibut. Cover and bake at 325° (162° C) for 20 minutes. Uncover and sprinkle with paprika. Bake another 10 minutes or until fish flakes easily with fork.

Baked Halibut Fillets

4 fresh halibut fillets	
2 tablespoons lime juice	30 ml
1 (10 ounce) can diced tomatoes and green chilies	280 g
1 cup salsa	240 ml
6 green olives, thinly sliced	
3 tablespoons butter, melted	45 ml
Hot, cooked rice	

- Preheat oven to 350° (176° C). Place fillets on shallow plate and spoon lime juice over fillets. Let stand 5 minutes.

- Place tomatoes and green chilies in 9 x 13-inch (23 x 33 cm) baking dish. Stir in salsa and olives and season with salt and pepper to taste. Place fillets on top of sauce and drizzle with melted butter. Bake for 15 minutes or until fish flakes easily with fork. Serve over rice, spooning sauce over each fillet.

Salmon Patties

1 (15 ounce) can pink salmon with juice	425 g
1 egg	
½ cup cracker crumbs	120 ml
1 teaspoon baking powder	5 ml

- Pour off juice from salmon and set juice aside. Remove bones and skin. Stir in egg and cracker crumbs with salmon.

- In small bowl, add baking powder to ¼ cup (60 ml) salmon juice. Mixture will foam. After foaming, add to salmon mixture. Drop by teaspoons into hot oil in skillet. Brown lightly on both sides. Serve hot.

Lemon-Baked Fish

1 pound sole or halibut fillets	.5 kg
2 tablespoons (¼ stick) butter	30 ml
1 teaspoon dried tarragon	5 ml
2 tablespoons lemon juice	30 ml

- Place fish fillets in greased, shallow pan with butter. Sprinkle with a little salt, pepper and a butter. Bake at 375° (190° C) for 8 to 10 minutes. Turn and bake another 6 minutes or until fish flakes. Melt butter with tarragon and lemon juice. Serve over fish fillets.

Home-Fried Fish

1½ pounds haddock, sole or cod	.7 kg
1 egg beaten	
2 tablespoons milk	30 ml
2 cups corn flake crumbs	480 ml

- Cut fish into serving-size pieces. Combine egg and milk. Dip fish in egg mixture and coat with corn flakes on both sides. Fry in a little oil in skillet until brown on both sides.

Ginger Salmon Steaks

¾ cup prepared teriyaki marinade and sauce	180 ml
3 tablespoons brown sugar	45 ml
1 teaspoon freshly peeled and grated ginger root	5 ml
4 salmon steaks	

- Combine teriyaki marinade, brown sugar and grated ginger and place in baggie; reserve ¼ cup (60 ml) of this mixture for later use. Place steaks in baggie and seal, pressing air out of bag. Turn bag over several times, coating well. Marinate 30 minutes.

- Grill salmon 5 inches (13 cm) from heat for 5 minutes on each side, brushing occasionally with reserved sauce.

Salmon and Green Beans

4 (6 ounce) salmon steaks	4 (168 g)
¼ cup soy sauce	60 ml
2 tablespoon lemon juice	30 ml
1 (10 ounce) package frozen whole green beans	280 g
Hot, buttered rice	

- Place a little oil in skillet over medium to high heat and add salmon steaks. Combine soy sauce and lemon juice and pour over steaks.

- Cover and cook about 5 minutes. Turn salmon and place green beans over salmon with 2 tablespoons (30 ml) water. Cover and steam 5 minutes or until beans are tender-crisp. Season green beans with a little salt and pepper and serve over rice.

Broiled Salmon Steaks

4 (1-inch) thick salmon steaks	4 (2.5 cm)
Garlic salt	
Worcestershire sauce	
¼ - ½ cup butter, melted	60 ml

- Place salmon steaks on baking sheet and sprinkle both sides with garlic salt. Splash Worcestershire and butter on top of each steak and broil for 2 to 3 minutes. Turn steaks and splash Worcestershire and butter on top and broil for 3 minutes. (Fish will flake, but should not be dry inside.) Top with melted butter.

Alfredo Salmon and Noodles

3 cups uncooked medium egg noodles	710 ml
1 (16 ounce) package frozen broccoli florets, thawed	.5 kg
1 cup prepared alfredo sauce	240 ml
1 (15 ounce) can salmon, drained, boned	425 g

- Cook noodles in large saucepan according to package directions. Add broccoli last 5 minutes of cooking time and drain. (Discard broccoli stems.) Stir in alfredo sauce and salmon and cook on low heat, stirring occasionally, until mixture heats through. Pour into serving bowl.

Tuna-Tomato Bowl

2 tablespoons olive oil	30 ml
1 teaspoon minced garlic	5 ml
¼ teaspoon cayenne pepper	1 ml
2 teaspoons dried basil	10 ml
1 (15 ounce) can stewed tomatoes	425 g
1 (12 ounce) can water-packed tuna, drained	340 g
¾ cup pitted green olives, sliced	180 ml
¼ cup drained capers	60 ml
1 cup favorite pasta, cooked	240 ml

- In saucepan, heat olive oil and add garlic, cayenne pepper and basil; cook on low heat for 2 minutes. Add tomatoes and bring to a boil, reduce heat and simmer 20 minutes. In serving bowl, combine tuna, olives, capers, cooked pasta and salt and pepper to taste. Stir in sauce and toss. Serve immediately.

Tuna Toast

1 (10 ounce) can cream of chicken soup   280 g
1 (6 ounce) can water-packed tuna, drained   168 g
2 slices thick Texas toast
1 tomato, cubed

• In saucepan, combine soup and tuna; stir to break up chunks of
  tuna. Brown Texas toast on both sides. Pour soup mixture over
  toast; sprinkle tomatoes over soup mixture. Serve immediately.

Tuna-Pasta Casserole

1 (8 ounce) package elbow macaroni   227 g
1 (8 ounce) package shredded processed cheese 227 g
1 (12 ounce) can tuna, drained   340 g
1 (10 ounce) can cream of celery soup   280 g
1 cup milk   240 ml

• Preheat oven to 350° (176° C). Cook macaroni according
  to package directions. Drain and stir in cheese until cheese
  melts. Stir in tuna, celery soup and milk and spoon into greased
  7 x 11-inch (18 x 28 cm) baking dish. Cover and bake 30 minutes.

Tuna-Stuffed Tomatoes

4 large tomatoes
2 (6 ounce) cans white meat tuna, drained   2 (168 g)
2 cups chopped celery   480 ml
½ cup chopped cashews   120 ml
1 small zucchini with peel, chopped
½ - ⅔ cup mayonnaise   120 ml

• Cut thin slice off top of each tomato, scoop out pulp and discard.
  Turn tomatoes over on paper towels to drain. Combine tuna,
  celery, cashews, zucchini, salt and pepper to taste and mix well.
  Add mayonnaise and blend. Add more mayonnaise if needed.
  Spoon mixture into hollowed-out tomatoes and chill.

Short Order Fresh Tuna

4 (¾ -inch thick) tuna steaks	4 (1.8 cm)
1 small onion, thinly sliced	
1 cup orange juice	240 ml
¼ teaspoon dried dill weed	1 ml
2 tablespoons butter	30 ml

- Sprinkle both sides of tuna steaks with 1 teaspoon (5 ml) seasoned salt. Place in skillet that has been sprayed with non-stick cooking spray. Cover and cook on medium heat for 6 to 8 minutes, turning once or until tuna is slightly pink in center. Remove tuna from skillet and keep warm.

- Add onion slices and cook 4 to 5 minutes and stir in orange juice, dill weed and butter. Continue cooking another 5 minutes or until sauce is slightly thickened. Serve sauce over tuna.

Tuna-Asparagus Pot Pie

1 (8 ounce) package crescent rolls, divided	227 g
1 (6 ounce) can solid white water-packed tuna, drained, flaked	168 g
1 (15 ounce) can cut asparagus, drained	425 g
1 cup shredded cheddar cheese	240 ml

- Preheat oven to 375° (190° C). Form 7-inch (18 cm) square using 4 crescent rolls. Pinch edges together to seal.

- Place in 8 x 8-inch (20 x 20 cm) square, prepared baking pan. Spread tuna, then asparagus, followed by shredded cheese.

- Form remaining 4 crescent rolls into 1 square. Place on top of cheese. Bake 20 minutes or until top is brown and cheese bubbles.

Red Snapper with Salsa

6 (6 ounce) red snapper fillets	6 (168 g)
1 teaspoon ground cumin	5 ml
½ teaspoon cayenne pepper	2 ml
½ cup chopped fresh cilantro	120 ml
1 (15 ounce) can great northern beans, drained	425 g
1 (15 ounce) can Italian stewed tomatoes, drained	425 g
⅓ cup chopped green olives	80 ml
1 teaspoon minced garlic	5 ml

- Dry snapper with paper towels and rub a little oil on both sides of snapper and sprinkle cumin, cayenne pepper and ½ teaspoon (2 ml) salt. Grill snapper about 5 minutes on each side or until fish flakes easily when tested with fork.

- Combine fresh cilantro, beans, tomatoes, olives and minced garlic, mixing well. Serve with each red snapper.

New Mexico Red Snapper

1 (8 ounce) can tomato sauce	227 g
1 (4 ounce) can chopped green chilies	114 g
1 clove garlic, minced	
1 pound red snapper fillets	.5 kg

- In small bowl, mix tomato sauce, green chilies and garlic. Put snapper fillets on microwave-safe dish and brush tomato sauce mixture evenly over red snapper. Cover with plastic wrap. Microwave on HIGH about 3 minutes, rotate dish and microwave 2 minutes. Check snapper to see if it flakes easily. If not, microwave another 2 minutes and check if meat is flaky.

Broiled Red Snapper

2 tablespoons dijon-style mustard	30 ml
¼ cup Italian dressing	60 ml
4 (6 ounce) red snapper fillets	4 (168 g)

- Preheat broiler. Combine mustard and Italian dressing in small bowl. Place snapper, skin side down on foil-lined baking pan that has been sprayed with cooking spray. Brush mustard-dressing mixture over fillets and broil 8 minutes or until snapper flakes easily when tested with fork.

Crab Mornay

2 (6 ounce) cans crabmeat, drained, flaked	2 (168 g)
1 cup cream of mushroom soup	240 ml
½ cup shredded Swiss cheese	120 ml
½ cup seasoned breadcrumbs	120 ml

- Preheat oven to 350° (176° C). Combine crabmeat, soup and cheese.

- Pour into prepared 1½-quart (1.5 L) baking dish and sprinkle with breadcrumbs. Bake uncovered 30 minutes until breadcrumbs brown.

Baked Oysters

1 cup oysters, drained, rinsed	240 ml
2 cups cracker crumbs	480 ml
¼ cup (½ stick) butter, melted	60 ml
½ cup milk	120 ml

- Make alternate layers of oysters, cracker crumbs and butter in 7 x 11-inch (18 x 28 cm) baking dish. Pour warmed milk over layers and add lots of salt and pepper. Bake at 350° (176° C) for about 35 minutes.

Grilled Swordfish

4 (1-inch thick) pieces swordfish	4 (2.5 cm)
3 tablespoons olive oil	45 ml
½ teaspoon lemon pepper	

Sauce:

⅓ cup roasted red pepper	80 ml
1 tablespoon dijon-style mustard	15 ml
3 tablespoons mayonnaise	45 ml

• Rub swordfish with olive oil and sprinkle with ¾ teaspoon (4 ml) salt and lemon pepper. Grill over medium-high heat for about 10 minutes, turning once or until thoroughly cooked.

• For sauce, place all ingredients with ½ teaspoon (2 ml) pepper in blender; process until well blended. Serve over swordfish.

Marinade for Grilled Seafood

⅓ cup honey	80 ml
¼ cup soy sauce	60 ml
¼ cup orange juice	60 ml
1 teaspoon cayenne powder	5 ml

• Combine honey, soy sauce, orange juice and cayenne powder, mixing well. Use as marinade for grilled or broiled seafood.

Restaurant-Style Tartar Sauce

1 quart mayonnaise	1 L
1½ cups dill pickle relish, well drained	360 ml
½ cup very finely chopped onion	120 ml
1 teaspoon lemon juice	5 ml
1 teaspoon dry mustard	5 ml

• In large bowl, combine all ingredients, mixing well. Store in refrigerator.

Tartar Sauce for Fried Fish

½ cup mayonnaise	120 ml
2 tablespoons chopped sweet pickles	30 ml
2 tablespoons finely chopped onion	30 ml
1 teaspoon dried parsley	5 ml

• Combine mayonnaise, sweet pickles, onion and parsley and mix well. Serve with fish.

Red Sauce for Fried Fish or Shrimp

1 (10 ounce) bottle chili sauce	280 g
2 cups ketchup	480 ml
¼ cup prepared horseradish	60 ml
3 tablespoons lemon juice	45 ml

• In bowl, whisk all ingredients together; cover and chill until ready to serve.

Howlin' Good Sweets

Desserts
Cakes
Pies
Cookies and Bars
Candy

Quick, Easy Chocolate Mousse

1 packet unflavored gelatin	
½ cup light corn syrup	120 ml
1 (6 ounce) package semi-sweet chocolate chips	168 g
1 teaspoon vanilla	5 ml
1 pint heavy (whipping) cream, whipped	.5 kg

- In saucepan sprinkle gelatin over ¼ cup (60 ml) water and let stand 2 minutes. Add corn syrup and over low heat, cook, stirring constantly for 5 minutes. Remove from heat and stir in chocolate chips and vanilla, stirring until smooth.

- Gently fold in chocolate mixture into whipped cream and spoon into individual serving bowls. Refrigerate.

Crave That Chocolate Sandwich

4 large slices bakery walnut or raisin bread	
Butter, softened	
3 - 4 ounces of a bittersweet chocolate bar, grated	84 g
Powdered sugar	

- Lightly spread bread slices with butter. Top the unbuttered side of 2 slices evenly with the chocolate. Top with other slice, buttered side out. In a non-stick skillet, over medium-high heat, cook sandwiches until golden brown on both sides and chocolate is melted. Sprinkle with powdered sugar. Cut sandwiches in half or fourths and serve immediately.

Cranberry Pudding

1 (22 ounce) carton refrigerated tapioca pudding	624 g
¾ cup Craisins® (dried cranberries)	180 ml
1 (8 ounce) can crushed pineapple, well drained	227 g

- In bowl, combine tapioca pudding, cranberries and pineapple, mixing well. Chill for cranberries to blend into pudding.

Chocolate-Peanut Pizza

1 (18 ounce) roll refrigerated sugar cookie dough	510 g
⅔ cup creamy peanut butter	160 ml
1 (8 ounce) package peanut butter morsels	227 g
1 cup miniature candy-coated chocolate pieces	240 ml
Hot fudge ice cream topping (optional)	

- Preheat oven to 350° (176° C). Spread dough evenly on bottom and up sides of greased 12-inch (32 cm) pizza pan. Bake on bottom rack for 20 minutes or until crust is golden brown. Cool for 15 minutes.

- Spread peanut butter evenly on top of cookie crust and sprinkle with morsels and chocolate pieces. Cut into wedges to serve. Drizzle top of each serving with hot fudge sauce.

Granny's Baked Custard

4 eggs, slightly beaten	
⅓ cup sugar	80 ml
1 quart milk	1 L
½ teaspoon vanilla	2 ml

- Preheat oven to 325° (162° C). In large bowl, combine all ingredients and stir until sugar is dissolved. Pour into small custard cups and place in pan containing ½-inch (1.2 cm) warm water. Bake for 25 to 30 minutes or until custard is firm.

Fresh Fruit with Orange Sauce

2 cups cut-up pineapple	480 ml
2 cups cubed cantaloupe	480 ml
2 cups strawberries	480 ml
2 cups green grapes	480 ml
2 cups cut-up melon	480 ml
2 cups blueberries	480 ml

Orange Sauce:

1½ cups orange juice	360 ml
½ cup sugar	120 ml
1 teaspoon vanilla	5 ml

- Combine all fruit in bowl with lid.

- Place orange juice, sugar and vanilla in jar with lid and shake until sugar dissolves. Pour over fruit, cover and chill.

Cream Cheese Pastry

¼ cup (½ stick) butter, cut in small cubes	60 ml
½ (8 ounce) package cream cheese, cut in small cubes	½ (227 g)
1 cup flour	240 ml

- Preheat oven to 375° (190° C). Combine all ingredients and blend with pasty blender. With hands, knead and shape into ball, roll into round shape with rolling pin. Place in 9-inch (23 cm) pie pan. Bake 10 to 12 minutes or until lightly golden.

Fruit Cocktail

¾ cup slices strawberries	180 ml
¾ cup diced fresh pineapple	180 ml
¾ cup sliced green or red seedless grapes	180 ml
3 kiwis, peeled and diced	

Dressing:

2 tablespoons white rum	30 ml
2 tablespoons chopped fresh mint	30 ml
3 tablespoons sugar	45 ml
1 teaspoon fresh lime juice	5 ml

- In bowl, combine strawberries, pineapple, grapes and kiwis.

- Combine dressing ingredients and pour over fruit, tossing occasionally, let stand 10 minutes until juicy and sugar dissolves.

Fruit Crispy

6 cups peeled, sliced apples	1.5 L
3 tablespoon lemon juice	45 ml
½ cup flour	120 ml
⅓ cup oats	80 ml
⅓ cup packed brown sugar	80 ml
1 teaspoon cinnamon	5 ml
¼ cup (½ stick) butter	60 ml
⅓ cup chopped pecans	80 ml

- Preheat oven to 425° (220° C). Toss apple slices with lemon juice and place in buttered 7 x 11-inch (18 x 28 cm) baking dish. In bowl, combine flour, oats, brown sugar, cinnamon and a pinch of salt. Cut butter in with pastry blender and stir in pecans. Bake 30 minutes until fruit bubbles and top is brown.

Grape Fluff

1 cup grape juice	240 ml
2 cups miniature marshmallows	480 ml
2 tablespoons lemon juice	30 ml
1 (8 ounce) carton whipping cream	227 g

- In saucepan heat grape juice to boiling. Add marshmallows and stir constantly until they melt. Add lemon juice and cool.

- Fold in whipped cream and spoon into individual serving dishes. Chill.

Peanut Butter Sundae

1 cup light corn syrup	240 ml
1 cup chunky peanut butter	240 ml
¼ cup milk	60 ml
Ice cream or pound cake	

- In mixing bowl, stir corn syrup, peanut butter and milk until well blended. Serve over ice cream or pound cake. Chill.

Honey-Rice Pudding Parfaits

12 cinnamon graham crackers, crushed	
1 (22 ounce) carton refrigerated rice pudding	624 g
½ cup honey	120 ml
Fresh strawberries	

- Spoon about 2 heaping tablespoons (30 ml) crushed crackers in bottom of 5 sherbet or parfait glasses. In bowl, mix together rice pudding and honey and divide evenly into sherbet glasses.

- Sprinkle remaining crushed graham crackers over top of pudding and place 4 or 5 strawberries on top. Chill.

Quick Company Apple Crisp

1 (8 ounce) carton whipping cream	227 g
1 cup (2 sticks) butter	240 ml
1½ cups packed brown sugar	360 ml
⅓ cup light corn syrup	80 ml
1 (20 ounce) can cooked, sliced apples for pies	567 g
1 (16 ounce) package crushed pecan shortbread cookies	.5 kg

- In saucepan, combine whipping cream, butter, brown sugar and corn syrup. Bring to a boil for 7 to 8 minutes, stirring several times. Reduce heat and cook about 3 minutes. Cool and transfer to storage jar with lid. (Sauce can be served warm or stored in refrigerator for later use, but warmed before use.)

- Place apples in individual serving bowls or sherbets and drizzle with caramel sauce and top with crushed cookies.

Strawberries in the Clouds

1 (8 ounce) package cream cheese, softened	227 g
1 tablespoon amaretto	15 ml
1 (16 ounce) box powdered sugar	.5 kg
1 (8 ounce) carton whipped topping	227 g

- Blend cream cheese and amaretto, beat until creamy and add powdered sugar. Gently fold in whipped topping.

- You can serve dollop of this creamy mixture over a bowl of sweetened strawberries or use as a dip for whole strawberries.

Spicy Cherry Topping

1 (20 ounce) can cherry pie filling	567 g
¼ cup sugar	60 ml
¼ teaspoon each cinnamon and nutmeg	1 ml

- Place pie filling in saucepan and stir in sugar, cinnamon, nutmeg and ¼ cup (60 ml) water. Heat over medium heat, stirring several times until thoroughly hot. This topping is great served over pound cake, ice cream or creamy puddings.

Lemon Treat

1 (3 ounce) package lemon pie filling mix (not instant)	84 g
⅓ cup sugar	80 ml
1 egg	
½ (8 ounce) carton whipped topping	½ (227 g)

- Mix pie filling, sugar and egg with ¼ cup (60 ml) water until smooth. Slowly add another 1¾ cups (420 ml) water.

- Cook, stirring constantly, over medium heat until mixture comes to full boil. Remove from heat and cool completely.

- Fold in whipped topping and spoon into individual dessert dishes. Top with fresh fruit.

Caramel-Apple Delight

3 (2 ounce) Snickers® candy bars, frozen	3 (57 g)
2 Granny Smith apples, chopped	
1 (12 ounce) carton whipped topping	340 g
1 (3 ounce) package dry instant vanilla pudding	84 g

- Smash frozen candy bars in wrappers with hammer. Mix all ingredients and chill.

Spirit Sweet Fruit

2 cups each peeled, cubed ripe mango and kiwifruit	480 ml
2 cups peeled, cubed fresh pineapple	480 ml
½ cup sugar	120 ml
¼ teaspoon ground cinnamon	60 ml
¼ cup white rum	60 ml
3 tablespoons lime juice	45 ml
¼ cup flaked coconut	60 ml

- In large bowl, combine mango, kiwifruit and pineapple. Refrigerate until fruit is well chilled

- In saucepan, place sugar, cinnamon and ½ cup (120 ml) water; bring to a boil and cook 1 minute. Stir in rum and lime juice and cool completely. Pour syrup over fruit and gently toss. Sprinkle coconut on top.

Mother's Boiled Custard

½ cup sugar	120 ml
4 eggs, slightly beaten	
1 gallon milk	4 L
2 teaspoons vanilla	10 ml

- In bowl, combine sugar, dash of salt and eggs and mix well.

- In double boiler, scald milk and add a little into egg mixture. Pour egg-milk mixture into double boiler and cook. Stir constantly until mixture is thick enough to coat spoon. Remove from heat and add vanilla. Chill until ready to serve.

Sweet Crispies

1 (6 ounce) package semi-sweet chocolate chips	168 g
¾ cup crunchy peanut butter	180 ml
6 cups crispix cereal	1.5 L
1½ cups powdered sugar	360 ml

- In microwave-safe bowl, melt chocolate in microwave, stirring two times. Stir in peanut butter, mixing well. Gently stir in cereal, mixing until cereal is well coated. Place powdered sugar in large baggie and add cereal mixture. Seal and gently toss until cereal is well coated. Chill in airtight container.

Divine Strawberries

1 quart fresh strawberries	1 L
1 (20 ounce) can pineapple chunks, well drained	567 g
2 bananas, sliced	
2 (18 ounce) carton strawberry glaze	2 (510 g)

- Cut strawberries in bite size pieces. Add pineapple chunks and bananas. Fold in strawberry glaze and chill.

Coffee Mallow

3 cups miniature marshmallows	710 ml
½ cup hot, strong coffee	120 ml
1 cup whipping cream, whipped	240 ml
½ teaspoon vanilla	2 ml

- In large saucepan, combine marshmallows and coffee. On low heat, stirring constantly, cook until marshmallows melt. Cool mixture. Fold in whipped cream and vanilla.

- Pour into individual sherbet dishes and chill.

Dessert Fondue

1 (16 ounce) carton coconut-pecan frosting mix	.5 kg
½ cup dry milk powder	120 ml
¼ cup (½ stick) butter, cut in 1-inch slices	60 ml/2.5 cm

- In saucepan, combine frosting mix, milk powder, butter and ¼ cup (60 ml) water. Heat, stirring constantly until butter melts and ingredients are well blended. Add about ½ cup (120 ml) water, just enough to make fondue of dipping consistency. Keep warm over very low heat. For dippers, use apple chunks, banana chunks, angel food or pound cake chunks.

Caramel-Cinnamon Dessert

1 (4 ounce) package French vanilla instant pudding	114 g
3 cups milk	710 ml
1 (8 ounce) carton whipped topping	227 g
1 (14 ounce) box cinnamon graham crackers	396 g
1 (16 ounce) can caramel icing	.5 kg

- Combine pudding and milk and mix well. Fold in whipped topping. Line bottom of 9 x 13-inch (23 x 33 cm) glass dish with whole graham crackers.

- Put half pudding mixture over crackers and top with second layer of crackers. Spread remaining pudding over top. Top with remaining crackers (2 or 3 crackers should be left). Add caramel icing over last layer of graham crackers. Chill.

Sweet Surrender

1 (14 ounce) can sweetened condensed milk	396 g
¼ cup lemon juice	60 ml
1 (20 ounce) can coconut pie filling, chilled	567 g
1 (15 ounce) can pineapple tidbits, drained, chilled	425 g
1 (15 ounce) fruit cocktail, drained, chilled	425 g
1 (8 ounce) carton whipped topping	227 g

• In large bowl, combine condensed milk and lemon juice. Stir in coconut pie filling, drained pineapple tidbits and drained fruit cocktail. Fold in whipped topping and chill.

Apple Crescents

1 (8 ounce) can refrigerated crescent rolls	227 g
2 Granny Smith apples, peeled, quartered	
1 cup orange juice	240 ml
1¼ cups sugar	300 ml
½ cup (1 stick) butter	120 ml
1 teaspoon cinnamon	5 ml

• Preheat oven to 350° (176° C). Unroll crescent rolls and separate. Wrap each apple quarter with crescent roll. Place each apple crescent in greased 9 x 13-inch (23 x 33 cm) baking dish. In saucepan, combine orange juice, sugar, butter and cinnamon and bring to a boil. Pour over crescents and bake 30 minutes or until golden and bubbly.

Winter Peach Dessert

1 (15 ounce) can sliced peaches	425 g
¼ cup grenadine syrup	60 ml
¼ cup sugar	60 ml
1 cup crumbled coconut macaroon cookies	240 ml

- Drain peaches, reserving 1/4 cup (60 ml) juice. In saucepan, combine peach slices, reserve juice, grenadine syrup and sugar. Bring to a boil, reduce heat and simmer 6 minutes, turning peach slices to coat with syrup.

- Gently stir in crumbled macaroons over low heat until liquid is absorbed by macaroons. Serve warm in sherbert dishes.

Blueberry Fluff

1 (20 ounce) can blueberry pie filling	567 g
1 (20 ounce) can crushed pineapple, drained	567 g
1 (14 ounce) can sweetened, condensed milk	396 g
1 (8 ounce) carton whipped topping	227 g

- Mix pie filling, pineapple and condensed milk. Fold in whipped topping. Combine all ingredients and pour into parfait glasses. Chill.

Chilled Fruit Medley

2 cups halved red grapes	480 ml
2 cups cubed honeydew melon, chilled	480 ml
1 (20 ounce) can pineapple tidbits, drained, chilled	567 g
1 large banana, sliced, chilled	
¾ cup peach preserves	180 ml

- In salad bowl, combine grapes, melon, pineapple and banana. Whisk in peach preserves and toss to coat all fruits. Chill before serving.

Chocolate-Vanilla-Almond Parfait

1 (3 ounce) box instant chocolate pudding mix	84 g
1 (3 ounce) box instant vanilla pudding mix	84 g
4 cups milk	1 L
2 cups slivered almonds	480 ml

- Using 2 mixing bowls to prepare each pudding with milk according to package directions. Cover tightly with plastic wrap and refrigerate.

- Place slivered almonds in dry skillet over medium heat. Stir until almonds brown evenly.

- In parfait glasses, first spoon small amounts of chocolate pudding, then vanilla pudding to top of glass. Garnish with almonds. Chill.

Kid's Delight

¼ cup (½ stick) butter	60 ml
1 (10 ounce) package marshmallows	280 g
6 cups cocoa rice cereal	1.5 L
½ cup miniature chocolate chips	120 ml

- Prepare 9 x 13-inch (23 x 33 cm) baking pan with cooking spray. In large saucepan over low heat, melt butter and add marshmallows. Stirring constantly, mix until marshmallows have melted. Remove from heat. Stir in rice cereal and chocolate chips. Spoon into prepared pan, using spatula to level cereal mixture. When cool, cut into squares to serve.

Pick Your Fruit-Here's the Dressing

½ cup mayonnaise	120 ml
½ cup sour cream	120 ml
½ cup powdered sugar	120 ml
1 teaspoon lemon juice	5 ml
½ teaspoon ground cinnamon	2 ml

• In bowl, combine mayonnaise and sour cream and mix well; stir in powdered sugar, lemon juice and cinnamon to blend well.

• This dressing is wonderful over a medley of fresh fruit.

Creamy Topping for Berries

4 ounces (½ of an 8 ounce package) cream cheese, softened	114 g/227 g
¼ cup honey	60 ml
2 tablespoons orange juice	30 ml
¼ teaspoon ground cinnamon	1 ml

• With mixer, beat together cream cheese, honey, orange juice and cinnamon until creamy. Serve topping with an assortment of berries or fruit.

Pound Cake Deluxe

1 (10-inch) round bakery pound cake	(25 cm)
1 (20 ounce) can crushed pineapple with juice	567 g
1 (5 ounce) package coconut instant pudding mix	143 g
1 (8 ounce) carton whipped topping	227 g

• Slice cake horizontally to make 3 layers. Mix pineapple, pudding and whipped topping; blend well. Spread on each layer and top of cake. Coconut may be sprinkled on top layer. Chill.

Extreme Pound Cake

1 (9-inch round) bakery pound cake	23 cm
1 (20 ounce) can crushed pineapple with juice	567 g
1 (4 serving size) instant vanilla pudding or	
pie filling	
1 (8 ounce) carton whipped topping, divided	227 g

• Cut pound cake horizontally into 3 layers and place bottom
  layer on cake plate. In bowl, gently combine and mix crushed
  pineapple and pudding together. When well mixed, fold in half of
  whipped topping.

• Spread one-third pineapple mixture over top of bottom layer (not
  on sides). Place second layer on top and spread half remaining
  pineapple mixture. Top with third cake layer and remaining
  pineapple mixture. Top with remaining whipped topping. Chill.

Pound Cake Supreme

1 round bakery pound cake	
1 (20 ounce) can apple pie filling	567 g
⅓ cup sugar	80 ml
⅓ cup packed brown sugar	80 ml
1 teaspoon ground cinnamon	5 ml
¾ cup finely chopped pecans	180 ml

• Cut generous slices of pound cake (as many as you need) and
  place on individual dessert plates. In saucepan, combine apple
  pie filling, both sugars, cinnamon and pecans and heat, stirring
  several times. Spoon over pound cake slices and serve warm.

Spiced-Up Pound Cake

1 (10 ounce) pound cake loaf, sliced	280 g
2 cups applesauce	480 ml
½ cup sugar	120 ml
½ teaspoon cinnamon and allspice	2 ml
¾ cup finely chopped pecans	180 ml

- Place each slice of pound cake (as many as you need) on individual serving plate.

- Over medium-high heat, combine and heat applesauce, sugar, spices and pecans. Place heaping tablespoon (15 ml) applesauce mixture over pound cake slice.

O'Shaughnessy's Special

1 (10 ounce) pound cake loaf	280 g
1 (15 ounce) can crushed pineapple with juice	425 g
1 (3.4 ounce) box pistachio pudding mix	100 g
1 (8 ounce) carton whipped topping	227 g

- Slice cake horizontally and make 3 layers. Combine pineapple and pudding and beat until mixture begins to thicken. Fold in whipped topping and blend well. Spread on each layer and on top. Chill.

Delicious Lemon Sauce
for Pound Cake

1 cup prepared slaw dressing	
(from 16 ounce bottle)	240 ml/.5 kg
1 (8 ounce) package cream cheese, softened	227 g
¼ cup lemon juice	
¼ cup half-and-half cream	60 ml
1½ cups powdered sugar	360 ml

• In mixer, beat together slaw dressing and cream cheese until
  creamy. Add lemon juice, cream and powdered sugar and
  continue beating until creamy. Spoon sauce over pieces of pound
  cake. It is also good over apple pie or spice cake.

Pecan Cake

1 (18 ounce) box butter pecan cake mix	510 g
½ cup (1 stick) butter, melted	120 ml
1 egg	
1 cup chopped pecans	240 ml
1 (8 ounce) package cream cheese, softened	227 g
2 eggs	
1 (1 pound) box powdered sugar	.5 kg

• Combine cake mix, ¾ cup (180 ml) water, butter and egg, mixing
  well. Stir in pecans. Pour into 9 x 13-inch (23 x 33 cm) baking
  dish.

• With mixer, combine cream cheese, eggs and powdered sugar.
  Pour over cake mixture. Bake at 350° (176° C) for 40 minutes.
  Test with toothpick to make sure cake is done.

Pink Lady Cake

1 (18 ounce) box strawberry cake mix	510 g
3 eggs	
1 teaspoon lemon extract	5 ml
1 (20 ounce) can strawberry pie filling	567 g

- In mixing bowl, beat cake mix, eggs and lemon extract together.

- Fold in pie filling. Pour in greased, floured 9 x 13-inch (23 x 33 cm) baking pan. Bake at 350° (176° C) for 30 to 35 minutes. Test with toothpick to make sure that cake is done.

Hawaiian Dream Cake

1 (18 ounce) yellow cake mix	510 g
4 eggs	
¾ cup oil	180 ml
½ (20 ounce) can crushed pineapple with ½ juice	½ (567 g)

- With mixer, beat all ingredients for 4 minutes. Pour into greased, floured 9 x 13-inch (23 x 33 cm) baking pan. Bake at 350° (176° C) for 35 minutes or until cake tests done with toothpick.

Coconut-Pineapple Icing for Hawaiian Dream Cake:

½ (20 ounce) can crushed pineapple with ½ juice	½ (567 g)
½ cup (1 stick) butter	120 ml
1 (16 ounce) box powdered sugar	.5 kg
1 (7 ounce) can flaked coconut	198 g

- Heat pineapple and butter and boil 1½ minutes. Add powdered sugar and coconut. Punch holes in cake with knife. Pour hot icing over cake.

Lemon-Pineapple Cake

1 (18 ounce) box lemon cake mix	510 g
1 (20 ounce) can crushed pineapple with juice	567 g
3 eggs	
⅓ cup oil	80 ml

- In mixing bowl, combine all ingredients. Blend on low speed to moisten and beat on medium for 2 minutes. Pour batter into greased, floured 9 x 13-inch (23 x 33 cm) baking pan.

- Bake at 350° (176° C) for 30 minutes. Test with toothpick to be sure cake is done. When cake is baking, start topping for cake. Cool for about 15 minutes.

Topping for Lemon-Pineapple Cake:

1 (14 ounce) can sweetened condensed milk	396 g
1 cup sour cream	240 ml
¼ cup lemon juice	60 ml

- In medium bowl, combine all ingredients. Stir well to blend.

- Pour over warm cake. Chill.

Quick Summer Cake

1 (16 ounce) frozen loaf pound cake	.5 kg
1 (8 ounce) carton whipping cream	227 g
1 (20 ounce) can coconut pie filling	567 g
2 kiwifruit, peeled, halved, sliced	

- Split cake into three horizontal layers and place bottom layer on serving platter. With mixer, beat whipping cream until thickened and fold in coconut pie filling, mixing until well blended. Spread one-third mixture over bottom cake layer. Place second layer on top and spread half remaining cream mixture on top. Top with third layer and spread remaining cream mixture on top. Garnish with slices of kiwi. Chill.

Miracle Cake

1 (18 ounce) lemon cake mix	510 g
3 eggs	
⅓ cup oil	80 ml
1 (20 ounce) can crushed pineapple with juice	567 g

- In mixing bowl, combine all ingredients.

- Blend on low speed and beat on medium for 2 minutes.

- Pour batter into greased, floured 9 x 13-inch (23 x 33 cm) baking dish. Bake at 350° (176° C.) for 30 to 35 minutes until cake tests done with toothpick.

Topping for Miracle Cake:

1 (14 ounce) can sweetened condensed milk	396 g
¼ cup lemon juice	60 ml
1 (8 ounce) carton whipped topping	227 g

- Blend all ingredients and mix well. Spread over cake. Chill.

All You Can Eat Chocolate Cake

1 (18 ounce) box chocolate cake mix	510 g
1 cup mayonnaise	240 ml
3 eggs, slightly beaten	
1 teaspoon cinnamon	5 ml

- Preheat oven to 350° (176° C). In mixing bowl, beat together cake mix, mayonnaise, eggs, cinnamon and 1 cup (240 ml) water. Pour into 2 (9-inch/23 cm) cake pans and bake as directed on cake mix box. Ice each layer with a 16-ounce (.5 kg) can of prepared chocolate icing.

Shortcakes for Fresh Berries

⅔ cup flour   160 ml
¾ teaspoon baking powder   4 ml
2 heaping tablespoons shortening   30 ml
3 tablespoons milk   45 ml
Extra sugar
1½ cups mixed fresh berries   360 ml
¾ cup sugar, divided   180 ml
Whipped topping

- Preheat oven to 400° (204° C). In bowl, combine flour, baking powder, a little salt and cut in shortening with fork. Stir in milk, just until moistened. Drop heaping ¼ cup (60 ml) batter about 2 inches (5 cm) apart on greased baking pan. Using wet glass bottom, flatten each circle and sprinkle on a little sugar (extra sugar from the berries). Bake for about 12 minutes.

- Sprinkle remaining sugar over berries. Split shortcakes in half; spoon berries on bottom half and replace tops. Garnish with whipped topping.

Strawberry Shortcakes

2½ cups baking mix	600 ml
¼ cup sugar	80 ml
3 tablespoons softened butter	45 ml
½ cup milk	120 ml
1 (8 ounce) carton whipped topping	227 g

Strawberries Glaze:

1 tablespoon cornstarch	15 ml
1 teaspoon almond extract	5 ml
¾ cup sugar	180 ml
1 (16 ounce) container frozen strawberries, thawed	.5 kg

- Preheat oven to 350° (176° C). In mixing bowl, combine baking mix and sugar and cut in butter until mixture is crumbly. Add milk and stir just until soft dough forms. Drop heaping tablespoons of batter onto greased baking sheet. Bake about 14 minutes until light brown.

- For strawberries, place cornstarch, almond extract, sugar and 2 tablespoons (30 ml) water in saucepan, add strawberries and bring mixture to a boil, stirring constantly. Reduce heat, cook and stir until mixture thickens. Remover from heat and chill.

- When ready to serve, split shortcakes in half, spoon about ½ cup (120 ml) strawberry mixture over each shortcake, top with an ample amount of whipped topping and place top half of shortcake on top.

Shortcakes for Strawberries or Raspberries

2½ cups flour, plus 2 tablespoons	600 ml/30 ml
2½ teaspoons baking powder	7 ml
⅓ cup sugar	80 ml
½ cup (1 stick) butter, softened and cut into slices	120 ml
1 cup milk	240 ml

- Preheat oven to 400° (204° C). In bowl, combine flour, baking powder, sugar and butter. Stir and mix with fork until mixture resembles coarse meal.

- Add milk and mix until dough forms. Place dough on lightly floured surface and with lightly floured hands, pat dough into

4 x 6-inch (10 x 15 cm) rectangle. Cut dough into 8 squares and place on greased baking sheet. Bake 30 minutes or until light golden. To serve, cut biscuits in half and serve with sugared strawberries or raspberries and top with whipped topping.

Butter-Toffee Cake

1 (18 ounce) box butter pecan cake mix	510 g
1 cup almond toffee bits	240 ml
1 cup chopped pecans	240 ml
Powdered sugar	

- Mix cake mix according to package directions. Fold in toffee bits and pecans. Pour into greased, floured bundt cake pan. Bake at 350° (176° C) for 40 minutes or until toothpick inserted in center comes out clean. Allow cake to cool several minutes and remove cake from pan. Dust with sifted powdered sugar.

Apple Shortcakes

1 (7 ounce) package apple-cinnamon muffin mix	198 g
½ cup milk	120 ml
¼ cup sour cream	60 ml
⅓ cup chopped pecans	80 ml

Apple-Cinnamon Sauce:

1 (20 ounce) can apple pie filling	567 g
½ cup sugar	120 ml
¼ cup raisins	60 ml
¼ teaspoon cinnamon	1 ml

- Preheat oven to 425° (220° C). In bowl, combine muffin mix, milk, sour cream and pecans, stirring just until blended. Pour into greased and floured 9-inch (23 cm) cake pan and bake for 10 to 12 minutes or until toothpick inserted in center comes out clean. Cool completely and cut into squares.

- In saucepan over medium heat, combine pie filling, sugar, raisins, cinnamon and ¼ cup (60 ml) water. Stir until well blended and serve over shortcake squares.

Strawberry-Raspberry Shortcakes

Shortcakes:

2 cups baking mix	480 ml
¼ cup cornmeal	60 ml
½ cup sugar, extra sugar for topping	120 ml
1 (8 ounce) carton whipping cream	227 g

Fruit:

2 pints strawberries, sliced	1 kg
1 pint red raspberries	.5 kg
⅔ cup sugar	160 ml
1 quart vanilla ice cream	1 L

- Preheat oven to 400° (204° C). In bowl, combine baking mix, cornmeal and sugar. Stir in cream, mixing just until mixture is evenly moistened. Drop 8 mounds of dough 2-inches (5 cm) apart on ungreased baking sheet; sprinkle tops with slight tablespoon (15 ml) sugar. Bake about 15 minutes or until light brown. Remove to wire rack to cool.

- While shortcakes are baking, combine strawberries, raspberries, sugar and 1 tablespoon (15 ml) water; leave at room temperature while shortcakes bake.

- To serve, carefully cut shortcakes horizontally in half with a serrated knife. Place bottom on each individual dessert plate. Top with scoop of ice cream, then spoon on berries and juice; then replace shortcake tops.

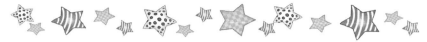

Fudge Cake Squares

1 cup plus 2 tablespoons flour	240 ml/30 ml
3 tablespoons cocoa	45 ml
1 cup sugar	240 ml
½ teaspoon baking soda	2 ml
⅓ cup oil	80 ml
1 large egg	
1 teaspoon vanilla	5 ml

• Preheat oven to 350° (176° C). Prepare 9-inch (23 cm) square baking pan with non-stick cooking spray.

• In large bowl, stir together flour, cocoa, sugar, baking soda and ½ teaspoon (2 ml) salt. Add ¾ cup (180 ml) water, oil, egg and vanilla and beat on low speed until well mixed. Then beat on medium speed another 2 minutes.

• Pour into prepared pan and bake 30 to 35 minutes or until toothpick inserted in center comes out clean; cool. Transfer cake to serving plate and cut into squares to serve.

White Chocolate-Almond Cake

1 (18 ounce) box white cake mix	510 g
4 egg whites	
¼ cup oil	60 ml
1 teaspoon almond extract	5 ml
1 cup chopped almonds	240 ml
6 (1 ounce) squares white chocolate, melted	6 (28 g)

- Preheat oven to 350° (176° C). In mixing bowl, combine cake mix, egg whites, oil, almond extract and 1½ cups (360 ml) water; beat until well blended.

- Stir in chopped almonds and melted white chocolate and pour into 2 (9-inch/23 cm) round cake pans. Bake 30 to 35 minutes or until toothpick inserted in center comes out clean.

- Spread each layer with half of 16-ounce (.5 kg) carton of caramel icing. Place second layer on top of first layer.

Coconut-Angel Cake

1 (14 ounce/10-inch) round angel food cake	396/25 cm
1 (20 ounce) can coconut pie filling	567 g
1 (12 ounce) carton whipped topping	340 g
3 tablespoons flaked coconut	45 ml

- Cut angel food cake horizontally to make 3 layers.

- Combine coconut pie filling and whipped topping. Spread one-third mixture on first layer. Top with second layer.

- Spread one-third mixture on second layer and top with third layer. Spread remaining whipped topping mixture on top of cake. Sprinkle coconut on top of mixture. Refrigerate.

Fruit Cocktail Crepes

4 (15 ounce) cans fruit cocktail, thoroughly drained	4 (425 g)
1 cup packed brown sugar	240 ml
1 cup butter, divided	240 ml
3 (8-inch) packages flour tortillas	3 (20 cm)

- Preheat oven at 325° (162° C). In small saucepan over low heat, stir constantly brown sugar and ⅓ cup (80 ml) butter until sugar melts and mixes well.

- Use remaining butter and brush flour tortillas on both sides. (If each tortilla is not soft enough to roll without breaking, heat 2 to 3 at a time wrapped in damp paper towel for 4 to 5 seconds in microwave oven.) For each crepe, place 2 teaspoons (10 ml) sugar mixture and 1 tablespoon (15 ml) drained fruit cocktail in middle of each tortilla.

- Roll each tortilla and place, seam-side down, in 7 x 11-inch (18 x 28 cm) baking pan. Spread remaining sugar mixture on top. Bake covered 15 minutes or until sugar mixture bubbles.

Peanut Butter Pie

1 (8 ounce) package cream cheese, softened	227 g
1 cup sugar	240 ml
1 cup creamy peanut butter	240 ml
1 teaspoon vanilla	5 ml
1 (8 ounce) carton whipping cream, whipped	227 g
1 (9-inch) graham cracker piecrust	23 cm

- In mixing bowl, combine cream cheese, sugar, peanut butter and vanilla and beat until creamy. Fold in whipped cream and spoon into graham cracker piecrust and chill.

Million-Dollar Pie

24 round, buttery crackers, crumbled
1 cup chopped pecans   240 ml
4 egg whites (absolutely no yolks at all)
1 cup sugar   240 ml

- Mix cracker crumbs with pecans. In separate mixing bowl, beat egg whites until stiff and slowly add sugar while still mixing.

- Gently fold crumbs and pecan mixture into egg whites. Pour into pie tin and bake at 350° (176° C) for 20 minutes. Let cool.

Individual Apple Pies

2 tart baking apples
⅔ cup sugar   160 ml
¾ teaspoon cinnamon   4 ml
2 tablespoons flour   30 ml
1 sheet of frozen piecrust (½ of 15 ounce package)   425 g

- Preheat oven to 425° (220° C). Peel, core and chop apples. In bowl, combine chopped apples, sugar, cinnamon and flour.

- Unroll piecrust flat and cut five circles and place each circle inside 5 spaces of muffin tin. Evenly divide apple mixture. Using remaining piecrust, cut into strips and place on top of apple mixture.

- Place about ⅓ cup (80 ml) water in extra muffin tin. Bake for 18 minutes or until bubbling and remove from tin when cool.

Apple Crumble

1 (20 ounce) can apple pie filling	567 g
½ cup packed brown sugar	120 ml
½ teaspoon ground cinnamon	2 ml
½ teaspoon ground ginger	2 ml

Topping:

1 cup flour	240 ml
¾ cup packed brown sugar	180 ml
¼ teaspoon ground cinnamon	1 ml
¼ teaspoon ground ginger	1 ml
½ cup (1 stick) butter	120 ml
⅓ cup slivered almonds	80 ml

- Preheat oven to 350° (176° C). In bowl, combine apple pie filling, ½ cup (120 ml) brown sugar, and ½ teaspoon (2 ml) each of cinnamon and ginger. Spoon into buttered 9-inch (23 cm) square baking dish.

- In bowl, combine flour, ¾ cup (180 ml) brown sugar and remaining cinnamon and ginger; cut in butter until mixture resembles coarse crumbs. Add almonds and sprinkle over apple mixture. Bake for 35 minutes or until filling is bubbly and topping is golden brown.

Holiday Pie

1 (8 ounce) package cream cheese, softened   227 g
1 (14 ounce) can sweetened condensed milk   396 g
1 (3.4 ounce) box instant vanilla pudding mix   100 g
1½ cups whipped topping   360 ml

- With mixer, beat cream cheese until smooth. Gradually add sweetened condensed milk and beat until smooth.

- Add ¾ cup (180 ml) water and pudding mix and beat until smooth. Fold in whipped topping. Pour into graham cracker piecrust. Top with crumbled holiday candies. Chill.

Banana-Vanilla Pie

1 banana, sliced
1 (9-inch) graham cracker piecrust   23 cm
2 cups cold milk   480 ml
⅓ cup sugar   80 ml
2 (4 serving size) packages vanilla instant pudding
1 (8 ounce) carton French vanilla whipped topping,
    divided   227 g

- Place banana slices in graham cracker piecrust. Pour milk in medium-size bowl and add sugar and pudding; beat about 2 minutes. Mixture will be thick. Fold in half of whipped topping and spoon into piecrust.

- Chill before serving. Top each serving with dabs of remaining whipped topping.

Cherry Crisp

2 (20 ounce) cans cherry pie filling	2 (567 g)
1 (18 ounce) box white cake mix	510 g
½ cup (1 stick) butter	120 ml
2 cups chopped pecans	480 ml

- Pour pie filling into greased 9 x 13-inch (23 x 33 cm) baking dish. Sprinkle cake mix over top of filling. Dot with butter and cover with pecans. Bake uncovered at 350° (176° C) for 40 minutes.

Pound Cake Cobbler

1 (10 ounce) bakery pound cake loaf	280 g
1 (20 ounce) can pineapple pie filling	567 g
½ teaspoon almond extract	2 ml
¼ cup sliced, toasted almonds	60 ml
3 tablespoons powdered sugar	45 ml
1 (8 ounce) carton whipping cream, whipped	227 g

- Cut cake into 1-inch cubes and place in a 7 x 11-inch (18 x 28 cm) glass baking dish. In bowl, combine pineapple pie filling, almond extract and ¼ cup (60 ml) water, mixing well. Spoon pie filling mixture over cake and microwave on HIGH for 2 to 3 minutes or until thoroughly hot.

- Stir powdered sugar into whipped cream. Spoon cobbler into individual sherbet glasses and top with whipped cream. Sprinkle almonds on top.

Cherry Cobbler

2 (20 ounce) cans cherry pie filling	2 (567 g)
1 (18 ounce) box white cake mix	510 g
¾ cup (1½ sticks) butter, melted	180 ml
1 (4 ounce) package slivered almonds	114 g

- Spread pie filling in greased 9 x 13-inch (23 x 33 cm) baking pan. Sprinkle cake mix over cherries. Drizzle with melted butter over top. Sprinkle almonds over top.

- Bake at 350° (176° C) for 40 minutes. Top with whipped topping.

Blueberry Cobbler Deluxe

1 (20 ounce) can blueberry pie filling	567 g
½ cup sugar	120 ml
1 tablespoon lemon juice	15 ml
1½ cups biscuit mix	360 ml
¼ cup sugar, plus 1 tablespoon	60 ml/15 ml
¼ cup (1 stick) butter, divided	60 ml
¾ cup sour cream	180 ml

- Combine blueberry pie filling, sugar and lemon juice, stir to blend. Spoon into buttered 9-inch (23 cm) square baking dish.

- In large bowl, combine biscuit mix and ¼ cup (60 ml) sugar; and cut in three-fourths butter until mixture is crumbly. Stir in sour cream, tossing with fork until mixture forms a ball.

- Roll out to fit top of baking dish and place pastry over filling. Melt remaining butter and brush over pastry. Sprinkle 1 tablespoon (15 ml) sugar over top.

Blueberry Bounce

1½ cups quick-cooking oats	360 ml
2 cups packed brown sugar	480 ml
1 (20 ounce) can blueberry pie filling	567 g
1 (18 ounce) box yellow cake mix (dry)	510 g
¾ cup chopped pecans	180 ml
½ cup (1 stick) butter, melted	120 ml

• Preheat oven to 350° (176° C). Spray bottom of 9 x 13-inch (23 x 33 cm) glass baking dish with vegetable spray. In medium bowl, combine oats and brown sugar and sprinkle half in bottom of prepared baking dish.

• Spoon blueberry pie filling over oat-sugar mixture and spread evenly, follow with cake mix, spread evenly. Combine pecans with remaining oat mixture and sprinkle over pie filling. Drizzle butter across oat-sugar mixture. Bake 35 minutes.

Gingerbread Cookies

¾ cup (1½ sticks) butter, softened	180 ml
2 egg yolks	
1 (18 ounce) spice cake mix	510 g
1 teaspoon ginger	5 ml

• In large bowl combine butter and egg yolks. Gradually blend in cake mix and ginger and mix well.

• Roll out to ⅛-inch (.4 cm) thickness on lightly floured surface. Use gingerbread cookie cutter to cut out cookies and place 2 inches (5 cm) apart on cookie sheet. Bake at 375° (190° C) for about 8 minutes or until edges are slightly brown. Cool cookies before transferring to cookie bowl.

Peanut Butter Cookies

1 cup sugar	240 ml
¾ cup light corn syrup	180 ml
1 (16 ounce) jar crunchy peanut butter	.5 kg
4½ cups chow mein noodles	1.1 L

- In saucepan over medium heat, bring sugar and corn syrup to boil and stir in peanut butter. Remove from heat and stir in noodles. Drop by spoonfuls onto wax paper and allow to cool.

Lemon Cookies

½ cup (1 stick) butter, softened	120 ml
1 cup sugar	240 ml
2 tablespoons lemon juice	30 ml
2 cups flour	480 ml

- Cream butter, sugar and lemon juice and slowly stir in flour. Drop by teaspoons onto ungreased cookie sheet. Bake at 350° (176° C) for 14 to 15 minutes.

Devil's Food Cookies

1 (18 ounce) package devil's food cake mix	510 g
½ cup oil	120 ml
2 eggs	
¾ cup chopped pecans, optional	180 ml

- Combine cake mix, oil and eggs in bowl and mix well.

- Drop by teaspoons onto non-stick cookie sheet. Bake at 350° (176° C) for 10 to 12 minutes. Cool and remove to wire rack.

Drop Cookies

1 cup (2 sticks) butter, softened	240 ml
¾ cup cornstarch	180 ml
⅓ cup powdered sugar	80 ml
1 cup flour	240 ml

- Mix butter, cornstarch, sugar and flour and mix well.

- Drop on cookie sheet in small balls and flatten slightly.

- Bake at 350° (176° C) for about 15 minutes but do not brown.

Icing for Drop Cookies:

1 (3 ounce) package cream cheese, softened	84 g
1 teaspoon vanilla	5 ml
1 cup powdered sugar	240 ml

- Blend all ingredients and mix well. Ice cool cookies.

Double-Chocolate Cookies

6 egg whites	
3 cups powdered sugar	710 ml
¼ cup cocoa	60 ml
3½ cups finely chopped pecans	830 ml

- Beat egg whites until light and frothy. Fold sugar and cocoa into egg whites and beat lightly. Fold in pecans.

- Drop by teaspoons on lightly greased, floured cookie sheet.

- Bake at 325° (162° C) for about 20 minutes. Do not over bake and cool completely before removing from cookie sheet.

Easy Peanut Butter Cookies

1⅔ cup powdered sugar	400 ml
1 cup crunchy peanut butter	240 ml
1 large egg	
1 teaspoon vanilla	5 ml

- Preheat oven to 325° (162° C). In bowl, combine powdered sugar, peanut butter, egg and vanilla, mixing well. Roll dough into 1-inch (2.5 cm) ball and place on greased baking sheet. Lightly press cookies with fork.

- Bake 10 minutes and cool several minutes before storing.

Chinese Cookies

1 (6 ounce) package chocolate chips	168 g
1 (6 ounce) package butterscotch chips	168 g
1 cup salted peanuts	240 ml
1 (3 ounce) can chow mein noodles	84 g

- In large saucepan, melt chocolate and butterscotch chips. Add peanuts and noodles and mix well.

- Drop by teaspoonfuls onto wax paper. Chill just to harden.

Butterscotch Cookies

1 (12 ounce) and 1 (6 ounce) package butterscotch chips	340 g/168 g
2¼ cups chow mein noodles	540 ml
½ cup chopped walnuts	120 ml
¼ cup flaked coconut	60 ml

- Melt butterscotch chips in double boiler. Add noodles, walnuts and coconut. Drop by tablespoonfuls onto wax paper.

Cheesecake Cookies

1 cup (2 sticks) butter, softened	240 ml
2 (3 ounce) packages cream cheese, softened	2 (84 g)
2 cups sugar	480 ml
2 cups flour	480 ml

- Cream butter and cream cheese. Add sugar and beat until light and fluffy. Add flour and beat well.

- Drop by teaspoons onto cookie sheet and bake at 350° (176° C) for 12 to 15 minutes or until edges are golden.

Chocolate-Crunch Cookies

1 (18 ounce) package German chocolate cake mix with pudding	510 g
1 egg, slightly beaten	
½ cup (1 stick) butter, melted	120 ml
1 cup crisp rice cereal	240 ml

- Combine cake mix, egg and butter. Add cereal and stir until they blend. Shape dough into 1-inch (2.5 cm) balls. Place on lightly sprayed cookie sheet.

- Dip fork in flour and flatten cookies in crisscross pattern. Bake at 350° (176° C) for 10 to 12 minutes. Cool.

Butter Cookies

1 pound butter	.5 kg
¾ cup each packed brown and granulated sugar	180 ml
4½ cups flour	1.1 L

- Preheat oven to 350° (176° C). Cream butter and sugars, slowly add flour and mix well. (Batter will be very thick.)

- Roll into small balls and place on ungreased cookie sheet. Bake for 15 minutes until only slightly brown.

Butter Cookie Special

1 (18 ounce) box butter cake mix	510 g
1 (3.4 ounce) package butterscotch instant pudding	
mix	100 g
1 cup oil	240 ml
1 egg, beaten	
1¼ cups chopped pecans	300 ml

- Mix by hand cake mix, pudding mix, oil and egg. Beat thoroughly. Stir in pecans. With teaspoon place cookie dough on cookie sheet about 2 inches (5 cm) apart. Bake at 350° (176° C) for about 8 minutes.

Brown Sugar Cookies

¾ cup packed brown sugar	180 ml
1 cup (2 sticks) butter, softened	240 ml
1 egg yolk	
2 cups flour	480 ml

- Cream sugar and butter until light and fluffy. Mix in egg yolk. Blend in flour. Chill dough. Form dough into 1-inch (2.5 cm) balls, flatten and criss-cross with fork on lightly greased baking sheet. Bake at 325° (162° C) for 10 to 12 minutes or until golden brown.

Macaroons

2 large egg whites	
3 tablespoons sugar	45 ml
½ teaspoon vanilla	2 ml
½ teaspoon almond extract	2 ml
½ cup sweetened flaked coconut	120 ml

- Preheat oven to 300° (148° C). Line large baking sheet with foil and spray with cooking spray and lightly dust with flour (shake off excess flour). In bowl, whisk together whites, sugar, vanilla, almond extract and a pinch of salt. Stir in coconut.

- Drop heaping tablespoons of mixture on prepared pan about 2 inches (5 cm) apart. Bake until tops are slightly brown in spots, about 18 minutes. Carefully lift foil with cookies from baking sheet and place on rack to cool. Peel macaroons off of foil.

Coconut Macaroons

2 (7 ounce) packages flaked coconut	2 (198 g)
1 (14 ounce) can sweetened condensed milk	396 g
2 teaspoons vanilla	10 ml
½ teaspoon almond extract	2 ml

- In mixing bowl, combine coconut, condensed milk and extracts; mix well. Drop by rounded teaspoons onto foil-lined cookie sheet.

- Bake at 350° (176° C) for 8 to 10 minutes or until light brown around edges. Immediately remove from foil to prevent sticking. Store at room temperature.

Marshmallow Treats

¼ cup (½ stick) butter	60 ml
4 cups miniature marshmallows	1 L
½ cup chunky peanut butter	120 ml
5 cups crispy rice cereal	1.3 L

- In saucepan, melt butter and add marshmallows. Stir until they melt and add peanut butter. Remove from heat. Add cereal and stir well. Press mixture into 9 x 13-inch (23 x 33 cm) pan. Cut in squares when cool.

Raisin Crunch

¾ cup light corn syrup	180 ml
1 cup sugar	240 ml
1 cup crunchy peanut butter	240 ml
1 (20 ounce) box raisin bran	567 g

- In saucepan combine corn syrup and sugar. Heat until sugar thoroughly dissolves. Remove from heat and stir in peanut butter. Place raisin bran in large container and pour sauce over top. Mix thoroughly. Pat mixture into 9 x 13-inch (23 x 33 cm) pan and completely chill. Cut into squares and store in airtight container.

Scotch Shortbread

½ cup (1 stick) unsalted butter, softened	120 ml
⅓ cup sugar	80 ml
1¼ cups flour	300 ml
Powdered sugar	

- Cream butter and sugar until light and fluffy. Add flour and pinch of salt and mix well. Spread dough in 8-inch (20 cm) square pan. Bake at 325° (162° C) for 20 minutes or until light brown. Cool shortbread in pan, dust with powdered sugar and cut into squares.

Strawberry Crumbles

2¼ cups baking mix	540 ml
1 cup oats	240 ml
1 cup packed brown sugar	240 ml
½ cup (1 stick) butter, softened	120 ml
1 cup strawberry preserves	240 ml

• Preheat oven to 375° (190° C). Mix together baking mix, oats and brown sugar. Cut in butter by using a pastry blender, until mixture is crumbly.

• Press half this mixture in bottom of greased 9 x 9-inch (23 x 23 cm) baking pan. Spread strawberry preserves over crumbly mixture to within ¼-inch (.6 cm) of edges. Sprinkle remaining crumbly mixture over and gently press into fruit. Bake 30 minutes or until light brown. Cool and cut into bars to serve.

Walnut Bars

1⅔ cups graham cracker crumbs	400 ml
1½ cups coarsely chopped walnuts	360 ml
1 (14 ounce) can sweetened condensed milk	396 g
¼ cup flaked coconut, optional	60 ml

• Place graham cracker crumbs and walnuts in bowl. Slowly add condensed milk, coconut and pinch of salt. Mixture will be very thick.

• Pack into greased 9-inch (23 cm) square sprayed pan. Pack mixture down with back of spoon. Bake at 350° (176° C) for 35 minutes. When cool cut into squares.

Toffee Bars

1½ cups (3 stick) butter, softened	360 ml
1¾ cups packed light brown sugar	420 ml
2 teaspoons vanilla	10 ml
3 cups flour	710 ml
1 (8 ounce) package chocolate chips	227 g

- Preheat oven to 350° (176° C). In mixing bowl, combine butter, brown sugar and vanilla; beat on medium speed for 3 minutes. Add flour and mix until completely blended and stir in chocolate chips. Place dough on a greased 9 x 13-inch (23 x 33 cm) baking pan and bake 25 minutes or until light brown. Cool slightly and cut into bars.

Snicker Brownies

1 (18 ounce) German chocolate cake mix	510 g
¾ cup (1½ sticks) butter, melted	180 ml
½ cup evaporated milk	120 ml
4 (3 ounce) Snickers® candy bars	4 (84 g)

- Combine cake mix, butter and evaporated milk in large bowl. Beat on low speed until mixture blends well.

- Add half batter into greased, floured 9 x 13-inch (23 x 33 cm) baking pan. Bake at 350° (176° C) for 10 minutes.

- Remove from oven. Cut candy bars in ⅛-inch (.4 cm) slices and place evenly over brownies. Drop remaining half of batter by spoonfuls over candy bars and spread as evenly as possible.

- Place back in oven and bake for 20 minutes longer. When cool, cut into bars.

Pecan Squares

1 (24 ounce) package almond bark	680 g
1 cup cinnamon chips	240 ml
1 cup chopped pecans	240 ml
8 cups frosted crispy rice cereal	1.8 L

- Melt almond bark and cinnamon chips in very large saucepan or roasting pan on low heat and stir constantly. After it melts, remove from heat and add pecans and frosted rice cereal. Mix well and stir into 9 x 13-inch (23 x 33 cm) pan. Pat down with back of spoon. Chill. Cut into squares.

Honey-Nut Bars

⅓ cup (⅔ stick) butter	80 ml
¼ cup cocoa	60 ml
1 (10 ounce) package miniature marshmallows	280 g
6 cups honey-nut clusters cereal	1.5 L

- Melt butter in large saucepan and stir in cocoa and marshmallows. Cook over low heat, stirring constantly, until marshmallows melt and mixture is smooth. Remove from heat and stir in honey-nut clusters. Pour into sprayed 7 x 11-inch (18 x 28 cm) pan. With spatula, smooth mixture in pan. Cool completely and cut into bars.

Easy Blonde Brownies

1 (1 pound) box light brown sugar	.5 kg
4 eggs	
2 cups biscuit mix	480 ml
2 cups chopped pecans	480 ml

- Preheat oven to 350° (176° C). Using mixer, beat brown sugar, eggs and biscuit mix. Stir in pecans and pour into sprayed 9 x 13-inch (23 x 33 cm) baking pan. Bake for 35 minutes. Cool and cut into squares.

Date-Pecan Bars

Filling:

2 (8 ounce) boxes pitted dates, chopped	2 (227 g)
1½ cups orange juice	360 ml
¼ cup sugar	60 ml
¼ teaspoon ground cinnamon	1 ml

Crust and Topping:

1½ cups flour	360 ml
1½ cups oats	360 ml
¾ cup brown sugar	180 ml
1½ cups finely chopped pecans	360 ml
1¼ cups (2½ sticks) cold butter, cut up	300 ml

- In saucepan, combine dates, orange juice, sugar and cinnamon and bring to boiling; reduce heat and simmer, stirring several times, for 15 minutes and until mixture thickens.

- Preheat oven to 350° (176° C). Spray 9 x 13-inch (23 x 33 cm) baking pan. Place flour, oats, brown sugar and pecans in mixing bowl; cut in butter until mixture is crumbly.

- Transfer 2½ cups mixture to another bowl and set aside. Press remaining crumbs over bottom of greased pan.

- Spoon filling over crust and spread up to ¼ inch (.6 cm) from edge. Sprinkle (set aside) crust mixture over top of filling and bake 35 minutes. Cool and cut into bars.

Chocolate-Cherry Bars

1 (18 ounce) devils food cake mix	510 g
1 (20 ounce) can cherry pie filling	567 g
2 eggs	
1 cup milk chocolate chips	240 ml

- In large bowl, mix all ingredients by hand and blend well.

- Pour batter into greased, floured 9 x 13-inch (23 x 33 cm) baking dish.

- Bake at 350° (176° C) for 25 to 30 minutes or until cake tester comes out clean.

Frosting for Chocolate Cherry Bars:

1 (3 ounce) square semi-sweet chocolate, melted	84 g
1 (3 ounce) package cream cheese, softened	84 g
½ teaspoon vanilla	2 ml
1½ cups powdered sugar	360 ml

- In medium bowl beat chocolate, cream cheese and vanilla until smooth. Gradually beat in powdered sugar.

- Pour over cool chocolate-cherry bars.

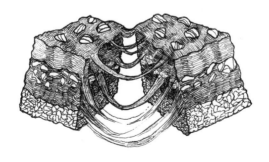

Chocolate Chip-Cheese Bars

1 (18 ounce) tube refrigerated chocolate chip cookie
   dough   510 g
1 (8 ounce) package cream cheese, softened   227 g
½ cup sugar   120 ml
1 egg

- Cut cookie dough half. For crust, press half dough onto bottom
  of sprayed 9-inch (23 cm) square baking pan or 7 x 11-inch
  (18 x 28 cm) baking pan.

- In mixing bowl, beat cream cheese, sugar and egg until smooth.
  Spread over crust. Crumble remaining dough over top.

- Bake at 350° (176° C) for 35 to 40 minutes or until toothpick
  inserted near center comes out clean. Cool on wire rack. Cut
  into bars. Refrigerate leftovers.

Chocolate Caramel Bars

1 (18 ounce) package chocolate chip cookie dough   510 g
1 cup chopped walnuts, divided   240 ml
1 (10 ounce) jar caramel ice cream topping   280 g

- Preheat oven to 350° (176° C). Press three-fourths cookie
  dough into greased 9 x 13-inch (23 x 33 cm) baking pan and bake
  10 minutes. Sprinkle half of walnuts over cookie dough and
  drizzle caramel topping over walnuts. Top teaspoonfuls of
  remaining dough and gently press into caramel topping. Top with
  remaining walnuts and bake for 16 minutes or until the edge of
  dough is set. Cool before cutting into bars.

Chocolate Cherry Squares

1 (4 ounce) package cook-and-serve chocolate	
pudding mix	114 g
1¾ cups milk	420 ml
¼ cup maraschino cherry juice	60 ml
1 (18 ounce) package chocolate cake mix	510 g
1 cup maraschino cherries, chopped	240 ml
1 (6 ounce) package chocolate chips	168 g
1 cup chopped pecans	240 ml

- Preheat oven to 350° (176° C). In saucepan, cook pudding mix, milk and cherry juice as directed on package.

- Stir pudding mixture into cake mix and cherries. Spread into 10 x 15-inch (25 x 38 cm) greased and floured baking pan. Sprinkle with chocolate chips and pecans and bake 30 minutes.

Apricot Bars

1¼ cups flour	300 ml
¾ cup packed brown sugar	180 ml
6 tablespoons (¾ stick) butter	90 ml
¾ cup apricot preserves	180 ml

- In mixing bowl, combine flour, brown sugar and butter and mix well. Place half mixture in 9-inch (23 cm) square baking pan. Spread apricot preserves over top of mixture. Add remaining flour mixture over top of dessert. Bake at 350° (176° C) for 30 minutes. Cut into squares.

Peanut Butter Balls

¾ cup light corn syrup	180 ml
2½ cups crunchy peanut butter	600 ml
2¼ cups graham cracker crumbs	540 ml
1¼ cups powdered sugar	300 ml

- In bowl, combine corn syrup, peanut butter, cracker crumbs and powdered sugar and mix until smooth. Shape balls (1-inch/2.5 cm in size) and place on wax paper lined baking sheet. Chill for about 30 minutes.

Chocolate-Peanut Butter Crisps

1 (10 count) package 8-inch flour tortillas	(20 cm)
8 (8 ounce) squares semi-sweet chocolate, coarsely chopped or 8 ounces semi-sweet chocolate morsels	227 g
⅓ cup creamy or chunky peanut butter	80 ml
1 (14 ounce) can sweetened condensed milk	396 g

- Cut flour tortillas into 8 wedges and place on baking sheet. Bake at 350° (176° C) for 10 minutes and cool on rack.

- In heavy saucepan, melt chocolate over low heat, stirring constantly. Stir in peanut putter, sweetened condensed milk and 2 tablespoons (30 ml) water and heat through. (If sauce is too thick, add 1 teaspoon (5 ml) water at a time, until sauce smoothly drizzles on foil.)

- Drizzle warm chocolate sauce over wedges or serve immediately in chafing dish or fondue pot and dip crisp tortilla wedges.

Nutty Fudgies

1 (18 ounce) package fudge cake mix	510 g
1 (8 ounce) carton sour cream	227 g
⅔ cup peanut butter chips	160 ml
½ cup chopped peanuts	120 ml

- Beat cake mix and sour cream until mixture blends and is smooth. Stir in peanut butter chips and peanuts.

- Drop by teaspoonfuls onto sprayed cookie sheet. Bake at 350° (176° C) for 10 to 12 minutes. Remove from oven and cool.

Peanut Butter Crunchies

1 cup sugar	240 ml
½ cup white corn syrup	120 ml
2 cups peanut butter	480 ml
4 cups crispy rice cereal	1 L

- In saucepan, mix sugar and syrup and bring to a boil. Remove from stove and stir in peanut butter. Add crispy rice cereal and mix well. Drop by teaspoonfuls onto wax paper. Chill.

Peanutty Cocoa Puffs

¾ cup light corn syrup	180 ml
1¼ cups sugar	300 ml
1¼ cups chunky peanut butter	300 ml
4½ cups cocoa puff cereal	1.2 L

- In large saucepan bring syrup and sugar to rolling boil. Stir in peanut butter and mix well. Stir in cocoa puffs.

- Drop on wax paper by teaspoonfuls.

Porcupine Clusters

¼ cup corn syrup	60 ml
1 (12 ounce) package white chocolate morsels	340 g
2 cups chow mein noodles	480 ml
¾ cup salted peanuts	180 ml

- On low heat, melt corn syrup and white chocolate chips. Pour over noodles and peanuts and mix well. Drop by teaspoonfuls on wax paper. Chill to harden. Store in airtight container.

Scotch Crunchies

½ cup crunchy peanut butter	120 ml
1 (6 ounce) package butterscotch bits	168 g
2½ cups frosted flakes	600 ml
½ cup peanuts	120 ml

- Combine peanut butter and butterscotch bits in large saucepan and melt over low heat. Stir until butterscotch bits melt. Stir in cereal and peanuts. Drop by teaspoonfuls onto wax paper. Chill. Store in airtight container.

Pumpkin Cupcakes

1 (18 ounce) package spice cake mix	510 g
1 (15 ounce) can pumpkin	425 g
3 eggs	
⅓ cup oil	80 ml

- With mixer, blend cake mix, pumpkin, eggs, oil and ⅓ cup (80 ml) water. Beat for 2 minutes. Pour batter into 24 paper-lined muffin cups and fill three-fourths full. Bake at 350° (176° C) for 18 to 20 minutes or until toothpick inserted in center comes out clean.

Caramel-Apple Cupcakes

1 (18 ounce) package carrot cake mix	510 g
3 cups chopped, peeled tart apples	710 ml
1 (12 ounce) package butterscotch chips	340 g
1 cup finely chopped pecans	240 ml

• Make cake mix according to package directions. Fold in apples. Fill 12 greased or paper-lined jumbo muffin cups three-fourths full. Bake at 350° (176° C) for 20 minutes or until toothpick comes out clean. In saucepan on very low heat melt butterscotch chips. Spread over cupcakes and sprinkle with chopped pecans.

Cracker Candy Bites

2¾ cups round buttery crackers, coarsely broken-up	660 ml
¾ cup (1 ½ sticks) butter	180 ml
2 cups packed brown sugar	480 ml
1 (12 ounce) package milk chocolate chips	340 g

• Preheat oven to 350° (176° C) degrees. Place crackers in greased 9 x 13-inch (23 x 33 cm) baking dish.

• In saucepan, combine butter and brown sugar and bring to boiling. Boil 3 minutes, stirring constantly. Pour over crackers.

• Bake for 5 minutes and turn oven off. Sprinkle chocolate chips over cracker mixture. Return to oven and let stand about 5 minutes or until chocolate melts. Remove from oven and spread chocolate evenly over cracker mixture. Cool, break into pieces.

Diamond Fudge

1 (6 ounce) package semi-sweet chocolate morsels	168 g
1 cup creamy peanut butter	240 ml
½ cup (1 stick) butter	120 ml
1 cup powdered sugar	240 ml

• Cook chocolate morsels, peanut butter and butter in saucepan over low heat, stirring constantly, just until mixture melts and is smooth. Remove from heat. Add powdered sugar and stir until smooth. Spoon into buttered 8-inch (20 cm) square pan and chill until firm. Cut into squares.

Peanut Butter Fudge

1 (12 ounce) jar chunky peanut butter	340 g
1 (12 ounce) package milk chocolate chips	340 g
1 (14 ounce) can sweetened condensed milk	396 g
1 cup chopped pecans	240 ml

• In saucepan, combine peanut butter and chocolate chips and condensed milk. Heat on low, stirring constantly, until chocolate melts.

• Add pecans and mix well. Pour into 9 x 9-inch (23 x 23 cm) buttered dish.

Microwave Fudge

3 cups semi-sweet chocolate morsels	710 ml
1 (14 ounce) can sweetened condensed milk	396 g
4 tablespoons (½ stick) butter, cut into pieces	60 ml
1 cup chopped walnuts	240 ml

- Combine chocolate morsels, condensed milk and butter in 2-quart (2 L) glass bowl. Microwave on MEDIUM 4 to 5 minutes, stirring at 1½-minute intervals. Stir in walnuts and pour into buttered 8-inch (20 cm) square dish. Chill. Cut into squares.

Raisin Fudge

1 (12 ounce) package semi-sweet chocolate chips	340 g
1 cup chunky peanut butter	240 ml
3 cups miniature marshmallows	710 ml
¾ cup raisins	180 ml

- In saucepan melt chocolate chips and peanut butter over medium to low heat. Fold in marshmallows and raisins and stir until marshmallows melt. Pour into 7 x 11-inch (18 x 28 cm) pan. Chill until firm. Cut into squares. Store where it is cool.

Easy, Fast Fudge

1 (14 ounce) can sweetened condensed milk	396 g
3 cups semi-sweet or milk chocolate chips	710 ml
1 teaspoon vanilla extract	5 ml

- Combine milk, chocolate chips and pinch of salt in medium saucepan over medium-low heat. Stir constantly until chocolate is melted.

- Remove from heat and stir in vanilla.

- Spread in buttered 8 x 8-inch (20 x 20 cm) pan and let cool.

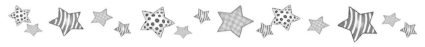

Hazel's Nutty Fudge

1 (12 ounce) package white chocolate chips	340 g
¾ cup hazelnut-cocoa spread	180 ml
1½ cups chopped hazelnuts, divided	360 ml
Coconut	

- In medium saucepan over low heat, melt white chocolate chips and add hazelnut spread. Cook and stir until mixture blends well. Remove from heat and stir in 1 cup (240 ml) hazelnuts.

- Drop by teaspoons on wax paper. Garnish with reserved hazelnuts. Chill.

Date Loaf Candy

3 cups sugar	710 ml
1 cup milk	240 ml
1 (16 ounce) box chopped dates	.5 kg
1 cup chopped pecans	240 ml

- Combine sugar and milk in large saucepan.

- Cook to soft-boil stage (234°/110° C on candy thermometer). Stir in dates. Cook to hard boil stage (260°/126° C), stirring constantly.

- Remove from heat, add pecans and mix well. Stir and cool until stiff. Pour mixture onto damp tea towel. Roll into log. Let stand until set. Remove tea towel and slice.

Dream Candy

2 (8 ounce) cartons whipping cream	2 (227 g)
3 cups sugar	710 ml
1 cup light corn syrup	240 ml
1 cup chopped pecans	240 ml

- In saucepan, combine whipping cream, sugar and corn syrup. Cook to soft-ball stage. Stir and beat until candy cools.

- Add pecans and pour into 9-inch (23 cm) buttered pan.

No-Bake Chocolate Drops

1 (6 ounce) semi-sweet chocolate baking chips	168 g
½ cup crunchy peanut butter	120 ml
1 (5 ounce) package chow mein noodles	143 g
1 cup salted, roasted peanuts	240 ml

- In saucepan, combine baking chips and peanut butter and heat on low, stirring constantly until chocolate chips have melted.

- Add noodles and peanuts and stir until ingredients are evenly coated with chocolate. Drop by heaping teaspoonfuls onto wax paper. Chill.

Tumbleweeds

1 (12 ounce) package butterscotch chips	340 g
¼ cup peanut butter	60 ml
1 (12 ounce) can peanuts	340 g
1 (4 ounce) can shoe-string potatoes	114 g

- In saucepan on low heat, melt chips with peanut butter and mix well. Stir in peanuts and shoe-string potatoes. Drop by tablespoonfuls on wax paper. Store in airtight container.

Chocolate Toffee

1 cup sugar	240 ml
1 cup (2 sticks) butter	240 ml
1 (6 ounce) package chocolate chips	168 g
1 cup chopped pecans	240 ml

- In heavy saucepan, combine sugar and butter. Cook until candy reaches hard-crack stage. Pour onto greased baking sheet.

- Melt chocolate in double boiler and spread over toffee.

- Sprinkle with pecans and press pecans into chocolate.

- Chill briefly to set chocolate. Break into pieces.

Pralines

1 (16 ounce) box light brown sugar	.5 kg
¾ cup unsweetened canned milk	180 ml
1½ cups pecan pieces or halves	360 ml
1½ teaspoons instant coffee or freeze-dried coffee	7 ml

- Mix all ingredients thoroughly in medium saucepan, cook slowly over low heat and stir constantly until mixture reaches soft-ball stage. Remove from heat and set aside 5 minutes.

- Beat with spoon until mixture is thick. Drop by teaspoonful onto greased foil. When cool and hard, peel foil from back and wrap each praline in plastic wrap.

Quick Pralines

1 (3 ounce) box butterscotch cook-and-serve pudding	84 g
1¼ cups sugar	300 ml
½ cup evaporated milk	120 ml
2 cups pecan pieces	480 ml

- In large saucepan, mix butterscotch pudding, sugar and milk.

- Bring to a boil, stirring constantly for 2 minutes.

- Add pecans and boil another 1½ minutes, stirring constantly.

- Remove from heat. Beat until candy begins to cool and drop by tablespoonfuls on wax paper.

Yummy Pralines

½ cup (1 stick) butter	120 ml
1 (16 ounce) box light brown sugar	.5 kg
1 (8 ounce) carton whipping cream, unwhipped	227 g
2½ cups whole pecans	600 ml

- In heavy saucepan, combine butter, brown sugar and whipping cream.

- Cook until temperature comes to soft-ball stage (about 20 minutes), stirring constantly. Remove from heat and set aside for 5 minutes. Fold in pecans and stir for several minutes until ingredients are glassy. With large spoon, drop onto wax paper and remove when cooled.

Index

457

Chocolate

D

Dessert

E

Index

463

Sandwiches

Soups and Stews

W

Y

Z

COOKBOOKS PUBLISHED BY COOKBOOK RESOURCES, LLC

The Ultimate Cooking
with 4 Ingredients

Easy Cooking with 5 Ingredients

The Best of Cooking
with 3 Ingredients

Gourmet Cooking with 5 Ingredients

Healthy Cooking with 4 Ingredients

Diabetic Cooking with 4 Ingredients

4-Ingredient Recipes for
30-Minute Meals

Essential 3-4-5 Ingredient Recipes

The Best 1001 Short, Easy Recipes

Easy Slow Cooker Cookbook

Easy One-Dish Meals

Easy Potluck Recipes

Essential Slow-Cooker Cooking

Quick Fixes with Cake Mixes

Casseroles to the Rescue

Easy Casseroles

Italian Family Cookbook

Sunday Night Suppers

365 Easy Meals

365 Easy Chicken

365 Soups and Stews

I Ain't On No Diet Cookbook

Kitchen Keepsakes/
More Kitchen Keepsakes

Old-Fashioned Cookies

Grandmother's Cookies

Mother's Recipes

Recipe Keeper

Cookie Dough Secrets

Gifts for the Cookie Jar

All New Gifts for the Cookie Jar

Gifts in a Pickle Jar

Muffins In A Jar

Brownies In A Jar

Cookie Jar Magic

Easy Desserts

Bake Sale Bestsellers

Quilters' Cooking Companion

Miss Sadie's Southern Cooking

Southern Family Favorites

Classic Tex-Mex and Texas Cooking

Classic Southwest Cooking

The Great Canadian Cookbook

The Best of Lone Star
Legacy Cookbook

Cookbook 25 Years

Pass the Plate

Texas Longhorn Cookbook

Trophy Hunters' Wild Game
Cookbook

Mealtimes and Memories

Holiday Recipes

Little Taste of Texas

Little Taste of Texas II

Southwest Sizzler

Southwest Olé

Class Treats

Leaving Home

To Order: **1001 Fast Easy Recipes**

Please send _____ paperback copies @ $19.95 (U.S.) each $ _____

Texas residents add sales tax @ $1.36 each $ _____

Plus postage/handling @ $6.00 (1st copy) $ _____

$1.00 (each additional copy) $ _____

Check or Credit Card (Canada-credit card only) Total $ _____

Charge to: ☐ MasterCard. or ☐ VISA

Account # _____

Expiration Date _____

Signature_____

Name _____

Address_____

City_____State_____Zip_____

Telephone (day_____(Evening)_____

Mail or Call:
Cookbook Resources
541 Doubletree Dr.
Highland Village, Texas 75077
Toll Free (866) 229-2665
(972) 317-6404 Fax

To Order: **1001 Fast Easy Recipes**

Please send _____ paperback copies @ $19.95 (U.S.) each $ _____

Texas residents add sales tax @ $1.36 each $ _____

Plus postage/handling @ $6.00 (1st copy) $ _____

$1.00 (each additional copy) $ _____

Check or Credit Card (Canada-credit card only) Total $ _____

Charge to: ☐ MasterCard. or ☐ VISA

Account # _____

Expiration Date _____

Signature_____

Name _____

Address_____

City_____State_____Zip_____

Telephone (Day)_____(Evening)_____

Mail or Call:
Cookbook Resources
541 Doubletree Dr.
Highland Village, Texas 75077
Toll Free (866) 229-2665
(972) 317-6404 Fax